Leadership in America

Consensus, Corruption, and Charisma

[**Edited by Peter Dennis Bathory**]

Livingston College
Rutgers, The State University of New Jersey

Longman

New York and London

For Peter D. Bathory, Sr.,
In the memory of Corinne Bathory

LEADERSHIP IN AMERICA
Consensus, Corruption, and Charisma

Longman Inc., New York
Associated companies, branches, and representatives
throughout the world.

Copyright © 1978 by Longman Inc.

Developmental Editor: Edward Artinian
Manuscript and Editorial Supervisor: Nicole Benevento
Design: Pencils Portfolio, Inc.
Manufacturing and Production Supervisor: Louis Gaber
Composition: Fuller Typesetting of Lancaster
Printing and Binding: Fairfield Graphics

Library of Congress Cataloging in Publication Data

Main entry under title:

Leadership in America.

   Includes index.
   1.   Elite (Social sciences)—United States—Addresses,
essays, lectures.   2.   Leadership—Addresses, essays,
lectures.   I.   Bathory, Peter D.
HN90.E4L4   301.15′53′0973   77–17714
ISBN 0–582–28039–7

Manufactured in the United States of America

Preface

The complexities of postindustrial and technological society have made the study of leadership in America increasingly difficult. While acknowledging these difficulties, the essays in this volume attempt to provide a common focus for the analysis of American leadership, public and private. It is our contention that the sustenance of democratic values requires careful analysis of the nature of leadership in America—its limitations as well as its possibilities. We worry that fascination with questions of economic justice and participatory democracy however central to the study of democratic leadership has too often blinded political actors and scholars alike to the importance of developing leaders and standards of leadership that will make the realization of democratic values more possible.

Moreover, it seems to us that the development of leaders and standards of leadership must proceed hand in hand. There are genuine disagreements among both leaders and scholars about the very nature of democratic values as well as about the role of particular leaders in particular circumstances. The essays that follow will address these disagreements through the analysis of particular leaders and the more general context of democratic values into which they fit.

This volume, therefore, represents an attempt to combine political history, political analysis, and political theory. It is an effort that was, in significant ways, begun in the early and mid-1960s at Oberlin College. Five of the contributors shared political and intellectual experiences at Oberlin then, and they have left an indelible mark on this work. More particularly, many of these essays are indebted to Professor John D. Lewis, whose commitment to democratic values and to the study of politics has inspired many generations of students. In addition, we owe a common debt to the Institute for the Study of Civic Values, of Philadelphia, which provides a continuing center for political analysis and political action dedicated to the development of democratic values. In particular, the Institute's concern with the problems of leadership through its Neighborhood Leadership Academies and its insistence on the importance of political education in America has provided sustenance to us all in the completion of this project.

Finally, I should like to express my personal gratitude for the hard work of each of my contributors, not only for their own essays but for their friendship and the painstaking editorial assistance they have given me. Thanks are due to Anita Neugeboren and Betty Van Aken as well for typing and editorial work, to Ed Artinian for his patience and encouragement, without which none of this would have been possible, and to my wife, Barbara Lewis, whose intellectual and moral support have, as always, kept me going.

P. D. B.

Contents

Part 1

The Science of
Politics and
the Art of Ruling

Chapter One

Political Leadership
A Common Search for the Possible

Ours is an "age of hyperbole,"[1] argues a recent commentator, an age
that moves all too easily from visions of the "heavenly city" to visions of
the "apocalypse." We must, insists another writer, move "beyond hope
and despair,"[2] avoiding the false prophecies of both. Both lament our
tendency to exaggerate and dramatize whatever we experience. Both in-
sist that this tendency leads inevitably to frustration—of citizens and
leaders alike. The cycles of hope and despair of the last fifteen years
surely indicate the good common sense of these and other analyses. Still,
we find ourselves with no easy response to their warnings.

The wild fluctuations of the 1960s—the promises of New Frontiers and
Great Societies, the specter of civil strife and global conflict—were, if
nothing else, exhausting. In this state of exhaustion, it is easy to be cynical
about promises of any sort, but it is also easy to be cynical about
prophecies of doom. Enervated by the spectacle of Watergate, morally
overwhelmed and then humiliated by defeat and withdrawal in Vietnam,
many will find the temptation to escape from public commitment of any
kind all the greater. It may be that a totally private world—one that is
also beyond hope and despair—is what we have most to fear. Alexis de
Tocqueville worried about one such vision of retreat when he spoke of
a democratic despotism "more extensive and more mild [which] would
degrade men without tormenting them."[3] More recently Philip Slater
has spoken of our "pursuit of loneliness"[4] with many of the same concerns. The challenge to modern democratic leadership is to energize
people without creating mania, to make them aware of human limitation
and imperfection without promoting depression and withdrawal.

POLITICAL LEADERSHIP AND POLITICAL THEORY

The modern democratic leader, no less than the classical Greek statesman,
must be a political educator. His task is to identify interests and principles

of common concern and to persuade his constituents of the importance
of these issues. A clear sense of the audience to whom a leader speaks is
crucial. He must understand the issues that can or might move them. He
must speak in a language that addresses these issues in clear and accessible form. He must develop rhetorical skills that will move people to
common support of the issues he has identified. These and other concerns
with the tactics and strategy of leadership were critical to earlier notions
of the leader as political educator and must be to ours.

Still, the task of the classical statesman, as the leader of a free people,
went far beyond such tactics and strategy. The art of persuasion was not
insignificant but its use was severely limited. Rhetoric was an art or a
knack for Plato.[5] As such, he worried that it could be used to subvert as
well as to nourish the fundamentals of a free people. Unless it was used
for proper public purposes, this knack would become an end in itself.
Public language judged solely on its persuasiveness could not guarantee
public virtue. For Plato, the statesman was judged to have been a success
only if he had "made better citizens of those who were worse before." [6]

The statesman's task was to mobilize *just* public action—action in
defense of the "Good [which] is one and the same for individuals and
communities." A citizen was "better" insofar as he recognized the pre-
dominance of that "Good" over partial and private interests and "worse"
insofar as those partial and private interests dominated. It was possible to
teach people to look beyond the short run and apparent desires, to teach
them the close relationship that existed between private and public interests and between individual and collective satisfactions.

Once these possibilities were understood, the potential statesman could
profitably begin to think about tactics and strategy. Such thought had to
be premised upon a discussion of public virtue and the common good.
It would take lengthy discussion in common together, warned Plato, before this point would be reached. Habits of heart and mind that lead
people to obey in a public-spirited fashion would develop, insisted
Aristotle, only if the proper end were kept in mind.[7] This, in turn, was
possible only if careful attention was paid to the nature of political
education—education that would identify and renew the bases of a civic
bond. Such a civic bond depended upon: (1) the emotional and personal
security of citizens, including their sense of moral security, (2) conditions which encourage trust, such as the keeping of pledges, (3) customs
and rituals that are shared and which mark one people off from others,
and (4) common meanings and uses of words, for the ability to communicate is the foundation of community.[8]

The classical statesman never took for granted the existence of the
civic bond. Its preconditions were delicate, fragile, and constantly in
need of support. However much he shared with the people, the leader of

a free people had a separate responsibility. His task was to take the first step even as he introduced and encouraged common interests and shared responsibilities. His special responsibility was to take the lead, so that those free citizens whom he led and educated might themselves some-day be ready to govern.

The modern democratic leader faces a world in which both the nature of persuasion and the nature of public virtue have been drastically al-tered. Caught in an endless stream of new campaign techniques—espe-cially the ever more "sophisticated" use of the media—leaders increasingly forget the special nature of their audience, neglect people's unique con-cerns and feelings, and speak in homogenized tones which make elected officials as close and as distant as Walter Cronkite. In much the same fashion, it becomes all the more difficult to identify common concerns except as they refer to private interests, on the one hand, or the most general and vague principles, on the other. The size and diversity of individual congressional districts—let alone the country itself—make it difficult to define common traditions and feelings. People are encouraged to see a distance between private and public, individual and collective interests. The maintenance of order is justified in terms of private inter-ests. Correspondingly, people are "taught" to obey or disobey in propor-tion to the security of private interests. A far cry, indeed, from Aristotle's concerns for the education of citizens and leaders.

In this context, it is tempting to reject as irrelevant the insights of the classics. (Indeed, Plato and Aristotle, as well as more recent defenders of democratic politics like Jean-Jacques Rousseau and Charles Louis de Montesquieu, would have found the enormous size of our country for-bidding.) It is in part the aim of the following essays to examine the force of this temptation. It would be foolhardy to suggest that theories and analyses designed to explain the workings of free government over two thousand years ago, in small, homogeneous communities, can easily be transported into the urbanized and industrialized mass societies of the twentieth century. It would, however, be equally foolish not to confront the seriousness with which earlier theorists examined the nature of a free people, its citizens, and its leaders. If an educated citizenry is in truth the heart of a free nation, then the modern democratic leader must seek to create an atmosphere in which political education can flourish and where some semblance of civic cohesion can be achieved.

Similarly, the study of political leadership in a modern democratic state must address these broader and more basic issues of political free-dom and civic cohesion. As Alvin Gouldner suggested in *Studies in Leadership*, it is incumbent upon the social scientist studying leadership to (1) adopt the "more gross, conceptual level, continually alert to dif-ferences of group, culture, situation and time . . . required for a social

science oriented to the needs of practice in a dynamic democracy," and
(2) to engage immediately in the encouragement of democratic action,
"whatever imperfect concepts and generalizations are now available or
risk delivery of a fully developed discipline, which, if not dead at birth,
will be born orphaned. Bereft of the democratic culture which conceived it, this social science will be unable to mature." [9]

Unfortunately, analysts of leadership have for the most part ignored
Gouldner's plea.[10] The studies of leadership in this volume attempt to
respond to Gouldner. They reexamine the relationship between political
education and political freedom, with an eye towards interpreting its
meaning for twentieth-century democratic leadership. They seek to
delineate both the limits and the possibilities which modern bureaucratic politics poses for political leadership conceived of as political
education. They hope to avoid the pitfalls of more narrowly conceived
research by reintroducing broader and more fundamental issues of democratic politics to the study of leadership. Finally, these studies explore the
problems of modern democratic leadership with an appreciation of the
inadequacy of our public vocabulary—political rhetoric and political
analysis alike. An adequate response to Gouldner's challenge depends
upon a vocabulary of both analysis and action which is clearly understood and which is sufficiently precise and rich in meaning to permit the
full expression of one's thought.

POLITICAL LANGUAGE AND POLITICAL LEADERSHIP

The poverty and imprecision of contemporary political vocabulary have
rendered the study of political leadership particularly difficult. To be
sure, our public vocabulary is filled with a series of words and phrases
which seem to offer insight into the workings of the political system,
but too often they mask as much as they convey. Many examples could
be cited. Three words are of particular interest here: *consensus, corruption,* and *charisma.* Each of these terms has been significant to both
analyst and leader in the past twenty-five years. Each is familiar to the
citizen. All three share the most general problem of our public vocabulary in their imprecision or, perhaps better, illusory precision. A more
careful look at each will help to introduce the problems at hand. Moreover, each of them serves as a tool of analysis for one or more of the
leadership studies presented here. The problem of *consensus* politics is
an integral part of the study of the leadership roles of George Meany and
Lyndon Johnson. The issue of *corruption* is central to an understanding of
James Michael Curley and John Lindsay, and Peter Drucker. Finally, the
nature of *charismatic* leadership is of implicit and explicit concern for
the studies of Martin Luther King, Jr., Cesar Chavez, and John Kennedy.

Despite the importance of these terms, each of the authors finds these words inadequate for explaining the most crucial aspects of the leadership role in question. A more detailed examination of these three concepts may help us to understand the reasons for their inadequacy and gain added insight into the problems that current political language poses for the understanding of leadership.

Consensus, hiding under the guise of the all-inclusive compromise, demands that we stifle conflict and opposition. Those who proclaim its virtues have often failed to realize the historical and conceptual dilemmas that accompany such pleas for harmony and unity. Michael P. Rogin tells us in *The Intellectuals and McCarthy* [11] that the original American *consensus* was based upon a Lockean vision of rural unity that was "splintered as the country urbanized and industrialized, as it filled with new immigrants and bureaucracies." As new groups emerged, cries for "legitimate conflict within consensus" resurfaced, but the substance of the new consensus became increasingly unclear.

However important the acceptance of diversity and conflicting interests has been to the development of the American polity, these realities have not been "the rallying cry of political debate." In the day-to-day process of winning adherents and discrediting opponents, appeals to the people against "vested interests" or against "outside agitators" are more effective. If the possibility of serious differences of opinion is dismissed, the possibility of an open discussion of political goals is correspondingly diminished. The reality of such differences must remain unexamined when the rhetoric of consensus dominates.

Gossip-column fascination with *corruption* may be understandable; but frequent exposure to the speculations of muckrakers (like exposure to consensus-mongers) produces unintended consequences. It is not merely the cynicism resulting from continual exposure to criticism that democracy has to fear. A far worse problem arises from the perverse effects that such preoccupation produces upon the expectations of the citizen—expectations of their leaders and of themselves as well. To define the public interest as the opposite of *corruption* is to establish a standard of civic virtue which is at once vague and unattainable. Frustration, despair, and withdrawal undermine the foundations of democracy as seriously as George Washington Plunkitt's "dishonest graft." [12]

To be sure, talk of *corruption* is not new to this country. It is at least as old as the eighteenth century,[13] when the issue served as an important basis for the colonists' increasingly anti-British attitudes. However, this earlier concern with corruption did not suffer from the same pitfalls as does contemporary preoccupation with the subject. Colonial pamphleteers and ministers considered cynicism in the face of corruption to be cynical in itself. In their eyes, such an attitude represented an inexcusable abdication of public responsibility. Though fear of corruption was great in earlier eras of American history, it seldom became the standard by which leaders were judged. Positive ideas of public virtue provided the standards of judgment. Our ancestors would have thought the contemporary treatment of the corruption issue to be a sad reversal of classical wisdom that viewed corruption as the absence of public virtue. Our inclination to define public virtue as the absence of corruption would have seemed strange and unwise to them.

The use of the word *charisma* generates a polarized view of politics and political leadership. The "opposite" of the charismatic personality is, after all, the commonplace, routinized bureaucrat. The absence of the former would seem to leave room for nothing but the latter.

Cynicism and doubt about the utility of the word *charisma* notwithstanding, we seem to be stuck with it. *Charisma*, whatever its contemporary meaning, is not so fleeting as the false promises that so often accompany it. We forget the inadequacies of a *charismatic* hero far more quickly than we remember the successes of less attractive leaders. Perhaps human nature, with the assistance of contemporary media, makes this situation inevitable. Still, the dominant part that the media have in creating contemporary heroes is itself symptomatic of a problem. Primary concern for "image" leads to a search for a savior devoid of any conception of salvation itself. In a cruel inversion of Platonic wisdom, political identity is created through identification with the hero. There is no obligation to know oneself or to know one's neighbor. Political action becomes the "action" of the leader; or perhaps better, the adrenalin that flows in response to the leader's image. Such "chemistry" is hardly the stuff of which political bonds are made.

The illusory precision of words like these is only part of the problem they generate. The unstated, but nonetheless exaggerated and extreme vision of politics and political leadership implicit in each is just as significant. Our words betray our public spirit. Our loss of a clear sense of ourselves as part of the public arena has accompanied a loss of a sense of the limitations that both collective action and human nature impose. We have come to expect either too much or too little and have lost our enthusiasm for a common search for the possible.

We would do well to take the words of James MacGregor Burns seriously. In *Roosevelt: The Lion and the Fox,*[14] he urges us to accept the "limitations on even the most creative leadership" and recognize that the leader brings about lasting change, not by intervening sporadically and casually in the stream of events, but only by altering the channels in which the stream of events takes place. Such leadership clearly requires more than the superficial analysis that is reflected in most popular discourse. To accept the "limitations" of which Burns speaks is, after all, to accept the necessity of a thoroughgoing examination of democratic values and the interaction among them.

His is not a plea for new categories, new boxes that describe new traits of new or old leaders. It is, instead, a plea for a return to simplicity, a plea that has not been heeded. What has been lost is indeed a sense of the "possible": What is possible in human terms? What can a leader be expected to do? What can the people do? What is possible in structural terms? What are the constraints of size and complexity? How do they affect leaders and followers?

A plea for simplicity is more than a plea for the revival of a discussion of democratic values—freedom, equality, and political participation. The reintroduction of a sense of the possible can allow the student of leadership a new perspective from which to view what a leader has done and can do. We can recognize again that an analysis of democratic values is central to an understanding of democratic politics. Likewise, a simpler and more frank discussion of human and political possibility can shape the expectations of citizens—expectations of themselves and of their leaders—in a more reasonable fashion. It can help them avoid both pessimistic and optimistic hyperbole and permit discussion of democratic values that is based on something more than negativisms and moralisms. Finally, for the potentially "creative leader," a search for answers to these questions is mandatory. Leadership requires an atmosphere in which citizens are willing to seek guidance, even as they seek opportunities for collective action. For a contemporary democratic leader to inspire such confidence and simultaneously to encourage public action is difficult enough. The task is rendered impossible without an improved common vocabulary through which citizen, leader, and scholar can analyze and judge their common problems.

NOTES

1. Steven R. Graubard, "Democracy and Its Critics" in *Excellence and Leadership in a Democracy*, ed. Steven R. Graubard and Gerald Holton (New York: Columbia University Press, 1962), p. 203.

2. John H. Schaar, "Power and Purity," in *American Review* (New York: Bantam Books, 1974), pp. 152 ff.

3. Alexis de Tocqueville, *Democracy in America*, ed. Phillips Bradley (New York: Vintage Books, 1954), 2:335.

4. Philip Slater, *The Pursuit of Loneliness* (Boston: Beacon Press, 1970).

5. Plato, *Gorgias*, tr. W. D. Woodhead, in *The Collected Dialogues*, ed. H. Cairns and E. Hamilton, Bollingen Series (Princeton, N.J.: Princeton University Press, 1969), p. 245.

6. Ibid., p. 297.

7. Aristotle, *The Politics*, ed. Ernest Barker (New York: Oxford University Press, 1962), p. 319.

8. Cf. P. D. Bathory and W. C. McWilliams, "The Nature of Leadership," Paper delivered at Time/Life Leadership Conference, Washington, D.C., September 1976.

9. Alvin Gouldner, *Studies in Leadership* (New York: Russell & Russell, 1965), p. 11.

10. There have, of course, been exceptions, notably, the work of James MacGregor Burns, especially *Roosevelt: The Lion and the Fox* (New York: Harcourt, Brace, 1956), Conclusion; and the more recent efforts of Glenn Paige, *Political Leadership: Readings for an Emerging Field* (New York: The Free Press, 1972), Introduction.

11. Michael P. Rogin, *The Intellectuals and McCarthy: The Radical Specter* (Cambridge, Mass.: MIT Press, 1967), p. 36.

12. William L. Riordan, *Plunkitt of Tammany Hall* (New York: Dutton, 1963), p. 3.

13. See, for example, Bernard Bailyn, *The Ideological Origins of the American Revolution* (Cambridge, Mass.: Belknap Press, 1973).

14. Burns, *Roosevelt*, p. 481.

Chapter Two

The Science of Politics
and the Art of Ruling
James Madison
and Alexis de Tocqueville

PETER DENNIS BATHORY

The rush of events of the twentieth century encourages us all to look for new syntheses, but it also tempts us to reduce seemingly inaccessible complexity to manageable proportions, to describe our politics in illusorily simple terms. All too often we have deluded ourselves by accepting the "solutions" that have followed on the heels of such "descriptions." To be sure, "solutions" are presented in a number of different forms. The cynic finds the wedding of politics and corruption inevitable, and so he simplifies the difficulties of public questions by retreating from them. The media analyst of the public "market" defines public opinion as the summation of private desires, and thereby simplifies collective/public questions by denying their existence. The social scientist searches for that last piece of the political systemic puzzle that will make our lives explicable and predictable, and simplifies public questions by reducing them to mechanics. Each one of these (and, no doubt, many others) may have discovered a way to cope with rapid change. None, however, offers a way to identify and study common or collective problems, much less a way to search collectively for answers to them. Rapid change demands that we engage in more, not less, of such analysis and action.

Facing the same social, political, and economic reality as their constituents, political leaders are no less fascinated with the discovery of new explanations and new procedures that allow them to cope with the unknown. Unnoticed by their constituents, however, our leaders face a new temptation that compounds the difficulties of our political language and the analysis that accompanies it. If the process of coping with the twentieth century has led many perilously close to the banal, it also threatens

11

to lure many of our leaders to the obscure, to the private language of the "expert," inaccessible to the general public. Thus a public language, imprecise and abstract (with pretensions to precision and concreteness) is wedded to the language of the expert, complex and obscurantist (with pretensions to specificity and technical clarity).

The press of day-to-day private business, whether it be the business of making a living or the business of writing a tax code, dominates naturally, for it is unchallenged. The work of democratic politics, in turn, has become far more difficult than even its most energetic classical critics could have imagined. Democratic citizens blissfully ignore politics until it interferes with specific private desires. Democratic leaders lose the ability to address *political* questions, for the people have forgotten how to listen to them.

The power of our private worlds is, in fact, so strong that we have lost the sense of what public or collective alternatives to them would be like. This is not, of course, to say that patriotism is dead. Flag decals on cars, Kate Smith singing "God Bless America," and that apotheosis of "patriotism," the Bicentennial, are constant reminders of its power and its fury. But is the surge of adrenalin that accompanies Kate Smith's performance directed at the United States of America or at the Philadelphia Flyers? Are the release and excitement of Fourth of July fireworks a symbol of the renewal of republican virtue, or a deafening and blinding moment that permits people to forget their day-to-day *private* existence —the "most important" and most difficult aspects of their lives? Symbols of public-spiritedness abound, but public actions that bespeak a renewal of principle and commitment are hard to find.

There are at least two reasons it would be hard to imagine an alternative to our private worlds. First, to remind people of a time when public virtue and common action were more central to people's lives is to heighten their own sense of inaction, to reemphasize their own political impotence, and to dramatize the chasm that exists between things public and private in their lives. There is, however, a second and more perplexing reason, that of *renewal* itself. What is involved in renewing old commitments? What is at stake in returning to the beginning, in remembering the reason for original being, in rededicating ourselves to the spirit of the Founding? Is it simply a matter of recounting the facts of the creation of our world, whether they be seventeenth- or eighteenth-century facts? Can we combine Bicentennial Minutes with public television and a dash of carefully written history and produce a renewal of public spirit?

These are difficult issues, but they have been made all the more difficult by the symbol manipulators. Lost in the "joy" of parades and picnics are the reality of the pain and difficulty surrounding the birth of the Republic, the responsibilities, commitment, and hard work that accompanied it. A society in which commitment to public virtue and public action is strong can afford the luxury of cathartic celebration. The renewal of commitments that sound foreign to the public ear or are lost to its memory requires stronger stuff.

Remembering only the glories of its past, a people risks far more than the distortion of historical reality. In much the same way that reverie about the simplicity and joy of one's childhood overlooks those resentments, conflicts, and pains that have been formative, the reveries of an entire people often slight that which made it a people—a collective entity—in the first place. Resentment, conflict, and pain must be understood and confronted if an individual is to be free and whole.[1] The same is true of a people. To "forget" that hardship is a part of the past of one's people is to forget the shared commitment and dedication of one's forefathers in meeting that hardship. Forgetting that shared commitment and dedication, we risk losing the ability to confront our own difficulties, let alone those of our children. Our ancestors knew that an honest assessment of the limitations as well as the possibilities of the human creature was a necessary precursor to both political analysis and political action. The framers of our government were certain that to proceed as though the potential of man were unlimited was to risk a "revolution of rising expectations"—the creation of false hopes and the inevitability of despair.

In both the seventeenth and eighteenth centuries, the founders of America faced the agonizing pain of separation—physical and spiritual—from their roots. They confronted internal conflict of massive proportions. Yet, in the midst of all of that, they never forgot that they were creating something for future generations. They were guided by a spirit of necessity, the necessity of common dedication and shared effort that came inevitably with the creation of something new, whether it was a new settlement or a new Republic. Dedication and effort were also the product of principle, of course, but that principle has been strengthened immeasurably by necessity and hardship. The easing of hardship would, they knew, make the necessity of common endeavor less compelling. Adaptation to changing circumstances would be required. None of our founding predecessors thought that it would be easy to sustain founding principles.

The problem was one to be shared by citizens and leaders alike. To sustain principle in the face of challenge to the public order would require prudence and courage of dedicated leaders. To maintain individual commitment to the common good in the midst of peace and prosperity would require temperance and justice of a vigilant citizenry. To combine the two would require a founding capable of more than any prior democracies and republics.

What is that tradition? What are its virtues and its limitations? How are they to be made available to the twentieth century? There is no simple answer. There are, however, questions to be raised anew, for even the questions, in many cases, have been forgotten. The language of public discourse was once more accessible than it is now. The language of political analysis was once more basic than ours has become. A public order that seeks to combine principle and practice, to interweave public and private worlds, must have these vocabularies available to it.

POLITICAL ANALYSIS AND POLITICAL ACTION: TWO VIEWS FROM THE PAST

The task here is not to rehash the history of our Founding. It is to attempt to recapture the spirit of inquiry—the elegance and force of style, the precision and simplicity of argument—characteristic of early American public discourse and debate. Complex questions were discussed, but in language that the public could understand. Many examples could be offered. I have chosen the work of two analysts—James Madison and Alexis de Tocqueville. They are men whose political analyses were systematic and thorough, men who were political scientists, careful empirical observers, pleaders for republican principle, and political actors. They combine (in significantly different ways) the art and science of politics: political action and political analysis. Each had a profound understanding of the language of public discourse and the need for both analyst and leader to be critically self-conscious of that language and of the problems of communication generally. Each recognized the power of history, tradition, and custom in the day-to-day life of the polity. Each saw the need to guard against the esoteric and excessively private, to speak in a language accessible to all, and to instill a set of expectations that promoted political engagement while ensuring political prudence. Their arguments are useful as guides to old and forgotten questions that are increasingly critical to our world.

Their differing points of view, though not all inclusive, cover a wide range of possibilities available to democratic politics and democratic politicians. Their separate views are, to be sure, in part products of their times and, of course, articulated with clear consciousness of the audiences to whom they spoke (in itself an increasingly lost art). At the same time, each man consciously sought to move beyond his time and argued in terms that would force his audience to take a more sweeping view of the problems of democracy.

Both sought to cultivate a stable democratic polity, but both insisted that democratic principles could not and need not be sacrificed in the name of stability. Such a combination of democratic order and democratic values required, in the terms of each writer, a keen sense of the limitations of action. A sense of the boundaries of political action lying between pure principle and pure act could, each felt, permit enthusiastic pursuit of attainable goals. The differing ways in which these boundaries were drawn suggest at least two dramatically different alternatives for the course of democratic politics.

MADISONIAN VIRTUE AND THE SCIENCE OF POLITICS

Madison's goal—and that of his opponents—was to establish "a deliberate sense of the community" that would firmly establish republican principle. Our own search for a combination of republican order and principle has much to learn from the character—the form and the substance—of Madison's argument. He spoke with a clear appreciation of the pressing concerns of his audience in a language that his audience could understand. In the end, it seemed (to Madison) advantageous to impose de facto limitations on the public activity of ordinary citizens, but the necessity of such limitations could—indeed, had to—be addressed openly. It would not do to disguise such designs in the language of future governors, in a private vocabulary suited to their understanding only.[2] On the contrary, the Federalist could address, in accessible and understandable language, dominant social and religious feelings even as they introduced a "new science of politics." A common recognition of human corruptibility sent Federalist and Anti-Federalist and their supporters in search of ways to shore up public virtue. Madison, no less than his opponents, knew that such a search had to be open and public. Even an argument cautiously limiting citizen participation had to be made in public and justified in terms of commonly held beliefs.

The critical point of disagreement between Madison and his opponents had little to do with disputes over the nature of political man, whether optimistic or pessimistic. The real debate centered on how best to contain excessive passion while maximizing liberty. For Madison and the Federalists the answer lay in the direction of a *national* leadership, "who could be expected to identify their own ambitions and sense of honor with an enlarged conception of the public good."[3] Madison's contention, in Federalist Letter Number 10, that it was "an advantage of large republics over small ones that more independent men would be found to represent the larger interests of the people"[4] was at the heart of a serious debate. His opponents argued that such national direction of government, far from promoting the national interest and controlling the passions of the multitude, would work against the representation of the common people, leaving them little chance to unite "unless in support of a popular but unprincipled demagogue."[5]

In an age in which cries for "community control" are heard, even as the necessity for more careful central planning becomes apparent, the issues raised in a debate of this kind are increasingly vital. We seem unable to bring either the substantive depth or the rhetorical clarity of these arguments to our own discussions. Madison's efforts to explicate assumptions about human nature and the nature of democratic institutions underlying even the most complex political dilemmas of his day are notable. As we examine his efforts to foster "the permanent and aggregate interests of the community," [6] the whole *national* community, and as we examine the problems inherent in the creation of such a "community" for our world as well as for his, we would do well to recognize and remember the depth and care of his analysis.

Previous "theoretic politicians," [7] said Madison, had ignored the advantages of large republics. Deluded by an exaggerated faith in political equality, the political theorists had failed to understand the difficulties inherent in maintaining an *ordered* liberty. "Reducing mankind to a perfect equality in their political rights," Madison argued, would not create a citizenry "perfectly equalized and assimilated in their possessions, their opinions and their passions." [8] Madison had no illusions about such perfection. On the contrary, he feared that the inevitability of certain inequalities of possession, opinion, and passion could well lead to disorder, threatening the security of the ordinary citizen and thereby rendering his liberty as well as his *political* equality empty.

What was required was the application—by founders and elected representatives alike—of a new science of politics that could order and balance interests while maintaining diversity in a passionless, deliberate spirit through a commonly applied set of rules. It would, he felt, be unwise to encourage direct participation. In fact, such participation flew in the face of republican principles. These principles were not, for Madison, merely expedient. Madison felt deeply about and highly valued them. His "pleasure and pride" at being a republican combined a fascination with the efficacy of the Republic and a belief in its righteousness. The new science would, he hoped, speak to both issues. The question that remains is one of application and the kind of leader Madison envisioned directing his Republic of ordered liberty.

The same sense of human limitation that made him suspicious of mass participation led him to an explicit recognition that "enlightened statesmen will not always be at the helm." [9] It was necessary, then, to think carefully about the recruitment of "appropriate" leaders, even as popular participation was being limited. Again, the new science of politics would solve his dilemma. Again, order and principle could be combined. In fact, the very scheme that had helped him to confront the dangers of mass participation would allow him to solve potential crises of leadership. The advantages of large republics were manifold! In the same way that a broadened focus of public debate would defuse local passion, it would, he felt, produce "representatives whose enlightened views and virtuous sentiments render them superior to local prejudices and to schemes of injustice." [10] His leaders were to become (due to the deliberate and reasonable spirit of representative assemblies, as well as to the nature of their diverse constituencies) "experts" on questions of the "public good" in ways that the "people themselves" could not. Removed from the passion generated by doting on "temporary or partial considerations," a national leadership stratum would emerge to guarantee the formal structures of representative institutions and the values of republicanism. It would in significant ways combine the "art of politics" with the "science of government."

In sum, Madison's argument is simple and direct. First, one must understand human nature, its weaknesses and its potential. That is, one must recognize that the temptation to turn to private, sometimes selfish, needs will always exist. Next, it was necessary to understand that the complex responsibilities of governance confronted the limitations of human nature to create an atmosphere of potential crisis that was continuous. The threat of public disaffection would be constant, Madison thought, if the public was taught to think that it ought to know about and constantly be a part of complicated decision-making processes. Finally, with these realities clearly in mind, an examination of the virtues of a republican form of government—the values it supports and the happiness that it can produce—became less forbidding. The solution was fairly simple: Attack public distrust by limiting public vision. Sustain republican principles by rendering them publicly distant.

After having proceeded in this manner, it was clear to Madison, as it should be to us, that there is a continuing tension between human nature and civic virtue. The world of politics, and so the world of the political leader, was thus a world of constant judgment between republican principle and human limitation. The questions posed by his investigation are the classic questions of the ancients: Can virtue be taught? If so, to what extent? By whom? To whom? Madison offers us one set of answers to these questions.

TOCQUEVILLEAN VIRTUE AND THE ART OF RULING

Alexis de Tocqueville shared many of Madison's concerns. Two are particularly interesting. First, Tocqueville too, was suspicious of an overly simple plea for political equality, and he was also aware of the threat to civil order that inequality posed as well. Moreover, he perceived the inadequacies of an egalitarian ideology for confronting some of democracy's most basic dilemmas.[11] He thought, however, that the human drive toward equality was far more basic and powerful than Madison had described it. Madison had noted that political equality would not *guarantee* equalized possessions, opinions, and passions, and that inequalities of this sort might create frustration, disaffection, and disorder. Tocqueville worried that passions and opinions would become more subdued as egalitarianism grew increasingly dominant, and that, while inequality would still exist, it would grow less apparent.[12] His central concern was with the hidden dangers lurking behind delusory egalitarian rhetoric—passivity and loss of public trust.

For Tocqueville, as for Madison, inequality was dangerous—almost always the source of "the great convulsions of the world." Both knew that the one must be eliminated if the other were to be avoided. Tocqueville, however, saw a relationship between passion, equality, and democratic principle that Madison either missed or ignored as irrelevant. Tocqueville worried that what we have described as "Madisonian virtue" masked more fundamental problems. Madison had opted for a politics mild and dependent in spirit, moderate and rational in action. Tocqueville described two conflicting but equally bothersome possibilities in such a politics. On the one hand, a people increasingly dependent on a centralized, removed government could begin to lose sight of inequalities and injustices that, festering and unrelieved, might explode. On the other hand, he worried that even were inequities met, the limitations of such a meek and mild "virtue" would be great.

Americans, argued Tocqueville, "by no means display revolutionary passions," but their absence was not a sign of political health. He worried that

> When social conditions are equal, every man is apt to live apart, centered in himself and forgetful of the public. If the rules of democratic nations were either to neglect to correct this fatal tendency or to encourage it from a notion that it weans men from political passions and thus wards off revolutions, they might eventually produce the evil they seek to avoid.[13]

Moreover, he continued, such a revolution would not be easily detected. It would be the result of long festering inequalities. Disturbances of the kind he prophesied would be the worst imaginable; they would be "revolutions unawares."[14] Unprepared for and not clearly understood, the revolutions that Tocqueville feared would be far more destructive than carefully planned disruptions. Though he does not directly address Madison, the irony that Tocqueville must see in Madison's argument is clear. Its privatization of political perceptions could well produce the very disorder that it sought to avoid.

Tocqueville's attack on the Madisonian positions was unyielding. He agreed, of course, that civil strife threatened the stability of the polity, but argued that the absence of an active sense of public virtue might destroy the very republican foundation that Madison had sought to guarantee. Tocqueville understood the need to direct and control passion, but he knew well that passion had first to be recognized—its limits and its potential. He feared a world that had lost a sense of the possibility of strong commitment to anything no less than disorderly passion.

Amid the ruins which surround me shall I dare to say that revolutions are not what I most fear for coming generations: If men continue to shut themselves more closely within the narrow circle of domestic interests and to live on that kind of excitement, it is to be apprehended that they may ultimately become inaccessible to those great and powerful public emotions which perturb nations, but which develop and recruit them. When property becomes so fluctuating and love of property so restless and so ardent, I cannot but fear that men may arrive at such a state as to regard every new theory as a peril, every innovation as an irksome toil, every social improvement as a stepping-stone to revolution, and so refuse to move altogether for fear of being moved too far. I dread, and I confess it, lest they should at last so entirely give way to a cowardly love of present enjoyment as to lose sight of the interests of their future selves and those of their descendants and prefer to glide along the easy current of life rather than to make, when it is necessary, a strong and sudden effort to a higher purpose.[15]

There were for Tocqueville two alternatives for a democratic age that systematically neglected the study of democratic values and the sustenance of public virtue: (1) regular civil disorder for which no one would be adequately prepared, or (2) a power that

is absolute, minute, regular, provident, and mild. It would be like the authority of a parent if, like that authority, its object was to prepare men for manhood; but it seeks, on the contrary, to keep them in perpetual childhood: and it is well content that the people should rejoice, provided they think of nothing but rejoicing. For their happiness, such a government willingly labors, but it chooses to be the sole agent and the only arbiter of happiness; it provides for their security, foresees and supplies their necessities, facilitates their pleasures, manages their principal concerns, directs their industry, regulates the descent of property, and subdivides their inheritances: what remains, but to spare them all the care of thinking and all

the trouble of living? Thus, it every day renders the exercise of the
free agency of man less useful and less frequent.[16]

"Such a power," Tocqueville continued, "does not destroy, but it pre-
vents existence; it does not tyrannize, but it compresses, enervates, ex-
tinguishes and stupifies a people, till each nation is reduced to nothing
better than a flock of timid and industrious animals, of which government is the shepherd." [17]

Though Tocqueville's fears of the potential "tyranny of the majority" [18] were at least as great as those of Madison, he still hoped for the
continuation of that spark of passionate commitment that might keep an
active sense of public virtue alive. Tocqueville was forced to confront
more directly and perhaps more realistically than had Madison's direct
opponents the existence of a vast Republic and the threat that size alone
could pose for civic values and citizen participation. He was, to be sure,
not excessively optimistic about the future of the institutions of which he
had grown so fond. What he seemed to dread most, however, was that
democratic citizens could be led astray *"unawares."* A flourish of political
rhetoric could, he feared, too easily lead democratic people—leaders and
citizens alike—to lose sight of, and then forget entirely, the nature of
their tenuous hold on political liberty.

Tocqueville's analysis follows the same pattern as that of Madison.
He, too, is pessimistic about the future of a politics dominated by the
masses. He, too, recognizes the inevitability of the tension between the
values and principles of democratic politics on the one hand and the human actors who must create and sustain that politics on the other. His
definition of political principle and his sense of human potential are,
however, significantly different from those of Madison. He hoped for a
freedom that could

> deliver the members of a community from that isolation which is the
> lot of the individual left to his own devices and, compelling them to
> get in touch with each other, promote an active sense of fellowship.
> In a community of free citizens, every man is daily reminded of the
> need of meeting his fellow men, of hearing what they have to say,
> of exchanging ideas, and of coming to an agreement as to the con-
> duct of their common interests. Freedom alone is capable of lifting
> men's minds above mere mammon worship and the petty personal
> worries which crop up in the course of everyday life, and of making
> them aware at every moment that they belong each and all to a
> vaster entity, above and around them—their native land. It alone
> replaces at critical moments their natural love of material welfare
> by a loftier, more virile ideal; offers other objectives than that of

getting rich; and sheds a light enabling all to see and appraise men's vices and their virtues as they truly are.[19]

Though not overly optimistic about the future of such a freedom, he was not, he insisted, ready to feel such contempt for those around him as to deny its possibility. "I trust," he asked, "that I be allowed to wait a little longer before being converted to such a view." [20]

Tocqueville hoped that the "science of politics" might serve the "art of ruling," that political science would be able to facilitate common discussion that could regenerate or sustain a common search for shared solutions to shared dilemmas. However cautious and even pessimistic he was, he seemed to hold to his concluding thought in *Democracy in America* that, "for democratic nations to be virtuous and prosperous, they require but to will it." He believed, to be sure, that "Providence has not created mankind entirely independent or entirely free." This recognition need not, however, lead to fatalism. On the contrary, for though

it is true that around every man a fatal circle is traced beyond which he cannot pass, . . . within the wide verge of that circle he is powerful and free; as it is with man, so with communities. The nations of our time cannot prevent the conditions of men from becoming equal, but it depends upon themselves whether the principle of equality is to lead them to servitude or freedom, to knowledge or barbarism, to prosperity or wretchedness.[21]

The "art of associating together must grow and improve," he insisted, "in the same ratio in which equality of conditions is increased," if in fact men were to remain civilized. The task of the Tocquevillean leader, recognizing the limits of his own efforts as well as those of his constituents, is clearly to promote that art. The task of the political scientist is to help make that task easier through investigations that clarify the possibilities inherent in human beings and the government structures that they create. Tocqueville did not assert that either could teach public virtue, but he felt that both could encourage circumstances in which citizens acting in common together might catch a glimpse of it.

TWO MODELS OF DEMOCRATIC LEADERSHIP

What we learn most significantly from both Tocqueville and Madison is that fundamental questions of democratic political theory can be raised in direct and simple terms. Indeed, both insisted that such basic questions about the origin of the American Republic—its principles and its governmental structure—must be addressed by all. Leaders, citizens, and

students alike must be aware of the nature of the origins or founding of
the Republic and of the relationship between that founding and the on-
going character of the government there created. Both understood
that this would be very difficult, that the press of everyday issues and
decisions would often turn public attention away from more basic historical and philosophical problems. Each argued that, in order to ensure
a system in which political liberty and public energy might be combined with political efficiency and social stability, attention to basic
principles must be continuous. Their goals were similar. They sought to
enhance liberty short of overzealous and unrestrained action, and to
maintain order consistent with the dictates of democratic principle.
Their *means* for pursuing these goals were, however, quite different. Two
broadly different models of democratic political leadership emerge
from these differences.

FOUNDATIONS AND RENEWALS

Their concerns with origins and foundations led Madison and Tocqueville to perceive and discuss three aspects of democratic political
leadership: the founding experience itself, the task of maintaining order
in an already-established polity, and, finally, the duty, in times of crisis,
of reminding citizens and leaders alike of the principles upon which political society is founded. First it was crucial to understand the nature of
the Founding.

Madison's argument was simple here; he felt that one could "ascer-
tain the real character of the government" only if one examined "the
foundation on which it is to be established." [22] Thus, even though fond
of pointing to the "improvement made by America on the ancient mode
of preparing and establishing regular plans of government," the latter
being the work of "some individual citizen of pre-eminent wisdom and
approved integrity," [23] he was by no means denying the significance of
the Founding nor its relevance to political leadership. On the contrary, he
argued that the "intervention of a deliberative body of citizens" shaped
the Founding and had created a "deliberate sense of community" that
would become the guidepost for all future leaders.

Tocqueville, likewise fascinated with origins, opened the second chapter of *Democracy in America* with the following:

> A man has come into the world; his early years are spent without
> notice in the pleasures and activities of childhood. As he grows up,
> the world receives him when his manhood begins, and he enters into
> contact with his fellows. He is then studied for the first time. . . .
> This, if I am not mistaken, is a great error. We must begin

higher up; we must watch the infant in his mother's arms. . . . The entire man is, so to speak, to be seen in the cradle of the child.

The growth of nations presents something analogous to this; they all bear some marks of their origin. The circumstances that accompanied their birth and contributed to their development affected the whole term of their being.[24]

It is in its seventeenth century origins that Tocqueville finds the cornerstone of the world that he examined in the 1830s.

Only after understanding these origins could the analyst proceed to an examination of the "operations of those powers" of government, of the "extent of them," [25] of the dilemma of those who followed the founders—the "stabilizing leaders," whose task was the "maintenance of orderly conduct." [26] It would not have occurred to either Madison or Tocqueville that there was not a significant relationship between the everyday tasks of maintaining a polity and its origins. In order to study or to act in the world of democratic politics, it was, each felt, necessary to understand its constituent parts—philosophical and historical, as well as mechanical or structural. This is not to say that, for either, all people were continually aware of these critical elements. Each insisted, however, that in time of crisis a way to reintroduce those elements must be found. It might be that, in ordinary times, the relationship between the history and the principles of the founding and the conduct of politics remained unperceived. Each felt, however, that if the very bonds that unite the polity were threatened, then recourse to such "memories" became mandatory. If such resource was not had, both the stability and the liberty of the republic would be threatened.

In our own frantic rush to explain every detail of our present and to predict the shape of the future, we have surely forgotten much of the past. It is, however, less detail and chronology of the past that is lost than its dynamic existence into our present and our future. It is that dynamic potential that led Madison and Tocqueville, albeit in different ways and with different results, to impress upon their audiences the need to study origins and founders as a necessary complement to an understanding of and action in the present. Our loss of a sense of this linkage of past and present will make the dynamic potential of our past seem remote, indeed, but both Tocqueville and Madison knew that such losses were likely. It was for this reason that each explored a third aspect of democratic leadership—the leader as political educator, the leader as teacher. Both anticipated situations that would necessitate a renewal of public commitment in the face of crisis. In addition to the problems of founding a polity and of maintaining it in an orderly fashion, it would from time to time be necessary—the third aspect of leadership—to revive that sense of shared purpose and commitment around which the nation had been formed. Circumstances would change as the nation expanded. Memories would become more vague as the founding moment grew more distant. To maintain both liberty and stability, the leader as political educator would have to refresh public memories and restore public commitment.

MADISONIAN STATECRAFT AND CIVIC EDUCATION

Madison found the origins of the American Republic unique. He had studied the foundings of many others and indicated that

> It is not a little remarkable that in every case reported by ancient history, in which government has been established with deliberation and consent, the task of framing it has not been committed to an assembly of men, but has been performed by some individual citizen of pre-eminent wisdom and approved integrity.[27]

Madison's Republic was, on the contrary, "a government wholly popular" that was "founded, at the same time, wholly on that principle." [28] What was critical for Madison in this argument was less the hint at popular participation than the avoiding of reliance upon a single person. He was, of course, anxious to shun any hint of monarchy, but his discussion is revealing of far more than defensive strategy. "History informs us," he allowed, "of the difficulties with which celebrated reformers [like Solon and Lycurgus] had to contend, as well as the expedients which they were obliged to employ to carry their reforms into effect." Forced to bend to popular "prejudices" and to employ "the authority of super- stition," they had lost from the beginning that spirit of deliberation and moderation of which Madison was so proud.[29] In the American Re- public, even as the dominance of a single man had been checked, a *national* spirit of *rational* discussion had been established.

The framers of the Constitution were able to subdue "fears of discord and disunion" in part, Madison insisted, because of the collective nature of their assembly.[30] They had established a government that could avoid classical pitfalls, for "the people"—through their representatives—were a part of the Founding. Henceforth leaders would not have to rely on prejudice, passion, or superstition to woo the people. They had sim- ply to recall and reestablish that spirit of national and rational discussion that had dominated the Founding and had been built into the govern- mental structures it had produced.

There were dangers, to be sure, but even these were confronted and addressed in a fashion that asserted the dominance of pragmatic, rational discussion. The document was not and could not be perfect. Madison, Hamilton, and the others were in clear agreement here. "The imperfections of the human faculties," "the complexity of objects" under study, and the limitations of language to express complex ideas in clear and straightforward terms [31] pushed Madison to "perceive the necessity of moderating . . . expectations" [32] in this founding endeavor.

The problem was simple for Madison:

> The novelty of the undertaking immediately strikes us. It has been shown in the course of these papers, that the existing Confederation is founded on principles which are fallacious; that we must consequently change this first foundation, and with it the superstructure resting upon it. It has been shown that the other confederacies which could be consulted as precedents have been vitiated by the same erroneous principles, and can therefore furnish no other light than that of beacons, which give warning of the course to be shunned, without pointing out that which ought to be pursued. The most that the convention could do in such a situation was to avoid the errors suggested by the past experience of other countries, as well as of our own; and to provide a convenient mode of rectifying their own errors, as future experience may unfold them.[33]

A fundamentally new order was to be created and this could occur, Madison felt, only in an atmosphere dominated by rational self-examination. Fortunately, he argued, the people of America "have not suffered a blind veneration for antiquity, for custom, or for names, to overrule the suggestions of their own good sense, the knowledge of their own situation, and the lessons of their own experience." [34] It was this "good sense," in fact, that defined what he had earlier called the "manly spirit" of the American people.

Pragmatic and reasonable, the people of America had only to be guaranteed an arena in which to demonstrate their skills and fulfill their experience. That arena was, for Madison, exemplified by the Constitutional Convention. "Stability and energy in government" had been and were to be guaranteed by a select group of individuals who "enjoyed . . . an exemption from the pestilential influence of party animosities" and, as a consequence, might with more regularity sacrifice "private opinions and partial interests to the public good." [35] Theirs was a national constituency, and so they could direct their attention to national problems. The day-to-day functions of government would be established and protected by such a group of leaders.

The example that had been set was unique. Madison hoped that the innovative spirit of the founders had been so deeply established that it would continue to dominate. He was not, however, naive about the possibility of its being lost. He knew that civic education would be necessary if both the stability and the energy, the order and the liberty, of the new government were to be maintained. Certain abuses could be checked mechanically. Vested power could be checked by restraining power vested elsewhere so that the ambition of one might counteract the ambition of another.[36] The careful separation of legislative, executive, and judicial power Madison defended for this purpose. Madison also insisted, however, that the spirit of the general public was critical to the success of the Republic. It was that spirit that, in the end, guaranteed its stability and its energy.

Madison's own writing was a form of civic education directed at a people incapable of moving "spontaneously and universally . . . in concert toward their object." [37] He was sure that such education would be needed in the future and thought that it too had been guaranteed by the new Constitution. In the principle of bicameralism, Madison had found the mechanism for civic education. Now, however, Madison had to rely not only on institutional safeguards, but on the wisdom of the people's elected representatives—both their prudence and their energetic support of liberty. The Senate and the House of Representatives were designed as checks on one another, he argued, but also as twin supporters of the spirit of the Republic. The Senate provided an "institution that will blend stability with liberty." The Senators had the responsibility of offering counsel and guidance to the people in times of crisis:

> To a people as little blinded by prejudice or corrupted by flattery as those whom I address, I shall not scruple to add that such an institution may sometimes be necessary as a defense to the people against their own temporary errors and delusions. As the *cool and deliberate sense of the community* ought, in all governments, and actually will, in all free governments, ultimately prevail over the views of its rulers; so there are particular moments in public affairs when the people, stimulated by some irregular passion, or some illicit advantage, or misled by the artful misrepresentation of interested men, may call for measures which they themselves will afterwards be the most ready to lament and condemn. In these critical moments, how salutary will be the interference of some *temperate and respectable body of citizens* in order to check the misguided career and to suspend the blow meditated by the people against themselves, until reason, justice, and truth can regain their authority over the public mind? [38]

The House of Representatives, meanwhile, assured the maintenance of principle in the face of these prudential "interventions." The Representatives closest to the people will keep alive that "communion of interests and sympathy of sentiments of which few governments have furnished examples." [39] Liberty will be guaranteed through that connection between "the rulers and the people" that unites duty and gratitude with interest and ambition.[40]

In each case, through the Senate and the House of Representatives, there is a return to the spirit of the origin of the Republic. In each case the example and the counsel of elected representatives, Madison hoped, would return the people to a sense of ordered liberty. It was a system that, at one and the same time, was conscious of the need for careful national planning "adequate to the national happiness" [41] and aware of the need to represent faithfully the interests and sentiments of a diverse people. Madison knew that the new system would produce some "masters of the public business" [42] who, within the bounds of principle, could lead the Republic to rational and deliberate decision-making. His genius is to have recognized that these new experts in the public good could function only so long as a spirit of ordered liberty was dominant. They then would have to be aware, as he was, of the need for civic education. In a strikingly Madisonian style, Walter Lippmann translated this understanding onto a twentieth-century framework:

The private citizen, beset by partisan appeals for the loan of his Public Opinion, will soon see, perhaps, that these appeals are not a compliment to his intelligence, but an imposition on his good nature and an insult to his sense of evidence. As his civic education takes account of the complexity of his environment, he will concern himself about the equity and sanity of procedure, and even this he will in most cases expect his elected representative to watch for him. He will refuse himself to accept the burden of these decisions, and will turn down his thumbs in most cases on those who, in their hurry to win, rush from the conference table with the first dope for the reporters.

Only by insisting that problems shall not come up to him until they have passed through a procedure, can the busy citizen of a modern state hope to deal with them in a form that is intelligible. For issues, as they are stated by a partisan, almost always consist of an intricate series of facts, as he has observed them, surrounded by a large fatty mass of stereotyped phrases charged with his emotion. According to the fashion of the day, he will emerge from the conference room insisting that what he wants is some soul-filling idea like Justice, Welfare, Americanism, Socialism. On such issues,

> the citizen outside can sometimes be provoked to fear or admiration,
> but to judgment never. Before he can do anything with the argument
> the fat has to be boiled out of it.[43]

Madison's legislators were charged not only with boiling out the "fat,"
but also with the task of civic education, which alerts the citizenry to
the dangers of partisanship and the virtues of rational judgment.

The delicate balance of Madisonian politics depends on a unity of analysis and action—a unity that Lippmann and many others fear has been
lost. In the process of guaranteeing the "safety and happiness" of the
people in routine decision-making, the leader must understand the need
to sustain the spirit of the Republic. Constant attention to opinion was
required—as that opinion became more diverse, analysis became more
complicated, but political action consistent with both the control of passion (local and parochial) and the support of principle (national and
rational) demanded it. The sustenance of founding principles and the
fulfillment of the founders' promises required political leaders who could
assure the day-to-day stability of the Republic and political educators
who could interpret and focus the decisions that were made in that
effort.

MADISONIAN LEADERSHIP: A SUMMARY

For Madison, the founding experience was notable for its calm and
reason. The Constitutional Convention had been a rational assembly. It
focused, he insisted, on a present and new creation without passion and
irrationality, without the sentiment bred of untoward attachment to antiquity, tradition, or custom.

In its form, the convention provided a model that future assemblies
and future generations would seek to imitate. In its substance, the Constitution offered encouragement to those future generations, providing
them public settings appropriate to the conduct of a "cool and deliberate" Republic.

Future leaders, encouraged to sustain these origins in a spirit of "ordered liberty," would be checked in their ambitions by the mechanics of
constitutional balance. Future citizens, guided by the decisions of their
assembled representatives, would be checked in their passion by the
prudence and moderation of legislative bodies.

Finally, a national leadership, unfettered by ambition and passion,
might, he hoped, plan for the future with an eye to the common good
that naturally avoided the private and the parochial.

TOCQUEVILLEAN STATECRAFT: POLITICAL EDUCATION AND THE ART OF ASSOCIATION

No less than Madison, Tocqueville feared the consequences of a too-sanguine reliance on popular partication. He did, however, find in democracy certain advantages that Madison had not examined. Tocqueville asserted,

> Democracy does not give the people the most skillful government, but it produces what the ablest governments are frequently unable to create, namely, an all-pervading and restless activity, a super-abundant force, and an energy which is inseparable from it and which may, however unfavorable circumstances may be, produce wonders.[44]

Unlike Madison, Tocqueville looked to localities and to the associational life within them as the source of this force and energy in America. Interests that Madison had labeled partial and private, Tocqueville found to be serving the common good and reinforcing commitment to public activity.

Tocqueville took issue with the Madisonian position on two different fronts. In the first place, he found private life and selfish interest supportive of the common good. Of democratic men's private concerns, he said:

> Certain men happen to have a common interest in some concern; either a commercial undertaking is to be managed, or some speculation in manufactures to be tried: they meet, they combine, and thus, by degrees, they become familiar with the principle of association. . . . Civil associations, therefore, facilitate political association. . . . When a people, then, have any knowledge of public life, the notion of associations and the wish to coalesce present themselves every day to the minds of the whole community; whatever natural repugnance may restrain men from acting in concert, they will always be ready to combine for the sake of a party.[45]

In the second place, he found Madison's concerns with political association or faction unsupported by the facts as he had observed them, and found an attack on them ironic. "Freedom of association in political matters is not so dangerous to public tranquility as is supposed, and . . . after having agitated society for some time, it may strengthen the state in the end." [46] In fact, Tocqueville insisted, far from provoking disunity,

associational activity and political involvement created a sense of national pride and commitment that grew from a merger of private and
public interests. Because of his personal involvement,

> The citizen looks upon the fortune of the public as his own, and he
> labors for the good of the state, not merely from a sense of pride or
> duty, but from what I venture to term cupidity.

> It is unnecessary to study the institutions and the history of the
> Americans in order to know the truth of this remark, for their man-
> ners render it sufficiently evident. As the American participates in
> all that is done in his country, he thinks himself obliged to defend
> whatever may be censured in it; for it is not only his country that
> is then attacked, it is himself.[47]

As private interest and public virtue combine, as affairs of business reinforce public activities and vice versa, political order was combined
with political principle.

Tocqueville, again like Madison, looked to the origins of America to
discover the source of its strength and principle. He found that source,
however, neither in the structure of its Constitution nor in the political
creation of the eighteenth century. Writing to a friend some twenty years
after he had visited America, he made clear the basis of the differences
between him and Madison:

> You are familiar enough with my ideas to know that I accord insti-
> tutions only a secondary influence over the destiny of men. I would
> to God that I believed more in the omnipotence of institutions! I
> would have higher hopes for our future, because chance could on
> some given day then allow us to fall upon the precious piece of
> paper that would contain the prescription for all our ills, or upon the
> man who knows the prescription. But, alas, it is not so, and I am
> thoroughly convinced that political societies are not what their laws
> make them, but what they are prepared in advance to be by the feel-
> ings, the beliefs, the ideas, the habits of heart and mind of the men
> who compose them, and what native disposition and education
> made these men to be.[48]

What had intrigued Tocqueville about America was the character of
its people—"the habits of heart and mind" that had dominated from its
origin. That character, he insisted, "was the result of two distinct elements, . . . which the Americans have succeeded in incorporating to

some extent one with the other and combining admirably. I allude to the *spirit of religion* and the *spirit of liberty*." [49] The philosophic expression of this spiritual merger was, for Tocqueville, expressed by John Winthrop in the following passage:

"The . . . kind of liberty I call civil or federal; it may also be termed moral, in reference to the covenant between God and man, in the moral law, and the politic covenants and constitutions, among men themselves. This liberty is the proper end and object of authority, and cannot subsist without it; and it is a liberty to that only which is good, just, and honest. This liberty you are to stand for, with the hazard not only of your goods, but of your lives, if need be. Whatsoever crosseth this, is not authority, but a distemper thereof." [50]

An image of liberty far more demanding than Madison's restrained advocacy of republican principle and a vision of leadership far more passionate than Madison's moderate "deliberative body of citizens" thus emerge from Tocqueville's study of origins.

Winthrop's speech was, however, more than a philosophical statement. It was offered to the entire community, and, as such, was an early signal for Tocqueville of the unity of principle and practice, political philosophy and political action, that had been the heart of the Founding. There "the boldest theories of the human mind were reduced to practice by a community so humble that not a statesman condescended to attend to it; and a system of legislation without a precedent was produced offhand by the natural originality of men's imaginations." [51] The focus of this practice, the physical and spiritual center of political originality, was the township:

The independence of the township was the nucleus round which the local interests, passions, rights, and duties collected and clung. It gave scope to the activity of a real political life, thoroughly democratic and republican. The colonies still recognized the supremacy of the mother country; monarchy was still the law of the state; but the republic was already established in every township. [52]

Republican principle in the township, he noted, turned quickly to practice—to the creation of stable and just political institutions.

In studying the laws that were promulgated at this early era of the American republics, it is impossible not to be struck by the legislator's knowledge of government and of advanced theories. The ideas there formed of the duties of society towards its members are evidently much loftier and more comprehensive than those of European legislators. . . . In the states of New England, from the first, the condition of the poor was provided for; strict measures were taken for the maintenance of roads, and surveyors were appointed to attend them; records were established in every town in which the results of public deliberations . . . were entered; . . . The law enters into a thousand various details to anticipate and satisfy a crowd of social wants that are even now very inadequately felt in France.[53]

The political freedom that produced these innovations was supported by the moral certainty of religious belief. Standards of judgment, firm and well known, were uncontested. Political practice, uncertain and controversial, was always debated. Uncertainty and controversy could be tolerated, even encouraged, once limits to politics had been established.[54] Knowing, on the one hand, that man's institutions were no more perfect than man himself, but, on the other, that man's duty to himself was to exercise his capacities and test his limits, these founding communities had made a lasting imprint on the American character and the politics that resulted from it. Future leaders would have to take the power of this experience seriously. To the extent that they neglected it, Tocqueville feared, they risked destruction of both the order and the principle, the stability and the justice that had been created there.

Tocqueville knew, of course, that such decay was possible. He saw in the people a love for security that might, over time, weaken their commitment to freedom.[55] He saw in their institutions a movement toward centralization that would make people more distant from, and so less committed to, public life.[56] He saw in their language a tendency toward ambiguity that threatened to make public action more difficult by making it harder for citizens to understand one another.[57] His experience in France had taught him that, "It is not a small undertaking to reunite fellow citizens who have lived . . . as strangers or enemies and to teach them to conduct their affairs in common. . . ."[58] For the Americans, the best remedy was then to prevent such a situation from arising, or at least to forestall the separation.

It had been the genius of the American founders, he argued, to suppose

that a general representation of the whole nation would suffice to ward off . . . disorder, they also thought that it would be well to infuse political life into each portion of the territory in order to multiply to an infinite extent opportunities of acting in concert for all the members of the community and to make them constantly feel their mutual dependence.[59]

It was "local freedom" that had led "a great number of citizens to value the affection of their neighbors and of their kindred" and that perpetually brought them together and forced them to help one another, "in spite of the propensities that sever them." [60] The answer to the problem of sustaining principle and order was simple—sustain local freedom. The problem was, he asserted, that "individual liberties and local liberties will ever be the work of art; centralization will be the natural government." [61]

It was then the task of democratic leaders to protect and encourage political freedom, to remember that "nothing but the love and the habit of freedom can maintain an advantageous contest with the love and habit of physical well-being. I can," he said, "conceive nothing better prepared for subjection, than a democratic people without free institutions." [62] The charge to the modern leader was to raise public attention and motivate public action.

> Leaders of modern society would be wrong to seek to lull the community by a state of too uniform and too peaceful happiness, [in fact] it is well to expose it from time to time to matters of difficulty and danger in order to raise ambition and to give it a field of action. [63]

There were, of course, established institutions that could aid such leaders. The myriad of public and private associations [64]—American public education, [65] the jury system, [66] and respect for the law itself [67]—each separately and all together promoted public commitment and public activity. Still, the task of teaching people "how to exercise political rights" [68] was never, he knew, an easy one. Yet, there were times when it would be required. In fact,

> If in the midst . . . of general disruption, you do not succeed in connecting the notion of right with that of private interest, which is the only immutable point in the human heart, what means will you have of governing the world except by fear? When I am told that the laws are weak and the people are turbulent, that passions are excited and the authority of virtue is paralyzed, and therefore no measures must be taken to increase the rights of the democracy, I reply that for these very reasons some measure of this kind ought to be taken. [69]

Without such teaching, the rule of fear followed by the destruction of old customs and beliefs was inevitable. The image Tocqueville painted of such a world is distressingly understandable. In such a time, he argued,

The country then assumes a dim and dubious shape in the eyes of the citizens; they no longer behold it in the soil which they inhabit, for that soil is to them an inanimate clod; nor in the usages of their forefathers, which they have learned to regard as a debasing yoke; nor in religion, for of that they doubt; nor in the laws, which do not originate in their own authority; nor in the legislator, whom they fear and despise. The country is lost to their senses; they can discover it neither under its own nor under borrowed features, and they retire into a narrow unenlightened selfishness. They are emancipated from prejudice without having acknowledged the empire of reason; they have neither the instinctive patriotism of a monarchy nor the reflecting patriotism of a republic; but they have stopped between the two in the midst of confusion and distress.[70]

Tocqueville hoped that proper warnings to "leaders of the modern society" could forestall such circumstances of confusion and distress. He knew that there were all too few leaders available to do the necessary educating, but he insisted that all, political actors and analysts alike, had the responsibility to encourage it.

CONCLUSION

Fascinated with American social and political institutions of the 1830s, Tocqueville found the source of their vitality and power in the origins of the people. It was the character and spirit of the seventeenth-century Founding, he thought, that had generated the moral strength and judgment still alive in the nineteenth. The moral strength and judgment of America's founding generation had permitted and supported truly free choice and clearheaded public action.

The "habits of heart and mind" of the American people, not their institutions, had made their political society what it was. That society could be maintained only if those habits continued to rule. Democratic man could cope positively with change, but, Tocqueville worried, he preferred not to.

Given these realities of history and of human nature, "leaders of modern societies" had always to make certain that their followers were schooled and reschooled in the arts of association, for association was "the mother of all action," and public action was in turn the basis of a healthy democratic society.

The primary duty of political leaders and political educators was the maintenance of free institutions. It was a duty that combined a responsibility to constituents with self-interest, for "only the interplay of free institutions can fully teach statesmen . . . how to judge what goes on in the mind of the masses and to foresee what will come of it." [71] The excellence of leadership depended upon mutuality and reciprocity, on a common understanding of basically shared language and principle, even in the midst of debate over specific policies.

In the end, Tocqueville hoped that modern leaders, aided by the public activity of democratic citizens, might confront the enervating, even debilitating, tendencies resulting from the centralization of power and the loss of local freedom.

NOTES

1. See, for example, Erik H. Erikson, "Identity and Uprootedness in Our Time," in *Insight and Responsibility* (New York: Norton, 1964).
2. See chapter 1. My aim is to discuss Madison's concern for political leadership. Madison's primary focus on the structure and mechanics of government should not, of course, be forgotten. There is, however, within that focus a strong interest in the problems of leadership, local and state, as well as national.
3. John D. Lewis, *Anti-Federalist versus Federalist* (Scranton, Pa.: Chandler, 1967), p. 37.
4. Ibid., p. 50.
5. Ibid., p. 22.
6. Ibid., p. 36.
7. James Madison, Number 10, in Alexander Hamilton, James Madison, John Jay, *The Federalist Papers* (New York: Mentor, 1961), p. 81.
8. Ibid., p. 82.
9. Ibid., p. 80.
10. See ibid., Number 10, pp. 83–84.
11. Alexis de Tocqueville, *Democracy in America*, ed. Phillips Bradley (New York: Vintage Books, 1954), 2:310 ff.
12. Ibid., pp. 334 ff.
13. Ibid., p. 270.
14. Ibid., p. 271.
15. Ibid., p. 277.
16. Ibid., pp. 336–37.
17. Ibid., p. 337.
18. Compare Madison's concerns in Number 10, Hamilton, Madison, and Jay, *Federalist Papers*, with those of Tocqueville, *Democracy in America*, 1:269 ff.
19. Alexis de Tocqueville, *The Old Régime and the French Revolution* (Garden City, N.Y.: Doubleday, 1955), p. xiv.

20. Ibid., p. xv.
21. Tocqueville, *Democracy in America,* 2:352.
22. Hamilton, Madison, and Jay, *Federalist Papers,* Number 39, p. 243.
23. Ibid., Number 38, p. 231.
24. Tocqueville, *Democracy in America,* 1:27–28.
25. Hamilton, Madison, and Jay, *Federalist Papers,* Number 39, p. 243.
26. Tocqueville, *Democracy in America,* 1:39.
27. Hamilton, Madison, and Jay, *Federalist Papers,* Number 38, p. 231.
28. Ibid., Number 14, p. 100.
29. Ibid., Number 38, p. 233.
30. Ibid.
31. Ibid., Number 37, p. 229.
32. Ibid., p. 228.
33. Ibid., p. 226.
34. Ibid., Number 14, p. 104.
35. Ibid., Number 37, p. 231.
36. Lewis, *Anti-Federalist versus Federalist,* p. 43.
37. Hamilton, Madison, and Jay, *Federalist Papers,* Number 40, p. 253.
38. Ibid., Number 63, p. 384. Emphasis mine.
39. Ibid., Number 57, p. 352.
40. Ibid., p. 353.
41. Ibid., Number 40, p. 249.
42. Ibid., Number 53, p. 335.
43. Walter Lippmann, *Public Opinion* (New York: The Free Press, 1965), p. 252.
44. Tocqueville, *Democracy in America,* 1:261.
45. Ibid., 2:123.
46. Ibid., p. 126.
47. Ibid., 1:253.
48. Richard Herr, *Tocqueville and the Old Régime* (Princeton, N.J.: Princeton University Press, 1962), pp. 35–36.
49. Tocqueville, *Democracy in America,* 1:45.
50. Ibid., p. 44.
51. Ibid.
52. Ibid., p. 42.
53. Ibid.
54. Ibid., p. 46.
55. Ibid., 2:99 f.
56. Ibid., pp. 310 ff.
57. Ibid., p. 71.
58. Herr, *Tocqueville and the Old Régime,* p. 53; see also, p. 61.
59. Tocqueville, *Democracy in America,* 2:110.
60. Ibid., p. 111.

61. Ibid., p. 313.
62. Ibid., p. 301.
63. Ibid., p. 261.
64. Ibid., vol. 1, chap. 12, pp. 198–206.
65. Ibid., pp. 43, 330.
66. Ibid., p. 295.
67. Ibid., p. 256.
68. Ibid., p. 255.
69. Ibid., p. 255.
70. Ibid., p. 252.
71. Herr, *Tocqueville and the Old Régime*, p. 57.

Chapter Three

Leadership in
the Twentieth Century
Private Language and Public Power

PETER DENNIS BATHORY

American industrialization rapidly transformed the worlds of Madison and Tocqueville. Sociologist Reinhard Bendix notes that, "from 1880 to 1910 the United States underwent the most rapid economic expansion of any industrialized country for a comparable period of time." [1] The aura of excitement and possibility that accompanied rapid change blinded many to the threat it posed to public order. There was, Bendix continues, a "widespread awareness of unlimited possibilities" and a growing belief that "success and riches were . . . signs of progress . . . and the reward of those who had proved themselves in the struggle for survival." Under the circumstances, new mandates were created for both leaders and citizens. Madison's rational political leader faced private interests and personalities of great new scope and power not anticipated by the "new science of politics," with its checks and balances and its mechanical rationality. Tocqueville's public order collapsed as people felt increasingly distant from the forces, public and private, that controlled their lives. In a sense, their worlds had been turned upside down. Men and ideas accountable neither to the institutions of Madison's world nor to the local political associations of Tocqueville's challenged the dominance of politics and politicians.

The events of the last decade of the nineteenth century reshaped the tasks of leadership in America. Large-scale private institutions seemed to require larger-scale public institutions to keep them in check. New skills were required to direct these institutions and new kinds of leaders emerged to help meet the imperatives of what has been called "the age of organization." [2] Leadership in America was increasingly defined by managerial and administrative necessity. A successful leader was one who achieved managerial and administrative goals efficiently. Too often, however, the definition of these goals was ambiguous or left imprecise. What were the goals of these new institutions? Who was to establish the ends toward which American society should work?

These questions of goals and purposes remain unresolved in critical ways. Both Madison and Tocqueville took the question of national goals very seriously. Their insight can be of great help to twentieth-century leaders. The great crises of the last quarter of the twentieth century— energy, the environment, employment, natural resources, health care— cry out for national planning. Such planning will require the "cool and deliberate" spirit of rationality and the careful attention to the "public interest" urged by Madison. At the same time, however, the atomization of American society (which Tocqueville foresaw) has made it more diffi- cult for citizens to identify the problems that we share. Isolated from one another and separated from our leaders, we are loath to grant po- tential planners the authority to plan for the future in new and creative ways. Thus, we also must heed Tocqueville's warning that a centralized government [3] and *democratic* national planning would require attention to political art and political association as well as to managerial science. We cannot ignore Tocqueville's advice without sacrificing the public trust—indeed, a public dedicated to the definition of shared goals and purposes—upon which democratic planning depends. What is striking about American society in the twentieth century, however, is that this "debate" between Madison and Tocqueville has taken place outside governmental institutions and very often apart from traditional political activities—in corporate boardrooms, trade union meetings, and the like. When goals were not clearly established by elected political leaders, new leaders arose to establish them. "Cool and deliberate" planning has more often than not been the result of decisions made by private leaders acting on the basis of private interest. Likewise the "art of association" has been nurtured by leaders of interest groups who were able to gain a trusted following by appealing to the shared concerns of a particular segment of the public. Sheldon Wolin summarizes the difficulty in the following discussion of post–World War II social scientific research:

> No longer do legislatures, prime ministers, courts and political parties occupy the spotlight of attention in the way they did fifty years ago. Now it is the "politics" of corporations, trade unions, and even uni- versities that is being scrutinized. This preoccupation suggests that the political has been transferred to another plane, to one that formerly was designated "private" but which now is believed to have overshadowed the old political system. We seem to be in an era where the individual seeks his political satisfactions outside the

traditional area of politics. This points to the possibility that what is significant in our time is the *diffusion of the political*.[4]

The "diffusion of the political" in America was forecast by the disorder of post–Civil War politics and by the development of a new American ideology distinct from, if not in opposition to, previously dominant political ideas. Calls for civil service reform and a return to civility followed widespread scandal in President Ulysses Grant's administration. "It looks at this distance," wrote one Republican senator at the time, "as though the Republican party were going to the dogs. . . . Like all parties that have an undisturbed power for a long time, it has become corrupt, and I believe that it is today the [most] corrupt and debauched party that ever existed."[5]

A simple attack on corruption was not, however, enough. As Geoffrey Blodgett points out, the "Gentle Reformers" of this period—the Mugwumps—failed utterly.[6] Outraged by urban corruption and frightened by the "blind enthusiasm" of Western farmers, these Boston gentlemen had helped to engineer the defeat of James G. Blaine in 1884. Then, however, having helped elect Grover Cleveland, the Mugwumps refused patronage and so refused a public forum through which they might have expounded their "goals." In fact, argued Blodgett, their "ordinance of self-denial" suggests more than a tactical or strategic flaw in their efforts at leadership. "Neither their legal conscience nor their party's commitments," he observes, "allowed them to formulate a notion of the general public interests above the clash of individual rights and private interests which obsessed them."[7] They chose to remain distant from the new social forces that were redefining America in the Gilded Age, and were in the end conquered by them. America was increasingly in need of a political renewal that enunciated positive standards of public conduct and commitment. In the absence of these standards, the "diffusion of the political" became inevitable.

LEADERSHIP IN THE GILDED AGE

Business leaders moved quickly to fill this political vacuum. They insisted that the pursuit of wealth through private initiative should become the new national goal. To be sure, their strident and powerful voices addressed the "business of the country," but for them the business of the country was not politics. They challenged both the style and the substance of American public discourse. The gentlemanly *consensus* yearned for in Boston gave way to the militancy of the "captains of industry," a militancy that grew naturally out of their struggle for existence. As the *American Journal of Sociology* pointed out in 1896:

It would be strange if the "captain of industry" did not sometimes manifest a militant spirit, for he has risen from the ranks largely because he was a better fighter than most of us. Competitive commercial life is not a flowery bed of ease, but a battlefield where the "struggle for existence" is defining the industrially "fittest to survive." In this country the great prizes are not found in Congress, in literature, in law, in medicine, but in industry. The successful man is praised and honored for his success. The social rewards of business prosperity, in power, in praise and luxury, are so great as to entice men of the greatest intellectual faculties. . . . The very perils of the situation have a fascination for adventurous and inventive spirits. In this fierce, though voiceless, contest, a peculiar type of manhood is developed, characterized by vitality, energy, concentration, skill in combining numerous forces for an end, and great foresight into the consequences of social events.[8]

The lack of gentility displayed by these financial corsairs was mirrored in the militant response they aroused among the losers of this financial contest. The Populist movement, drawing its strength from the rural backwaters of the West and South, mounted a challenge to the new corporate hegemony. In the words of the Kansas Populist, W. A. Harris:

How shall individual rights and freedom be preserved, in spite of the enormous capital and the monopolization of every field of industry? How shall our legislatures be freed from the influence which control and affect from one end of the country to the other every form of legislation? We cannot go back to the old ways, and the trusts themselves, by teaching the possibility of organization, are also pointing clearly to the only possible remedy. The power which is concentrated in the hands of a few people can only be met and defeated by concentrating and utilizing the power of all of the people. . . . In order to do all of these things essential to the general welfare, it is necessary to take it out of the grasp of the powers that have no thought for the welfare of the people.[9]

Thus, the breakdown of common, public values gave way to a major battle over what the new national goals would be. Its specific terms and the arena in which it was to be fought were yet to be determined.

POPULISM

Early business leaders seemed to call for a national scramble for the "acres of diamonds" around them. Populism's "grassroots, evangelical protestant mentality," [10] by contrast, sprang from the soil, recombining the "spirit of liberty" with the "spirit of religion" in a Tocquevillean democratic renaissance. Faced with new, unknown, and distant forces, its early leaders knew that the people needed fundamental reeducation —*political* reeducation. If they were to contend with those powers—both public and private—that sought to wrest sovereignty from them, they would have to relearn the basic lessons of economic and political self-government.

This attempt to reassert democratic participatory norms, in the "centralizing, culturally complacent nation of the Gilded Age," [11] is critical for our understanding of leadership in the twentieth century. In its confrontation with large-scale corporate organization, Populism developed new notions of political and economic organization, new styles of politics, and a new language of public discourse. The strategies of leadership it presented and the substantive goals it pursued offer us an historical bridge to the goals and strategies of earlier leaders and hint at both the possibilities and limitations of comparable leadership in the present.

Lawrence Goodwyn argues,

> Populism is the story of how a large number of people, through a gradual process of self-education that grew out of their cooperative efforts, developed a new interpretation of their society and new political institutions to give expression to these interpretations. Their new ideas grew out of their new self-respect.[12]

It was at base, he continues, a "cooperative crusade."

> The agrarian revolt cannot be understood outside the framework of the cooperative crusade that was its source. Amidst a national political system in which the mass constituencies of both major parties were fashioned out of the sectional loyalties of the Civil War, the cooperative movement became the recruiting vehicle through which huge numbers of farmers of the South and West were brought into an interest-group institution geared to a new kind of internal "political education." [13]

Group by group, neighborhood by neighborhood, this "cooperative crusade" attempted to restore the fundamental components of self-government. "Populism was, at bottom, a movement of ordinary Americans to gain control over their own lives and futures, a massive democratic effort to gain that most central component of human freedom —dignity." [14] After dignity had been restored, self-government would prosper. Only then, they thought, could the "populistic sense of public life" be reborn. A sense of "public life as shared experience of people" [15] was necessary, they felt, to any constructive economic and political action. Populism's early leaders knew that their followers "shared" a great deal. They were the common victims of "retailers, wholesalers, railroads, commission houses and bankers." [16] That sense of common victimhood had first to be highlighted and specifically defined. It had next to be translated into positive, collective action against the victimizers. This was the task of Populist political education.

The responsibility of the leader/organizer was to tap sentiments already powerfully felt and to redirect them. "The reality of their organizational feat," argues Goodwyn, "rested in the substance of the daily lives of millions of farmers." [17] The appeal of their leaders "emanated not so much from their rhetorical skill as it did from the grim realities in the lives of those who heard [their] lectures." [18] They created "a new political language for an industrial society," based on the belief "that government had fallen disastrously behind the sweeping changes of industrial society, leaving the mass of people as helpless victims of outmoded rules." [19]

They understood what the Mugwumps could not. It would not be sufficient merely to point out the indignities of the ruling order. Cries of moral outrage would not by themselves redress imbalance. Blind fury could too easily ignore the problems of day-to-day survival that plagued the farmer. New forms of local economic and political organization were required to cope with these problems—new forms that had to be developed even as the massive power of national corporate wealth was being defined. Buying and selling cooperatives were created to cope with everyday problems of subsistence. Then, and only then, could local groups turn to political organization.

It would be a mistake, argued one Populist leader, to plunge into politics with no clear sense of what political action was for. Existing "political machines," he worried, could too easily absorb their movement without confronting its most pressing concerns. An alternative to such self-defeating absorption was, however, possible. "There is a way," argued the same leader, "to take part in politics without having it [politics] in the order [the Farmer's Alliance]. Call each neighborhood together and organize anti-monopoly leagues . . . and nominate candidates for office." [20] First, having defined the end of political action, the farmers could pursue that action with a sense of individuality and self-respect that would allow them to "emancipate themselves from the grasp of political tricksters without pulling down the only organization they have for their mutual benefit." [21] The intensity of public life had diminished. The Populist leader sought to restore it with a full understanding of the subtlety and difficulty of his task.

Post–Civil War politics had combined with the private power of the Gilded Age to produce an inversion of Tocquevillean norms. In the 1830s, Tocqueville had marveled at the union of private and public interests in America.[22] The former seemed continuously to be in the service of the latter. If there was a union of private and public interests in the 1880s and 1890s, then surely the emphasis had changed. "Public" interests had increasingly become redefined by private interests. The Populist sought to redress the balance, knowing that civil and political associations could unite in the service of the public good only when the interests of the common man were seriously debated in a public forum. Insofar as those interests were ignored by powerful leaders—both public and private—their most pressing concerns remained unaddressed. Early Populist attempts to reintroduce the importance of "private" issues—the family farm, neighborhood organization, religious belief, and the dignity and self-respect of individual citizens—were all directed at creating a new public forum and a new public debate. The fundamentals of Tocquevillean politics were rediscovered and reintroduced.

The success of American politics, Tocqueville argued, depended upon the fact that "everyone, in his own sphere, takes an active part in the government of society." In this setting, he continued, people

are accustomed to regard . . . prosperity as the fruit of their own exertions. The citizen looks upon the fortune of the public as his own, and he labors for the good of the state, not merely from a sense of pride or duty, but from what I shall venture to term cupidity.[23]

The success of Populist political education depended upon the creation of a similar set of circumstances. On many fronts, in the Southeast and the Midwest, it did, in fact, succeed. In the end, however, it failed and we have as much to learn from its failure as from its success.

The failure of Populism was the result of its inability to sustain the debate it had initiated. The limitations of its leadership were implicit in the very fabric of its success. Unable to forge a working coalition with other "victims" of industrialization (especially the urban laborer) or to coordinate successfully the aspirations and interests of its own followers, the Populist movement was driven to fusion with the Democratic Party and to the campaign of 1896. William Jennings Bryan continued the evangelical style of early local leaders. However, the national arena into which he was thrust and the central issue of his campaign were both at odds with the substantive message of his local predecessors. Pleas for inflationary monetary policy turned to debate over a distant and abstract symbol—the free coinage of silver. Cries for a renewed "public life" and collective action in response to immediate economic and political depri-

vation faded with the collapse of the "cooperative crusade" and compromise with the leadership of the national Democratic Party. The warnings of an early leader were ignored. His predictions proved to be both
clear and accurate. He argued that

> To degrade the Alliance to a political machine will subvert its pur-
> poses, ruin the order, and fail to accomplish any thing in politics.
> It will only divide the order into factions, one against the other, and
> all outsiders against the order.[24]

Populism had failed, on its own terms, before William Jennings
Bryan's loss in 1896 to William McKinley. As it lost touch with the con-
crete grievances of specific groups of people, its original mission disappeared. Internal political education gave way to national proselytiz-
ing, and the vitality of the neighborhood got lost in the shuffle. Once
again, the pressing concerns of day-to-day living were subordinated to a
national politics whose rhetoric depended upon general issues more
easily framed by the whim of "political tricksters." That "union of private
with public interests" sought by earlier Populist political educators did
not survive.

The failure of the Populists was perhaps inevitable. Goodwyn argues
persuasively that

> The irony of what befell the agrarian radicals was that they would
> have failed even if they had made no tactical errors of any kind,
> for their creed centered on concepts of political organization and
> uses of democratic governments that—even though still in a formative
> stage—were already too advanced to be accepted by the centraliz-
> ing, culturally complacent nation of the Gilded Age.[25]

Despite their failure, their paramount political objective, that of trans-
lating grass-roots organization into a nationally viable force, must remain
of central concern to us, if we are to explore the possibilities of revitaliz-
ing political democracy in the modern context. Goodwyn states the issue with vigor and eloquence:

> That more mature concepts can conceivably be attained within the
> less provincial but even more centralized environment of modern
> America remains the open question that describes the range of po-
> litical possibility in our own time. Presumably, the quest for an
> answer begins with an attempt to understand the failure of this
> society's sole previous attempt to bring democratic structural reform
> to a triumphant industrial system. Such an inquiry would, of course,

also seek to discover something about the forces and values that prevailed over Populist objections to shape social and political relations in the twentieth century. The issues of Populism were large. They dominate our world.[26]

The attempt to answer Goodwyn's "open question" is the fundamental theme that unites all the essays in this volume. As he suggests, this attempt must probe not only the implications of Populism but also of the forces which triumphed over it. Those forces did not represent a simple return to the undisciplined rapacity of the "robber barons." Rather, new forces were stirring. These were more compatible with the orderly industrial system that was rapidly rendering obsolescent the piratical plundering of post–Civil War enterprise. The campaign of 1896 produced a leader capable of articulating the principles and purposes that underlay these forces, and of giving them a powerful political voice. In the process of orchestrating the Republican victory, Marcus Alonzo Hanna succeeded in reshaping the American political landscape and in transforming the style and substance of American political leadership.

CORPORATE IDEOLOGY AND POLITICAL LEADERSHIP

However formidable the early grass-roots sentiments of the Populists, Hanna sensed that Bryan's national appeal could be challenged. In the first place, Bryan had failed to forge a coalition between the Western farmers and the urban workers who had also been victims of rapid industrialization. Hanna knew that the increasing insecurity of the latter could be exploited. As one commentator notes,

> Under the whiplash of their debts farmers were increasingly concentrating on demands for inflation, particularly for inflation by the alluringly simple method of free silver, and this emphasis was decidedly counter to the urban trend. Most industrial workers were coming to believe that they would be more hurt than helped by any type of inflation, and they generally shared the businessman's feeling that inflation by free silver was something out of a cracked pot.[27]

Hanna exploited these feelings, but he did not stop there. He sensed as well that Bryan's *charisma* could be used against him in two different ways. Bryan's rhetoric could be cited to promote fear of mass passion and mob violence, while, at the same time, his personal style and his ability to communicate with the common man could be adopted and adapted to promote his opponent's point of view. Hanna was a genius in both regards.

Hanna grew up with the new industry but without either the aristocratic pretensions of the Eastern establishment or the preoccupation with "spoils" characteristic of the followers of Ulysses S. Grant and Blaine. His role as political leader and campaign manager was the natural outgrowth of his desire to bring added maturity and respectability to both business and politics.

Hanna was as wary of the "political machine" as were the early Populists. Like the Mugwumps, he was unhappy with the functioning of his party throughout Grant's first term. He, too, would bolt the party. Indeed, in 1873, he helped "elect a reputable Democrat mayor of Cleveland." [28] Unlike the "Gentle Reformers," however, Hanna knew that the future of his party depended upon organization. It would not do to ignore the influx of laborers and immigrants into urban areas like Cleveland. He quickly understood the potential that such groups offered an enterprising political organizer. He realized that the future of his city depended upon political skills that many wealthy Republicans took too lightly. Hanna was laughed at by friends who thought politics a "dirty game" and his attendance at caucuses and meetings a waste of time. Still, Hanna was relentless. Beginning in Ohio, he laid the foundation for a new national political organization.

The election of 1896 climaxed four years of machine-building that would label Hanna as the nation's foremost political engineer. He had begun to build McKinley's future in 1892. Recognizing that an Easterner could not be the foundation of a Republican resurgence, he saw McKinley as an appropriate focus of reorganization. Thomas Beer tells of his having brought an Easterner, Thomas Reed, to Ohio to speak for McKinley's congressional campaign in 1891:

> Cleveland gave the celebrity a good time, but rural Ohio did not like his speeches. The people laughed and applauded and were not won to him. There was nothing Lincolnian about Reed, obese, dapper, and sarcastic. He wasn't too friendly when they came to shake hands after meetings. He was an Eastern product.[29]

Perhaps Western Populism affronted the sensibilities of the middle class, but Eastern Republicans, Hanna insisted, offered no one who could beat Bryan. Hanna had his own machine—he did not need the power of the Eastern establishment. Its moralisms were out of keeping with the fight that was at hand. He was sure that, had the Republicans been allowed to nominate Tom Reed, Bryan would have walked all over them.

So the machine swept against the Democrats in an explosion of pamphlets, blue and gold emblems, placards, and voices. A dynamo whirred inside Mark Hanna's head. This man knew how to carry West Virginia? Send him speakers or money to hire them! Crowds in California liked a lot of music? Give it to them. . . .[30]

Indeed, as Goodwyn notes, "the advertising campaign organized by Mark Hanna in behalf of William McKinley was without parallel in American history. It set a creative standard for the twentieth century." [31] Hanna rallied corporate interests, newspapers, and any other group who shared his fears of Populism. Even the power of the church was invoked in an appeal to the morality of "sound money" and the "nation's honor," to "cultural intuitions about respectability, civic order and the sanctity of commerce. . . ." [32] Hanna had a sense of the dramatic reality of human emotion. He recognized that emotion must be appealed to in order to justify the position of big business, and so win votes for it. Beer again offers an illustration. "Dollar Mark," Cleveland's "Red Boss," had gone out West to prove a point in the country of the Populist:

What about the Trusts? Well what about 'em? All you boys have got foolish reading the papers. You'll see that big combinations of capital end up forcing down prices. Why's one wagon ten dollars cheaper than the next one? That's what comes of these big combinations in the long run. . . . Any old Grangers in the crowd here? Good morning. . . . I ask you this. Didn't the Grangers combine to run prices up, so's your families could live comfortably and didn't you fight the railroads like Sam Hill, to get rates regulated? Of course you did! It was sound business and good practice. Anybody abusin' you people now? All right, combine and smash 'em! Combination is the life of business, and of politics, too! Huh? Yes, I believe in capitalism. Set something up against it as a better system for promoting prosperity and I'll believe in that, when it works. . . . And now listen to Mr. Dolliver a minute. He makes a lot better speech than I do.[33]

Hanna was an unabashed "advocate of pioneer economics." [34] He asked his audience "to vote for the system under which they and their country had become prosperous and which could not be attacked or modified without a certain sacrifice of prosperity." He knew that his audiences understood him. "He must," says Herbert Croly, "have embodied in his own life and purposes some vital American social and economic tradition, which gave his personality, individual as it was, something more than an individual meaning and impulse. . . ." [35] The tradition, argues Croly, was that "of the pioneer."

Still, there was more than the pioneer in Hanna. In much the same way that he had adapted quickly to the challenges of the 1880s and '90s, he adapted yet again to the new crises of the twentieth century.

Appointed to the United States Senate in 1897 and then elected in 1898, Hanna recognized that the complexity of twentieth-century industrialization brought with it new responsibilities for the businessman and the political leader alike. He saw early on that it was necessary to move beyond the sterile tactics and strategy of the Mugwumps. In addition, there was a firm substance to his rhetoric—a belief in capitalism, a mandate to its leaders, and a vision of its future—that went far beyond the electoral hoopla he had devised for McKinley.

Hanna had challenged the Populists on their own rhetorical terms. He defeated not only their candidate but the most significant principles for which they stood. Moreover, he was able to appeal to a national constituency that had evaded the grasp of the most careful Populist leaders. In the midst of his senatorial campaign in 1898, Hanna laid the foundation for what would become a carefully articulated appeal to both urban laborers and businessmen.

> Mr. Bryan said just one thing in his big speech in Chicago last year that strikes me as true. He said that farmers and workingmen are businessmen just as much as any banker or lawyer. Well, that's true. I like that. If you men will study business methods and learn how to look after your interests we won't have to hear any more wishy-washy stuff about how Wall Street's abusin' you. Now Johnny McClean went to the trouble to bring Mr. Bryan all this long way from Nebraska—hope he got a pass on the railroad for him—to tell you that Mark Hanna is a labor crusher and God knows what all. My brothers and I employ six-thousand men. Some of them are here in this crowd. Let any of them come forward and say that he hasn't had a square deal from M.A. Hanna and Company and I'll shut up.[36]

These were people whom he understood. "Oh my friends," he said, "you have to be with these men, among them and a part of them to understand this labor question thoroughly." [37] He felt as though he were a part of them and he sought to persuade others of his perspective. To this end, Mark Hanna began to see himself as more than the representative of business interests. "He proposed," suggests Croly, "to represent the whole country. . . ." [38]

In pursuit of broader cooperative goals Hanna moved toward a policy of conciliation and mediation to bring labor and business together. "I believe," he said, in a speech to the Ohio State Convention in May 1903,

"I believe in organized capital as an auxiliary." Hanna's analysis was a far-reaching and sophisticated one, as Croly suggests:

> The labor program did not engage his support merely because it might sweeten the corporation pill for the palate of the American people. He was one of the first of our public men to understand that the organization of capital necessarily implied some corresponding kind of labor organization. He saw clearly that the large corporations could not survive in case their behavior towards their employees was oppressive, and that they would in the end strengthen themselves by recognizing union labor.[39]

The mechanism through which this cooperation was to be accomplished illustrates yet another facet of Hanna's "political salesmanship." Now, through the National Civic Federation (NCF), Hanna turned his impressive skills toward the education of businessmen and workers in hopes of teaching the "two contending parties how far they could properly go without destroying a fair basis of conciliation and cooperation." [40] Born in 1893 as the Chicago Civic Federation, the NCF, under Hanna's leadership from 1901 to 1904,

> took the lead in educating businessmen to the changing needs in political economy that accompanied the changing nature of America's business system. In its membership the NCF originated the principle of tripartite representation that was later to become a feature of various government boards and agencies. The Federation was organized in three nominal divisions, representing business, labor and an undefined public. Business leaders were of central importance but the leading trade unionists of the day were members, as were professionals . . . political leaders, university presidents, newspaper editors, . . . and leaders of conservative farm organizations.[41]

Once again Hanna's common sense had combined with uncommon political and economic vision to chart a course for the twentieth century. The mix is never more apparent than in his article on "Socialism and Labor Unions":

> Every man is vulnerable in some part and it is a rare thing to find any man proof against methods of kindness and justice. If every man is treated as a *Man*, and an appeal is made to his heart as well as to his reason, it will establish a bond of confidence as a sure foundation to build upon. This is the condition aimed at by the Civic

Federation—absolute confidence on both sides. Many of the ills that
have crept into labor organizations are importations from older
countries and will not live here because they are not fitted to our
conditions. While labor unions may have proved a curse to England,
I believe that they will prove a boon to our own country when a
proper basis of confidence and respect is established. We have,
perhaps, been too busy and too engrossed in our rapid expansion to
look upon the ethical side of this question, and have forgotten that
two factors contributed to the prosperity of our nation—the man who
works with his hands and the man who works with his head—
partners in toil who ought to be partners in the profits of that toil.[42]

In establishing a mutual respect between laborer and employer, Hanna
announced that he aimed to "lay the foundation stone for a structure that
will endure for all time." He, along with men like Andrew Carnegie,
Charles Francis Adams, and others, sought to consolidate the gains they
had made in 1896 and to wrest control from any who would continue the
agitation that had marked those years. "The Federation sought to establish an extra-political system of rationalization, conciliation, and reform
based on cooperation with representatives of organized workers, farmers,
academics and reformers." [43] Through this "extra-political system," they
hoped, new directions for the twentieth century could be charted, cooly
and deliberately, by those who best understood the complexities of that
world.

Hanna had in significant ways begun to fill the political vacuum of
the late nineteenth century. He engineered the defeat of the one serious
political movement of rebellion. He then moved with others to define the
basis of a new American *consensus*—its language and its policies.

Supported by emerging theories of "scientific management," Hanna and
his associates had prepared the way for a new Madisonianism. New qualities of business leadership were regularly discussed—qualities "necessarily different from, and less self-evident than those required for success in
the struggle for survival." [44] *The Management Review*, for example,
characterized a "leader" in these terms: "He should be worthy of his
authority, eager to acquire new information, willing to learn from sub-
ordinates, anxious to see them develop, able to take criticism and
acknowledge mistakes. . . ." [45] In addition, it was pointed out that
such qualities "are not necessarily inherited, but . . . can be developed
by training." [46] All of this was a long way indeed from the militancy of
early business leaders and from the bitterness of 1896 as well.

A spirit of deliberation and rationality had been reintroduced in an
effort to restore collective social responsibility to America's most powerful

social institutions. New checks and balances of "scientific management" were introduced to guard against excessive ambition. To be sure,
these were new "masters of the public business," different from those
described by Madison. Social responsibility was linked to public accountability only insofar as these new "leaders" agreed voluntarily. There was a
self-conscious effort to keep "social questions out of the arena of public
debate." Madisonianism was truly turned upside down. Still, the assumption of these new leaders, that social and economic problems "were essentially technical, that the framework of the political economy need only
be rationalized and that 'experts' applying their skills in the assumed
common interest could best do the job," [47] has strikingly Madisonian
overtones. Representation of the "public good" was now dependent on a
combination of general good will and the good sense of a neutral aris-
tocracy. It was the responsibility of the business leader to recognize that
his own success was tied to the general welfare of the whole nation.

To ensure the success of these new "scientific" standards of the "public
good," Hanna succeeded in redefining the meaning of the "art of
association." As was Madison's, Tocqueville's vision of democratic politics
was to be turned on its head to achieve new purposes. The civic association, which Tocqueville had envisaged as a bulwark against centralization and privatism, was to be transformed into the modern interest group
whose central purpose is to foster just those attitudes of dependency and
self-concern that Tocqueville had hoped most to keep in check.

For all of Tocqueville's brilliance, argues Reinhard Bendix,

> There is a lacuna in [his] approach. He failed to see that men
> would associate together not just for the "vast multitude of lesser
> undertakings" performed every day, but specifically for the purpose
> of enlisting governmental assistance in the advancement of their
> major economic interests. . . . That is to say, he did not connect the
> two tendencies he observed: the growth of voluntary associations and
> the "craving for governmental assistance." [48]

Tocqueville had hoped that voluntary associations would check centralization and provide a source of public commitment. He insisted that
private interests and desires must be directed toward public ends.

The remarkable fact of American associational life, argued Tocqueville, was that civil or private associations were closely related to and in
many cases the direct result of political association. He argued that, "Civil
associations . . . facilitate political associations; but, on the other hand,
political association singularly strengthens and improves associations for
civil purposes." [49] He continued:

I do not say that there can be no civil associations in a country
where political association is prohibited, for men can never live in
society without embarking in some common undertakings: but I
maintain that in such a country civil associations will always be few
in number, feebly planned, unskillfully managed, that they will
never form any vast designs, or that they will fail in the execution
of them.[50]

Though he was more concerned to highlight the relationship between
civil and political associations and to note the advantages of freedom of
political association, Tocqueville surely underestimated the cunning of
men like Hanna. Hanna was able to maintain the relationship between
civil and political associations, but to reverse the relative strength and
priority between them. Civil or private associations were to dominate in
his world. Political associations—political parties—were meant to respond
to the demands of private associations. Subsequent attempts to revive
public leadership and direction of American social and economic policy
cannot be understood apart from this ingenious reversal of public and
private power initiated by Hanna and his cohorts.

PROGRESSIVISM AND BEYOND

"Progressivism arose," argues Michael P. Rogin, "as a response to the
growing power of . . . urban machines, private interests and giant corporations."[51] These new powers threatened to produce confusion and
disorder. A new order was clearly and desperately needed. The nature of
that order was, however, to be hotly debated. Like Hanna, the Progressives knew that "the spontaneous workings of society could no longer
produce harmony. But [they thought] harmony could be created from
above by a neutral, administrative state. The state could eliminate conflict or at least limit it to the petty inessentials of narrow group squab-
bling. . . ."[52] Theirs was a well-conceived attack against the political
associations put together by men like Bryan. The real struggle for control
would, however, not be waged on this front.

It was clear, for the Progressives, that neither the grass-roots political
organizing of the Populists nor Tocqueville's local political associations
could respond adequately to the new powers that Progressivism sought
to check. On the contrary, the specter of civil strife struck fear in the
hearts of men like Theodore Roosevelt. Time and again he spoke of the
evils of mob politics and of the need for discipline and control—law,
order, and justice—in their place.[53] Discipline and order could be restored only through the "neutral state" and its expertise. To involve the

people directly would surely make that neutrality more difficult and reduce the potential force of the expert. There was, to be sure, concern voiced for the victims of industrial society. The plight of those victims could, however, he felt, be ministered to best by "experts."

It appears, then, that we have witnessed the birth of a second "new Madisonianism" in the Progressive response to industrialization. In fact, however, the Progressives succeeded in extending the "new Madisonianism" of the private sector. Mark Hanna and friends had won the day.

The problem, as Michael P. Rogin reveals it, was that the Progressives' preoccupation with "efficiency" had led them to neglect more fundamental questions. "They did not," he argues, "fully comprehend that one had to counterpose more than honest and scientific administration to business power and business values. Their faith in harmony made them innocent of the fact that the norms of efficiency and expertise could not supply values." [54] The political vacuum left by the Mugwumps was yet to be filled by a public force. Into this vacuum came Hanna and others; the pervasive force of their "power and values" remained, to a significant degree, unnoticed by the Progressive reformers.

> The result has been the parceling out of government to organized groups, which do not compete with each other but rather divide pieces of power. What would have surprised and dismayed the Progressives is not the pervasiveness of conflict but rather the current locus of power. They did not see that power would reside in the organized groups far more than in the State.[55]

If, however, they had looked more carefully at Hanna et al., their surprise might have been diminished.

The New Deal offered a more serious challenge to the preeminence of private power. Its active intervention into the spheres of industrial organization, agriculture, and electrical power generation appeared to signal a willingness to restore the preeminence of public over private power. However, the refusal of the Supreme Court to ratify the New Deal's comprehensive attempts to provide public direction combined with the exigencies of wartime preparedness and President Franklin Roosevelt's own ambivalences prevented this restoration of public direction from reaching fruition. Instead, the accomplishments of the New Deal—most notably, social security, the creation of the modern labor movement, and the belated acceptance of Keynesian principles of fiscal management—led to the establishment of a revised form of the Progressives' neutral state.

The New Deal did not guarantee everyone a floor for his or her income. But civic association was no longer solely the preserve of the rich and the powerful. Indeed, the working class's civic association quickly acquired a degree of political leverage that rivaled that of the older business-oriented interest groups. In this new context, the role of the state could remain an essentially passive one: balancing the demands of Big Business against those of Big Labor and checking the excesses of both. It was to exercise real initiative only when general prosperity was endangered. Then its initiative could be limited to a "quick fix" of fiscal stimulus, followed by a hasty retreat to its passive "umpire" function.

Obviously, such a state could do nothing to protect the interest of those—like the migrant worker, the urban poor, and the family farmer—who were not subject to the protection of the large interest groups. This grave defect was, to a significant extent, redressed by the bountiful programs of the Great Society. However, the inability of either the Progressive movement or the New Deal to restore a proper balance between Tocqueville's political associations and Hanna's private ones ensured that this latest and most generous attempt at reform would likewise fail to revive political democracy.

The directions of leadership, public and private, continued to vacillate in the postwar period. New voices spoke on behalf of the private sector and its "new Madisonianism." Leaders and analysts of private interest groups (see part two, chapters four and five) revised and developed the techniques for the "age of organization." Businessmen and labor leaders alike sought to construct a social order that would meet a broad range of social and economic problems while serving the needs of stability and efficiency as well.

At the same time, there were other group leaders who found the confines of the "new Madisonianism" inadequate. Clamor for direct participation and more clearly defined representation reintroduced Tocquevillean principles onto the national scene (see chapters five and six). Prophets and organizers of the unorganized and often the disenfranchised strove to reshape the public interest. They hoped not merely to include those who had been excluded, but to reassert *democratic* principles—political and economic—as the foundation of public action and the goal of public planning.

Finally, elected political leaders, local (see part three, chapters eight and nine) and national (see chapters ten and eleven), had to confront the complex and often contradictory advice and pressure brought by new nongovernmental leaders. The real possibilities of reasserting the public priorities, the necessities of national planning, *and* the requirements of democratic politics lie ultimately in the realm of the judgment and the direction of these elected leaders.

NOTES

1. Reinhard Bendix, *Work & Authority in Industry* (Berkeley: University of California Press, 1974), p. 254.
2. Sheldon S. Wolin, *Politics and Vision: Continuity and Innovation in Western Political Thought* (Boston: Little, Brown, 1960), chap. 10, pp. 352 ff.
3. Alexis de Tocqueville, *Democracy in America*, ed. Phillips Bradley (New York: Vintage Books, 1954), 1:89 ff.
4. Wolin, *Politics and Vision*, p. 353.
5. S. E. Morrison and H. S. Commager, *The Growth of the American Republic* (New York: Oxford University Press, 1962), 12:69.
6. Geoffrey Blodgett, *The Gentle Reformers* (Cambridge, Mass: Harvard University Press, 1966), p. 21.
7. Ibid., p. 140.
8. C. R. Henderson, "Business Men and Social Theorists," *American Journal of Sociology* 1 (1896):385–86, cited in Bendix, *Work & Authority in Industry*, p. 256.
9. Walter Nugent, *The Tolerant Populists* (Chicago: University of Chicago Press, 1963), p. 97.
10. Michael P. Rogin, *The Intellectuals and McCarthy: The Radical Specter* (Cambridge, Mass.: MIT Press, 1967), p. 179.
11. Lawrence Goodwyn, *Democratic Promise: The Populist Movement in America* (New York: Oxford University Press, 1976), p. xxiii.
12. Ibid., p. 88.
13. Ibid., p. 110.
14. Ibid., p. 197.
15. Ibid., p. 209.
16. Ibid., p. 172.
17. Ibid., p. 113.
18. Ibid., p. 117.
19. Ibid., p. 379.
20. Ibid., p. 67.
21. Ibid., p. 69.
22. Tocqueville, *Democracy in America*, 1:252.
23. Ibid., p. 253.
24. Goodwyn, *Democratic Promise*, p. 67.
25. Ibid., p. xxiii.
26. Ibid.
27. Eric Goldman, *Rendezvous with Destiny* (New York: Vintage Books, 1962), pp. 45–46.

28. Thomas Beer, *Hanna* (New York: Alfred A. Knopf, 1929), p. 69.
29. Ibid., p. 131.
30. Ibid., p. 162.
31. Goodwyn, *Democratic Promise*, p. 529.
32. Ibid., p. 521.
33. Beer, *Hanna*, p. 231.
34. Herbert Croly, *Marcus Alonzo Hanna: His Life and Work* (Hamden, Conn.: Archon Books, 1965), p. 472.
35. Ibid., p. 465.
36. Beer, *Hanna*, p. 186.
37. Croly, *Hanna*, p. 408.
38. Ibid., p. 386.
39. Ibid., p. 409.
40. Ibid., p. 406.
41. James Weinstein, *The Corporate Ideal and the Liberal State* (Boston: Beacon Press, 1968), p. 7.
42. Croly, *Hanna*, pp. 406–7.
43. Weinstein, *The Corporate Ideal and the Liberal State*, p. 7.
44. In defense of the principles of scientific management, Frederick W. Taylor made the following speech before the Special House Committee to Investigate the Taylor and Other Systems of Shop Management, noted in Bendix, *Work & Authority in Industry*, pp. 275–76:

> It becomes the duty of those on the management's side to deliberately study the character, the nature and the performance of each workman with a view to finding out his limitations on the one hand, but even more important, his possibilities for development on the other hand; and then, as deliberately and as systematically to train and help and teach this workman, giving him, wherever possible, those opportunities for advancement which will finally enable him to do the highest and most interesting and most profitable class of work for which his natural abilities fit him, and which are open to him in the particular company in which he is employed.

> "And by maximizing the productive efficiency of each worker," continues Bendix, "scientific management would also maximize the earnings of workers and employers. Hence, all conflicts between capital and labor would be resolved by the findings of science."

45. Ibid., p. 301.
46. Ibid.
47. Croly, *Hanna*, pp. 406–7.
48. Bendix, *Work & Authority in Industry*, p. xxxv.
49. Tocqueville, *Democracy in America*, 2:123.

50. Ibid., p. 126.
51. Rogin, *The Intellectuals and McCarthy*, p. 193.
52. Ibid., pp. 193–94.
53. Theodore Roosevelt, *The New Nationalism* (Englewood Cliffs, N.J.: Prentice-Hall, 1961), pp. 150–60.
54. Rogin, *The Intellectuals and McCarthy*, p. 202.
55. Ibid., p. 204.

Part 2

Private Interests
and
Public Values

EDITOR'S INTRODUCTION

Businessman, labor leader, social prophet, or organizer, none can escape the complex and often contradictory realities of the twentieth century. Each of the four leaders examined in part two attained a position of great influence without having been elected to office. Still, none has escaped the impact of the debate between private and public power sketched in chapter three. Similarly, each leader has had to address the reality of centralized social, economic, and political institutions in the twentieth century. They have in turn all recognized the need for those institutions to foster that combination of efficiency and commitment to democratic principle discussed in chapter two.

The businessman is no longer afforded the luxury of privacy, suggests Henry Plotkin in chapter four. Indeed, with changes in the structure of twentieth-century political economy, he argues, "Political leadership could not simply be seen as existing within the public sphere alone, it had clearly extended itself to the private economic sector. . . ." Making reference to the writings of Peter Drucker, Mr. Plotkin examines the nature of the business leader's political responsibilities and the ways in which he must be held accountable for those responsibilities. Mr. Plotkin concludes with the suggestion that "Drucker represents the clearest and most extreme reformulation of the Madisonian ideal." That ideal, translated from the public to the private sector, is based on Drucker's firm opinion that, "Modernity has its own logic, and to ignore that logic is to run the risk of economic and social decay." Only a leadership with roots in that logic, the business executive or the manager, suggests Drucker, can overcome those risks.

George Meany's "vision of leadership is [also] strikingly Madisonian in concept," declares Marc K. Landy. "The success of Meany's leadership strategy is . . . totally dependent upon the organization that has been fashioned to carry it out. He conceives of leadership, not as ministering to the needs of the flock," continues Mr. Landy, "but rather as preserving the strength and integrity of an institution." Nonetheless, Meany has a distinctive personality and style, argues Mr. Landy, that have given him great flexibility. In part, because of this style and personality, Meany has been able to use his office both to strengthen his organization and to educate his membership politically. Once again, the translation of Madisonianism into the twentieth century has been accomplished outside of public office. And, again, we see created a conception of leadership that is an "amalgam of public/private man." Meany's success as a leader, suggests Mr. Landy, is at once a benchmark from which to judge the quality of leadership in America generally and an example of the possibilities of personal leadership in the face of organizational imperatives and institutional limitations.

In startling contrast to these leaders, Martin Luther King, Jr., offers a conception of leadership that speaks to the spirit and feelings of people rather than to the imperatives of large-scale organization. The Reverend Willie Smith eloquently tells the "story" of Dr. King's political successes from the perspective of the black Baptist Church, its preaching tradition, and its powerful ability to speak directly to people's feelings. King knew "secrets" of that tradition, suggests Mr. Smith, that allowed him to become the dominant figure he was in the black movement. Reaching back to the roots of his people, to their culture, and to their local communities, King was able to mobilize a people. "Dr. King humbled himself and he became a leader of people," claims Mr. Smith. "Was Martin a leader?" Mr. Smith asks. "Yes! He was a leader because the people proclaimed him a leader. He was a leader because the movement laid claim to him." In the end, Mr. Smith insists, one had to experience King directly. Mr. Smith recreates the words of one man's experience and concludes with them: "Funny things happen when he talks. I hope Luther King come back. He put into words what I feel and think. He's good! Never heard a man who sounds like I feel."

Ed Schwartz suggests that, much as Martin Luther King, Jr., "exemplified the leader as prophet," Cesar Chavez "shows us the leader as organizer." Chavez' roots are significantly religious, but, argues Mr. Schwartz, Chavez, the organizer, "reflects the tradition of David," whereas King, the prophet, stood in the tradition of Moses. Both roles are significant, but the two must be separated. Unlike the prophet, Mr. Schwartz insists, the "organizer is content only when the people come together within a permanent organization." He concludes by suggesting that, "Chavez knows better than anyone what a Populist faces today —corporate dominance of the economy, bureaucratic dominance of the polity, and materialistic perversion of our basic civic values." His success should "remind us that when Divine inspiration brings a people together, even their slingshots can become powerful weapons."

The Tocquevillean image of America, with its "spirit of religion" and its "spirit of liberty," is surely very much alive in each of these movements. Again, however, it is notable that its messengers are not elected governmental officials. As we will see in part three, the advice of neither Madison nor Tocqueville finds such clear expression in the public sector. It may be that the possibilities of leadership in the private sector have far outstripped those of the public sector. In any case, we have lessons to learn as well as warnings to heed from their successes.

Chapter Four

The Businessman as Leader
Peter Drucker and
the Folklore of Managerialism

I confess I believe democratic society to have much less to fear from boldness than from paltriness of aim. What frightens me most is the danger that, amid all constant trivial preoccupations of private life, ambition may lose both its force and its greatness, that human passions may grow gentler and at the same time baser, with the result that the progress of the body social may become daily quieter and less aspiring.

—Alexis de Tocqueville, *Democracy in America*

HENRY A. PLOTKIN

The rapid increase in the scale of modern business raises significant questions about its role in political leadership. There is little doubt that much of American politics has been shaped by the development and concentration in the corporate sector. Most orthodox business ideologists place great emphasis on the autonomy of the private economic sector with its roots firmly placed in nineteenth-century capitalist theory. The justification for private property, these proponents argue, lay in a constitutional system that protects the right to own and control what one has produced.[1] This Lockean vision of property remains one of the essentials of a liberal dogma which is pervasive in modern-day America. With its commitment to the ultimate rationality of the marketplace, contemporary liberal political economy persists in seeing the intervention of the state as the exception and not the rule.[2] Belief in the efficacy of the marketplace is necessary to a system of thought, which is committed to a natural equilibrium of forces that are beyond the ability of any faction to control. It is the modern equivalent of James Madison's world of shifting coalitions of small factions, none of which are able to coalesce into any permanent elite.

In this vision of the economic world, the business of business is clearly to maximize its profits. The genius of the system, it is asserted, lies in the fact that the net result of individual self-interest is the good of the whole. Among adherents to this notion, the marketplace is hailed as the great alternative to political leadership: a wondrously symmetrical system which leaves to an anonymous natural force the responsibility for economic decisions.[3] Since Hobbesian/Lockean man possesses an aggressive nature which will lead, if unchecked, to political tyranny, the best solution is to subordinate real ego to the discipline of the market.

As political and economic institutions become more complex, the role of the marketplace becomes more tenuous. While twentieth-century liberalism held up the standard of antitrust legislation against monopoly and oligopoly, it soon became apparent that the most powerful corporations were able to supersede the iron law of supply and demand and create their own markets, based on their capacity to manipulate the demand curve. The force of technology has propelled many firms into control of their markets with relative impunity from consumer demands. Technological innovations have made modern business into private planning sectors where a predictable and malleable market is the precondition for sophisticated innovations.[4] A firm will simply not risk great amounts of capital to develop goods which may not sell; the rationality of the consumer must be shaped by the values and techniques of marketing researchers.

Once it becomes apparent that business can transgress the traditional laws of the market and, in fact, make autonomous decisions, a new foundation must be laid which will justify this new role for business. With the publication of *The Modern Corporation and Private Property*, by Adolph A. Berle and Gardiner C. Means,[5] came the realization that traditional liberal political economy was no longer viable in a world of oligopolistic and managerially dominated corporations. If the old public ideology of private profits was no longer valid, it then became necessary to discern a new way of analyzing state/economy relations. One could no longer render unto the Caesar of the limited state what was his and keep the rest; it was now necessary to reconcile great private economic power held by a new managerial class with the power of the state. Political leadership could not simply be seen as existing within the public sphere alone; it had clearly extended itself to the private economic sector and transformed private man pursuing a private morality into an amalgam of public/private man who existed in a curious limbo between the City on the Hill and the accountants' ledger sheet.

Perhaps the most significant exponent of the need for a new role for the managerial elite is Peter F. Drucker. While he has neither headed a large corporation nor been a major stockholder, Drucker has written most extensively about the changed status of the modern business enterprise. Indeed, one author's recent account of the influence of Drucker's writings states with some awe:

> Who else writes on the new politics of the 1970's for *The Public Interest*—perhaps America's most important platform for cerebral and influential analysis of the public scene—and in the same month appears . . . in *Dun's Review?* Who else is so prolific and so pertinent in what he says about such a wide range of topics? [6]

Most of Drucker's work has focused on the role of the corporation in modern society. While Drucker earns his living as a business consultant, his most important role has been as an educator of the corporate manager and the general public. From the publication of his first book, *The End of Economic Man*,[7] Drucker has attempted to teach the American public about the significance of the modern business enterprise. His teachings have been concerned most with discarding the old shibboleths of capitalist economic theory. For Drucker, the world of nineteenth-century laissez faire economics has come to an end and has been replaced by a far more complex structure of relationships. It is the task of the contemporary theorist to describe and explain these new relationships without being limited by intellectual paradigms, the appeal of which is more to sentiment than to the new practicalities.

> We have neither political nor social theory for the society of institutions and its new pluralism. . . . We still use as political and social model what the great thinkers of the late sixteenth and seventeenth centuries, Bodin, Locke, Hume and Harrington, codified: the society which knows no power centers and no autonomous institutions, save only one central government. Reality has outgrown this model—but it is still the only one we have.[8]

While Drucker concedes that a new social theory will take a long time to evolve, he believes it is possible to establish a fresh perspective on the problem. Central to that perspective is the concept of management. What is most known about modern societies is their reliance on large-scale institutions for their functioning. Increased complexity brought about by industrialization, technology, the division of labor, and an increase in sheer social scale have made the role of institutions crucial. At the heart of these modern organizations is the manager. For Drucker, institutions are mere fictions or simply accounting realities; they do not perform; they have no will of their own. The decisions made in these structures are made by individuals who are performing the management functions. Therefore, if one is concerned with the level of efficiency and stability in a social system dominated by large-scale institutions, the most appropriate area to focus on is that of the manager.

It is Drucker's basic thesis that the modern corporation is the central institution of modern American life.[9] The corporation is the most recent and significant example of the progress of western civilization. The corporation not only served as a vehicle for amassing large sums of capital, but its very form altered the social organization of work. As Abram Chayes has pointed out, the modern corporation allowed social wealth to be concentrated in large and stable combinations of fixed assets.[10] In addition, the corporation allowed, through the transfer of stock, wealth to remain liquid, a necessity in a society based on private property. It is also the case that the corporation provided the hierarchy and authority necessary for the rational allocation of resources. And, by shrouding itself in the American tradition of private property rights, it was able to retain its aloofness from both external and internal demands for democratic control.

The importance of the modern corporation and of managerial leadership is related directly to Drucker's understanding of contemporary society. For Drucker civilization is defined by the dominance of economic values.[11] In much the same way as James Madison, Drucker understands human nature as essentially self-interested. Human beings are weak, governed by an imperfect spirit that is conceived in sin. Reflecting an almost Calvinist sensibility to human desires, Drucker believes that it is naive to assume the perfectibility of human beings. What is most crucial for any society is to constrain human passions by channeling them into socially acceptable directions. Therefore, Drucker places great faith, not in the malleability of human nature, but in the potential of institutions which can restrain the darker side of man's nature. The modern corporation is most admirable in its capacity to do just that.

THE SUBLIMATION OF POLITICAL LEADERSHIP

If the modern corporation, based on the maximization of rational economic values, is the twentieth century's most impressive contribution to civilization, the rise of the totalitarian political state, based on the irrational search for demons, was the antithesis of civilized life. The advantage of the Total State was that it seemed to satisfy human needs which were not simply economic. It offered human beings a sense of place, commonality, and purpose that had been absent from Western societies since the breakdown of feudalism. The need to feel part of an organic whole, where one's status is assured by the forces of blood and tradition, is for Drucker as real a human need as that of material satisfaction. The problem with totalitarian states is that they offered the mere symbols of organic solidarity and not its substance.[12]

The role of Drucker's manager and the institution he heads is to provide the leadership necessary to restore a sense of connectedness for a fragmented society. Drucker's thought echoes that of John Dewey in the Progressive Era. Dewey was obsessed with the twin dangers to human freedom of dictatorship and anarchy. In Dewey's terms, the doctrine of laissez faire offered little hope of providing an equitable distribution of resources or of social stability. The alternative of a powerful state's controlling economic affairs was equally unacceptable because of its potential for descending into tyranny.[13] Dewey hoped that society would remain open and flexible enough to allow for intelligent experimentation with various forms of social engagement. Drucker's basic argument is that the modern corporation is the intermediate institution between the extremes of unregulated individualism and advanced collectivism. The exploration of how the heads of these institutions can understand their new social positions and act on that knowledge is at the heart of Drucker's work. "If he [the corporate manager] is to remain—as he should—the manager of an autonomous institution, he must accept the moral responsibility of organization, the responsibility of making individual strengths productive and achieving." [14]

The leadership needed for the realization of this task must come from the increased consciousness on the part of the business executive of his new social role. The manager as public man does not imply that he replaces the politician, but that he recognizes his social function as extending beyond the profitability of his business. Drucker is quite clear about the guidelines for corporate leadership. He wants the manager to be accountable for his performance, along three specific dimensions. The first measure of accountability is how his performance contributes to the interest of the economy in terms of "the market for goods and services, the market for capital and investments and the market for careers and jobs." [15] These are objective criteria, and it is vital that the manager be judged on his capacity to expand all three markets.

The second dimension of accountability is how well the manager contributes to a strong and effective government. The extent to which business performs its task well minimizes the necessity for state intervention. Drucker is skeptical about the capacity of the state to make rational economic decisions.[16] As the government increases in size, as it takes on more and more tasks, it seems to become less effective. Frequently, the state seems paralyzed, caught between the conflicting demands of an insatiable public and its own inability to deliver on the promises it has made. This breeds increased citizen mistrust of government and alienation from the political process. It makes the future of liberal democracy more problematic: more likely to fall prey to the appeal of the demagogue and the tyrant.

Drucker's final standard of accountability is how well the manager's performance conforms to the interests of society. This involves his ability to anticipate the needs of a changing society. Drucker has little patience for those businessmen who constantly criticize governmental regulation. The state intervenes, Drucker argues, when businessmen have failed to do their job. The new manager will have to learn not only to do his traditional job better, but to extend his enterprise into new areas where there is little experience to draw on:

> We will increasingly be responsible for . . . "the quality of life," which is simply a new word for community. We will increasingly have to take responsibility for our social impacts, that is, for the things we do, not because we have the slightest urge to do them, but because we cannot make shoes or build ships . . . without implications outside our four walls.[17]

If business is concerned with maintaining its autonomy, it will have to face its responsibility as a leader in society. The rationality of the allocation of social and economic goods will be the criterion upon which management is judged. Drucker believes that the corporate manager who ignores this task will do so at his own peril and that of the wider society. The alternative to managerial leadership is economic and social disaster: a world of totalitarian political states, which are unable "to perform anything except to wage war and depreciate the currency." [18]

In Drucker's view, leadership in modern society is not the exclusive province of politics. Indeed, political leadership can at best be tentative, because it is ultimately dependent on the capacity of the private business sector to perform its tasks. Drucker is not at all bothered by this fact. He does not believe that political institutions must be at the center of man's loyalty. Nor does he see politics as the primary integrative social force. Drucker views political institutions in their relation to other social institutions as, simply, the chairman of the board, the first among equals.[19]

The Druckerian vision of modern society is one in which all members recognize the centrality of institutions. The era of the individualist has ended; there are no Bonapartist leaders who will redeem the human soul. Indeed, it is the very quest for "the leader" or the "savior" that deflects societies from understanding the task ahead. That task involves the management of complexity. This is not to be accomplished by abstract theories of history or by nostalgic calls for a return to a pastoral past. It will be accomplished by cool, rational decisions about what is humanly possible.

In significant ways Drucker's notion about the role of management is reminiscent of the Madisonian ideal brought to its modern conclusion. While the Federalists were concerned with a science of politics that would avoid the pitfalls of man's lusty and greedy nature, Drucker seeks to construct a science of management that will accomplish the same end. Unlike theorists such as C. Wright Mills, who worried about the potential of institutions for coalescing into a power elite that would rule society,[20] Drucker sees institutions as contributing to diversity. The specific task of managerial leadership is to provide diversity and flexibility. For Drucker is calling for a society based on a plurality of organizations, and it is the leaders of those organizations to whom he speaks. He speaks to them, not as democratically chosen representatives, but as the servants of those institutions. Their purpose and function lie in their fidelity to a broad social definition of their role. Drucker says of modern managers,

> They have to serve their own institutions and the common good. If society is to function, let alone if it is to remain a free society, the men we call managers will remain private in their institutions. No matter who owns them and how, they will maintain autonomy. But they will have to remain "public" in their ethics.[21]

In Drucker's world, there is no call for the "statesman" executive: He does not think it at all desirable for the manager to perform political functions. Indeed, the integrity of a pluralistic society demands that leadership functions be sharply demarcated according to the purposes of the various institutions. In the case of business, its social authority lies, not in its capacity to educate, provide medical care or welfare, but in the fact that the wider society has ceded to it the use of economic resources with the expectation that innovation and progress will occur. For business to attempt to perform functions beyond its own logic would be akin to state bureaucrats attempting to perform brain surgery. Personal freedom can only exist in a world of institutional diversity, where purposes are specified and individuals are held accountable.

What Drucker is plainly arguing for is the maintenance of many centers of social power. These centers of social power are based ideally on their performing specific functions for the society. The specificity of these functions is one of the fundamental tasks of definition that falls within the province of the modern manager. Complex societies require a clear sense of what their primary tasks are. The old politics of balancing off interest-group demands will no longer work. The political leader is severely hampered by those very constituents who have elected him. He or she must serve their interest as they define it, and this frequently leaves the leader without the capacity to make intelligent decisions. Drucker believes that, just as the old economic marketplace no longer functions, neither does the political marketplace. The stakes in modern society are simply too high to be left to the vagaries of interest-group bargaining and political logrolling.

In significant ways, Drucker's argument is much like that of Theodore Lowi in his estimable book, *The End of Liberalism.*[22] Lowi asserts that what will surely not emerge from the conflict of interest groups ("interest group liberalism") is justice. For Drucker, it is equally clear that efficiency and rationality will not result from the quagmire which is modern politics. An efficient society requires, not political leaders, but well-managed institutions.

Drucker's purpose as a consultant to large corporations is to educate the executive for managing his business intelligently. This process does not involve complicated assessments of the corporation's financial structure or its organizational chart. Drucker emphasizes the corporation's social function and from that attempts to formulate a clear assessment of the appropriateness of managerial behavior. Drucker is likely to ask the simplest questions of managers:

What do you really want to do?
Why do you want to do it?
What are you doing now?
Why do you do it that way? [23]

Drucker forces managers to check their assumptions constantly and not to allow the proximate pressures of everyday decisions to engulf them so that they forget the purposes of the organization. An executive who tells Drucker that the purpose of the corporation is to make a profit shows a basic misunderstanding of managerial objectives. While profits are needed to fuel the corporation, they are not the primary goal. The purpose of the corporation inheres in its own logic, in its wider social consequences. Concentration on the mere maximization of profits ignores the overall economic and social function of the enterprise.

The whole thrust of Drucker's consulting approach is to concentrate on the future, not the past, strength not weakness, people not systems. He emphasizes objectives, strategies, contributions. He demands that the right, simple questions be faced—and answered. And he works on the assumption that the answers are already there.[24]

The answers for Drucker lie in the nature of an industrial society. It is essential for the corporation to understand that its fundamental purpose lies in helping to maximize society's material progress through innovation and the intelligent use of resources. This means that an individual corporation must see itself as performing vital social functions, not simply producing a product or providing a service. The managers of railroads, for instance, would have been much shrewder had they seen their purpose not as simply running railroads, but as providing society with cheap and efficient transportation. This might have allowed them to adapt more rapidly to the changing needs of the society, instead of attempting to sustain an industry that was increasingly becoming anachronistic in the face of competition from the private automobile and the trucking industry.

THE END OF POLITICAL MAN

Of primary concern for Drucker is the need for social solidarity. Drucker does not believe that political institutions can accomplish the task of making whole a society as fragmented as American society. Political leaders are simply incapable of performing this task. While they may lead, they are incapable of governing. Drucker would agree with James Madison's famous comment:

> It is in vain to say that enlightened statesmen will be able to adjust these clashing interests, and render them all subservient to the public good. Enlightened statesmen will not always be at the helm. Nor, in many cases, can such an adjustment be made at all without taking into view indirect and remote considerations, which will rarely prevail over the immediate interest which one party may find in disregarding the rights of another or the good of the whole.[25]

The primary task of the theorist is to help define the objectives of major social institutions. Drucker believes that the perfection of institutions is essential for a smoothly functioning society. It is archaic and dangerous to depend on the *charisma* of a leader to cure social ills which are fundamentally managerial. In Drucker's view, it is only a comprehensive science of managerialism that can serve as an adequate remedy for the social sickness which pervades modern societies.[26]

Republican self-government will ultimately degenerate, because citizens feel their opinions do not matter, and because it is more convenient to trust the expert to make decisions. Indeed, Drucker's argument, taken to its logical conclusion, would posit that people care more about results than they do about process. It is a mistake to assume that people have an instinct for politics. They care more about their status and function; security is more important to them than participation. It is Drucker's ultimate purpose to persuade the general society to grant managers the legitimacy to provide precisely that status and function to citizens. It is only those who are at the helm of large-scale institutions who can perform this vital task. For, if a society whose landscape is dominated by large organizations persists in denying them their appropriate social role, then only chaos and confusion will result. Too, if the managers of these institutions do not understand that they occupy key social positions and acknowledge their accountability to the general public, they will surely lose their legitimacy.[27]

The central theme of Drucker's work concerns the impossibility of achieving a more meaningful politics and the necessity for developing a more public-regarding corporation. Drucker represents the clearest and most extreme reformulation of the Madisonian ideal. In the background of almost all of Drucker's writings is the dark presence of the totalitarian state. His pluralism represents an attempt to circumvent the pitfalls of a coercive political system made more dangerous by the achievements of a sophisticated and awesome technology. The individual's interest is best served by a clear understanding of his place within the fabric of institutional life. One may speak of the *polis* or of republican virtue, but only as a poet, and not as a citizen of managerial society. Indeed, political freedom cannot be preserved by the politicians—but may be by the managers. Political leaders can exercise the passions; they cannot deliver goods and services. Modernity has its own logic, and to ignore that logic is to run the risk of economic and social decay.

Drucker's view of the limits of politics and the possibilities of managerial leadership stands as a testimony to the failure of American public thought. It becomes increasingly clear that political faith is at a low ebb in America. What is certainly lacking is the political will necessary to chart a common direction for the nation. The public purpose has become defined as the satisfaction of private purpose, with the state being reduced to a mere vehicle of private interests. Drucker's attempt to redefine the role of the manager represents, in significant ways, the moribund state of republican thought. While Drucker is cautious about the amount of authority he would grant to the manager, nevertheless, he advocates significant redefinition of the public and private division of authority. The ideal of the consent of the governed as the basis of a political society must give way to one in which efficiency and innovation are the main criteria for social authority.

What is perhaps most ironic about Drucker's work is that the group that would be most resistant to this new distribution of social responsibility is the managers themselves. It has been a rare time in American history when the business classes have evinced any understanding or interest in the public purpose. Indeed, businessmen have consistently seen themselves as the best results of a political system that protects and defends private property and private morality. Despite Drucker's stated goal of protecting freedom, one of the very likely consequences of his position might be giving managers a legitimacy they have no right to, because they exist independently of the citizenry.

A generation ago, Thurman Arnold argued that the problem with the antitrust laws was that they gave business the symbols of legitimacy for their activities.[28] These laws brought the behavior of oligopolistic firms within the concept of free competition. This was for Arnold the "folklore of capitalism," a belief that the mere existence of laws to ensure competition could mask the reality of oligopolistic and monopoly control. This social folklore has been used effectively to insulate the structure of the American economy from any serious intrusion on the part of the state, and has also prevented citizens from gaining any clear understanding that the modern corporation is not merely a larger version of the local grocery store. One wonders if Drucker has not presented the public with a "folklore of managerialism," which will invest private men pursuing private ends with the political leadership of modern America.

In Drucker's work there is a serious inversion of traditional democratic theory. There was a time in the American past when it was believed that an efficient economic structure served the purposes of democracy and not the reverse. Bishop Potter had once argued that the "supreme vice of commercialism is that it is without ideal." It may well be argued now that Drucker's managerial society is also without an ideal, save that of its own organizational logic. The promise of American life will not be met in the boardrooms of modern corporations. Leadership will have to come to America through its own traditions and experiences, tempered as always by the imperfections and difficulties of political life.

NOTES

1. This argument is drawn from classical, liberal political economy. The primary text for this position is Adam Smith, *The Wealth of Nations* (London: P. F. Collier, 1902). See also, for a more contemporary adaptation of this theme, F. A. Hayek, *The Road to Serfdom* (Chicago: University of Chicago Press, 1944).

2. See Milton Friedman, *Capitalism and Freedom* (Chicago: University of Chicago Press, 1962).

3. See Theodore Lowi, *The End of Liberalism* (New York: Norton, 1969), for an informed discussion of the intellectual origins of this notion. Of particular interest is the extension of this economic model into the political arena. See also, Robert A. Dahl, *Pluralistic Democracy in the United States: Conflict and Consent* (Chicago:

Rand McNally, 1967), and John Kenneth Galbraith, *American Capitalism: The Concept of Countervailing Power* (Boston: Houghton Mifflin, 1952), for two recent works that utilize this concept.

4. John Kenneth Galbraith, *The New Industrial State* (Boston: Houghton Mifflin, 1967).

5. Adolph A. Berle and Gardiner C. Means, *The Modern Corporation and Private Property* (New York: Macmillan, 1932).

6. Theodore Levitt, "The Living Legacy of Peter Drucker," in *Peter Drucker: Contributions to Business Enterprise*, ed. Tony H. Bonaparte and John E. Flaherty (New York: New York University Press, 1970), p. 6.

7. Peter F. Drucker, *The End of Economic Man* (New York: John Day, 1939).

8. Peter F. Drucker, *Management: Tasks, Responsibilities, Practices* (New York: Harper & Row, 1973), p. 5.

9. Peter F. Drucker, *The Future of Industrial Man* (New York: John Day, 1942).

10. Abram Chayes, "The Modern Corporation and the Rule of Law," in *The Corporation in Modern Society*, ed. Edward S. Mason (Cambridge, Mass.: Harvard University Press, 1960).

11. Drucker's *The End of Economic Man* represents the clearest expression of Drucker's views on the role of economic values and his fear of the totalitarian state.

12. Ibid. See also, Peter F. Drucker, *The Age of Discontinuity* (New York: Harper & Row, 1969).

13. John Dewey, *The Public and Its Problems* (Chicago: Swallow Press, 1959). See also, John Dewey, *Liberalism and Social Action* (New York: Putnam, 1963).

14. Drucker, *Management*, p. 811.

15. Ibid., p. 362.

16. Drucker, *The Age of Discontinuity*, esp. chap. 10, "The Sickness of Government."

17. Peter F. Drucker, "Management's New Role—The Price of Success," in *The Future of the Corporation*, ed. Herman Kahn (New York: Mason and Lipscomb, 1974), p. 66.

18. Ibid., p. 59.

19. Drucker, *Management*.

20. C. Wright Mills, *The Power Elite* (New York: Oxford University Press, 1956).

21. Drucker, *Management*, p. 375.

22. Lowi, *End of Liberalism*.

23. Quoted in John J. Tarrant, *Drucker: The Man Who Invented the*

Corporate Society (Boston: Cahners Books, 1976), p. 124. This book is the best overall assessment of Drucker's work.

24. Ibid., p. 126.
25. James Madison, Number 10, in Alexander Hamilton, James Madison, and John Jay, *The Federalist*, ed. Benjamin F. Wright (Cambridge, Mass.: Belknap Press of Harvard University Press, 1961).
26. Peter Drucker. *The Practice of Management* (New York: Harper, 1954).
27. Drucker, *Management*. See also, Peter F. Drucker, *The Landmarks of Tomorrow* (New York: Harper, 1959).
28. Thurman Arnold, *The Folklore of Capitalism* (New Haven, Conn.: Yale University Press, 1937).

Chapter Five

The Political Imperative
George Meany's
Strategy of Leadership

MARC K. LANDY

As recently as a decade ago, the most noteworthy attribute of postwar labor leadership appeared to be its failure. Despite the promise it had offered during the Depression decade, it had not taken the lead in restructuring postindustrial society, and it had been unable to stem the burgeoning materialism and privatism of the American worker. The symbol of this failure was the president of the nation's only labor federation, George Meany. His cautiousness, reinforced by advancing age, was held by many to be responsible for labor's inability to meet the challenges of the times.

Today, Meany remains the unchallenged head of the American Federation of Labor–Congress of Industrial Organizations (AFL-CIO), and is undoubtedly the oldest major leader in American public life. Nonetheless, the image projected by organized labor is no longer one of failure, but one of substantial success. Massive organizing efforts among public employees, coupled with rejuvenated efforts among farm and textile workers, have significantly widened the base of the union constituency. The decisive role played by organized labor in winning passage of the landmark pieces of social welfare and reform legislation of the 1960s marked it as the nation's most powerful congressional lobbying organization. Enactment of the Occupational Safety and Health Act of 1971 was evidence of the extension of labor's political concerns beyond the issues of wages and hours, with which it was traditionally associated. Finally, its sustained advocacy of social welfare and civil rights goals during the Richard Nixon–Gerald Ford years, coming as it did in the face of a massive retreat from such issues on the part of liberal politicians, intellectuals, college students, and other opinion-molders, made the earlier

charges of conservatism and selfishness levied against the labor movement appear petulant indeed.

This change in the image of labor leadership in no way represents a
"greening" of George Meany. His approach to the problems of leadership
has remained remarkably consistent over the years. The change stems
rather from our predilection to evaluate public figures by comparing
them to their contemporaries. In an earlier period, when leaders like
Adlai E. Stevenson and Martin Luther King, Jr., were engaged in pro-
tean efforts to improve the quality of public life and language, Meany's
efforts appeared clumsy and timid. However, his ability to sustain
those efforts in recent years stands in bold contrast to the pusillanimous
posture adopted by other leaders of national stature. This record of con-
stancy allows us to use Meany's version of leadership as a standard
against which to measure the accomplishments of other public men. An
understanding of it not only gives us insight into the nature of contemporary labor leadership, but helps us to assess the general quality of
American political leadership as well.

LIMITS AND POSSIBILITIES

The limits on the possibilities available to labor leadership stem directly
from the historic failures and successes which the labor movement has
experienced. The worst failing of the American labor movement, and of
working-class movements around the world, has been its inability to gain
a significant measure of control over the pace and direction of industrial
development itself. Unions have no meaningful say over those issues
which most profoundly affect the work and community life of their members. For the most part, unions cannot influence the rate at which automation is adopted; the content and scope of corporate long-term planning, budgeting, or merger activity; or decisions concerning the shift of
production facilities from one locality, region, or even nation to another.
Labor leadership's inability to address these sources of rank-and-file
anxiety and resentment severely restricts the degree of trust and enthusiasm it is capable of generating among its constituents.

Paradoxically, labor's most significant achievement, the enactment of
stable collective bargaining arrangements with much of American industry, has proven to be an equally important source of leadership limitation. Once a union has won its fight for recognition, the role of the
leader becomes one of a manager of discontent. In order to negotiate
effectively with management, he must mobilize discontent on the part of
the members by promising them more than he can possibly hope to
achieve. Then, after completing the bargaining process, he must seek
to dampen their discontent and coax them to accept the package he has

negotiated, a package which inevitably delivers far less than he promised initially. Once the contract is agreed to, he becomes its primary
enforcer. He continually finds himself in the position of coercing members to "go along" with contract provisions that they either do not understand or do not agree with.

The achievement of a "mature" bargaining relationship creates other
sorts of tensions between leader and member. To protect the rights of
members adequately, the leader must spend his time in virtually continual formal and informal talks with management. He thus spends a
greater portion of his time and attention in talking to corporate officials
than he does in fraternizing with his own members, who begin to wonder what is actually going on "behind closed doors." Their fears attain
a certain degree of justification as a result of the uniquely precarious
situation faced by a labor leader. Continually confronted with the real
possibility of being voted out of office, he lacks the comfortable option enjoyed by his counterparts in government of returning to a pres-
tigious and lucrative white-collar job. Instead, he has little choice but to
return to the manual trade he practiced prior to his election. The pros-
pect of such a drastic change in life-style gives the labor leader a powerful incentive to find means, fair or foul, of staying in office and/or of
squirreling away sufficient funds to provide for premature retirement.
Recognition of the leader's plight serves to underscore the rank and file's
skepticism concerning his behavior.

Between leader and member a further wedge is driven by the increasingly specialized nature of the leadership function itself. To ensure that
the hard-won provisions of the contract actually result in improved benefits for members, the leader must learn to speak a variety of esoteric
private languages. Enforcement of grievance procedures demands an
understanding of the fine points of labor law. Adjustment of cost-of-living
provisions requires him to fathom the netherworld of macroeconomics.
Administration of multimillion-dollar pension funds obliges him to learn
to think and act like an investment banker. These languages are exceedingly difficult to master and still more difficult to transcend. It is the
rare leader, indeed, who can learn to speak them fluently while retaining
the capacity to speak plainly and meaningfully in the ordinary language
of his members.

Perhaps the greatest price of all, which labor leaders have had to pay
for the achievement of "mature" relations with management, has been
the loss of the strike as the major weapon for accomplishing their goals.
The relative affluence of the contemporary worker has served to dampen
his enthusiasm for striking. When the worker lived on the edge of subsistence, deprivation of wages caused him little additional hardship. The
modern worker, whose attempts to lead a middle-class existence force

him to go deeply in debt to pay off mortgages, car loans, and tuition bills, has a much harder time "affording" a strike. It is still possible to persuade him to strike to protect those things nearest and dearest to his heart—job security and wages—but he is no longer willing to endure the loss of income brought on by a strike for any lesser goal.

The labor leader suffers also from his inability to inspire confidence among the public at large. This failure is due in large part to the inordinately high expectations which the public holds of him. In the words of one leading social critic, "The labor leader whose vision is not loftier than that of the average businessman or doctor or lawyer should get out of the movement. Organized labor should function as the conscience of an industrial society. . . ." [1]

At the same time that he is functioning as the "conscience of an industrial society," he is expected to remain faithful to the wishes of the rank and file. No one seriously expects a large corporation to be run democratically by its stockholders, yet this expectation is held of international unions. Nonetheless, when labor leaders respond to rank-and-file demands for increased wages and ironclad job security, they are accused of featherbedding and sacrificing the well-being of the consumer. Meany aptly described the dilemma faced by labor leadership when he was asked to comment on Secretary of Labor George P. Schultz' contention that labor's wage demands were creating an inflationary spiral damaging to the economy:

> I don't buy it. I think there is some logic to it. But let me say this. If Shultz was the leader of a big steelworkers union and made those sorts of observations to his members, he wouldn't be head of the union next year. Now this is a very practical situation. [2]

The public's unwillingness to consider the "practical situation," which rank-and-file democracy imposes upon the labor leader, causes it to be excessively cynical with respect to his activities. The public is unable to discern when he is, in fact, taking substantial risks in order to act in the public interest and is therefore in need of, and deserving of, its support.

George Meany's great accomplishment has been to develop a means for exercising public-spirited leadership in this harsh context. He reconciled his vision of the common good with the severe constraints upon his freedom of action by devising a whole new set of strategic principles, along with a new form of organizational structure capable of implementing those principles.

Like the strike, the new strategy relied for its effectiveness upon the sheer size of the working populace and its ability to remain unified. It did not, however, require a similar degree of risk and commitment. Instead of asking workers to man the barricades and endure loss of income, all that Meany's "social unionism" required of them was to contribute a few dollars to a political education fund, to ring a few doorbells and, most important of all, to vote. Meany proposed to shift the locus of labor's activity from the bargaining table to the halls of Congress. He would mobilize the union vote to elect public officials who were sympathetic to the union's political point of view and who could be relied upon to pass legislation which embodied his social welfare goals.

Meany was acutely aware that the most spectacular previous attempt by a labor leader to influence his constituents' vote had been a humiliating failure. In 1940, John L. Lewis, then the head of both the CIO and the United Mine Workers (UMW) and the most powerful labor leader in America, had urged his members not to support President Franklin Roosevelt's bid for a third term. His advice was blithely ignored. Meany's realism allowed him to see that Lewis' mistake had been to personalize the matter, forcing working people to choose between Roosevelt and himself. Instead, Meany would rely on a more detached appeal to the workers. Through intensive political education efforts, he would try to acquaint union members with the issues at stake in particular elections and try to persuade them that certain candidates were taking positions on those issues which made them worthy of labor's support.

This new strategy had two structural requirements. First, it necessitated the creation of a centralized bureaucracy staffed by experts in research, publicity, the mechanics of campaigning—and the art of lobbying among union-endorsed politicians in order to ensure that they did not forget their liberal principles upon crossing the Potomac. Second, the political action strategy required unity. If labor was to become a truly effective political force, it needed to speak with one voice. The rivalry and acrimony that characterized the relationship between the two existing labor federations, the CIO representing the newly organized industrial unions and the AFL speaking for the older, more conservative craft unions, would have to be overcome. A single central authority would have to be created to act as the sole spokesman for organized labor.

These two strategic imperatives dictated that a single merged federation be created and that the leadership of that body be given wide authority to represent labor in the corridors of power. They also required that the budget allocated to the central body be sufficiently large to enable it to assemble the expert talent needed to staff a national campaigning and lobbying operation. These considerations impelled Meany to struggle to overcome the divisive ideological and personal forces, which had split the labor movement two decades earlier, and to bring about the creation of a new merged organization.

Meany's vision of leadership was strikingly Madisonian in concept. As a powerful, centralized institution, the merged federation was to be created to fulfill a moral purpose, the betterment of the worker and the poor through political action. The fact that it was national in scope would permit it to transcend the parochial passions and prejudices which afflict local institutions. The fact that its leaders were chosen by representative election would ensure that they would be responsive to the needs of the rank and file, while still preserving sufficient detachment from rank-and-file scrutiny to allow them to function in the rational and calm manner needed to formulate intelligent policies and preserve ordered liberty.[3]

The success of Meany's leadership strategy is thus totally dependent upon the organization that has been fashioned to carry it out. He conceives of leadership, not as ministering to the needs of a flock, but rather as preserving the strength and integrity of an institution. If that task is accomplished, then he can rely upon the organization's mechanisms and procedures to filter out the irrational demands and disorderly passions of the flock, and to identify and promote its best interests. When asked how he assures himself that the rank and file is behind his leadership, he replied:

> I don't. I go by what happens in the organization. . . . He [a rank and filer] might not have attended a union meeting for ten years. So he is pretty hard to reach. But still you will find that from his union, from the local level, these problems come into the movement and I am not looking over my shoulder to see if the rank-and-file is following. I am quite sure that if we are doing things the rank-and-file don't want we will learn it in the very same way we find out about the things they do want. . . . *I don't go searching out and hold a referendum here and a referendum there because these things have a way of coming to the trade union structure. . . .*[4]

His belief in the primacy of organization allows him to greet the fact that the union movement represents only a minority of workers with a yawn of indifference. This problem is "solved" by the principle of representation: Just as the union official speaks for the union member, so the organized workers, in general, will speak for the unorganized.

> Why should we worry about organizing groups who do not appear to want to be organized? If they prefer to have others speak for them and make the decisions which affect their lives without effective participation on their part, that is their right. . . . I used to worry about . . . the size of the membership. But quite a few years ago I just stopped worrying because to me it doesn't make any differ-

ence. *It's the organized voice that counts,* and it's not just in legislation, it's anyplace. The organized fellow is the fellow that counts.
That's human nature.[5]

More than any other individual, George Meany has been responsible
for setting the tone, pitch, and volume for labor's "organized voice." He
has conducted the three critical performances of the AFL-CIO's postwar
career: its founding, its attainment of stability despite external hostility
and internal schism, and the education of its members to support and
sustain its founding principles.

THE FOUNDING

The decisive impact that George Meany had upon the creation of the
AFL-CIO highlights the inadequacy of the term *charisma* as a tool for
analyzing the effects of an individual's personality on his role as a leader.
Meany is the antithesis of the charismatic leader. His appearance so lacks
distinction that, even after twenty years at the helm of the Federation, his
portrait would not be recognized by a majority of the public or even by
large numbers of his own members. He is incapable of producing the sort
of spellbinding and emotionally charged oratory that made John L. Lewis
simultaneously the most loved and most hated man in the nation.

Despite this lack of panache, Meany has interjected his personality in
the way a founding leader must: to obscure points of potential discord
and to reinforce perceptions of commonality. By assiduously cultivating
his Bronx plumber *persona,* he was able to persuade his AFL comrades
to accept a constitution for the merged Federation that included powerful centralist principles inherited from their former antagonist, the CIO.
Logic alone would never have persuaded members to abandon the principle of autonomy and to allow the central labor body to intrude on
internal union affairs. They gave in to Meany, not because of what he
said, but because of who he was—a building tradesman, a local business
agent, a state federation president, and a man who had served them
loyally for sixteen years as a national AFL official.

Meany talks like the Bronx plumber he has been. His own native intelligence and his years of hobnobbing with Presidents, cabinet members,
academicians, and the highly educated and cosmopolitan members of his
own staff have enabled him to acquire a high degree of sophistication
and polish. Yet he goes to great lengths to hide these qualities from his
own members and the public at large. A typical Meany public statement is terse, gruff, blunt, and hostile toward anything or anybody that
smacks of pretense or effeteness. Addressing a legislative conference of
the Building and Construction Trades Department in 1968, he said:

"We have some loudmouth critics on our own side who say we are
not doing well. . . . The AFL-CIO is decadent, it is the custodian of
the status quo, it is moribund. I looked that up. That means in the
process of extinction. . . . it has failed to display an adequate sense of
social consciousness, whatever the hell that means." [6]

While there is no doubt that Meany knows exactly what "social consciousness" means, and had no need to resort to a dictionary for the
meaning of "moribund," his plain speech and constant ridicule of those
who do not speak plainly are a great help in reducing the psychic distance that lies between leader and member.

Meany also vacations like a Bronx plumber. The virtually continual
round of departmental conventions, executive council meetings, and other
labor gatherings which he attends are held in Bal Harbour, Florida, and
similar cement-covered, semitropical ex-paradises. His schedule remains
flexible enough to allow for plenty of time on the golf course and at the
card table. Such an ambience does not alienate the rank and file. Rather,
it serves to reassure them that their leader's aspirations mirror their own.

Meany's fun in the sun serves another vital purpose. Since his vacations
are always taken in the company of other labor chieftains, they serve both
to ingratiate him with them and to keep him aware of their activities. It
takes a truly heartless courtier to stage a *coup d'état* against the King
whom he has just beaten at gin rummy. The House of Labor is not the
House of Medici. Meany's willingness to fraternize with the leaders of
important unions, regardless of whether they emerged from the old AFL
or CIO, has allowed him to maintain the loyalty and affection of men
whose personal politics diverge far to the left and to the right of his
own.

The term *consensus* is as inadequate for describing Meany's objectives
vis-à-vis the founding of the merged Federation as *charisma* was for
analyzing his personal leadership style. Meany's overriding concern in
pursuing merger was not simply to bring about some sort of pleasant
harmony within the House of Labor, but rather to fashion a centralized
organization capable of exercising real authority. Unity was therefore a
necessary but hardly sufficient goal.

Had Meany simply been interested in reuniting the labor movement, he
had the option of pursuing an alternative strategy that contained fewer
risks and that his AFL allies would have found far more congenial. Strong
indications existed that the CIO was about to dissolve of its own ac-
cord. Walter Reuther's election as president of the CIO had created
powerful discord. The president of the Steelworkers, David McDonald,
who had championed an opposing candidate, hinted broadly that he was
considering withdrawing from the organization and was willing to enter-

tain the idea of joining the AFL. Had Meany chosen to treat with McDonald, he might well have succeeded in destroying the CIO and bringing its affiliates back into the Federation one by one. His refusal to do so was based on his desire to maintain the authority of existing labor organizations, so as to maximize his ability to strengthen them in the future.

> "I don't want them to fall into my lap. I think if the CIO disintegrates it's going to be bad for labor, it's going to be bad for everybody to have a national trade union center sort of fall apart. It wouldn't even work to the interest in the long run of the unions in the AFL to pick them all up. *If this would be the way they were assimilated, this could be the way they leave too.* I wasn't interested in that." [7]

Meany was aware that the manner in which a political body is founded will have a determining effect upon its future. If his goal was to create a powerful centralized federation, he could ill afford to destroy the organization which most closely approximated that ideal.

Similar considerations determined his approach to the problem which posed the greatest obstacle to merger, jurisdictional conflict. Such conflicts arose as a result of the competition for members between AFL and CIO affiliates. They reflected the deeply rooted ideological gulf separating the adherents of craft and industrial unionism. To the CIO industrial unions, it was obvious that the men who built scaffolding inside steel plants should belong to the Steelworkers, since they were part of the steel industry. It was just as clear to the AFL craft unions that such men, since they were carpenters by trade, belonged in the Carpenters Union.

In the face of such a clear-cut difference in principle, *consensus* within the labor movement appeared an impossible dream. Indeed, it was. Meany's "solution" to the problem was classically Madisonian. Just as Madison had considered some degree of factional strife to be the inevitable price of liberty, so Meany felt that a measure of interunion competition for members was the inevitable price of a free labor movement. The proper course of action was, therefore, not to try to "solve" the problem of jurisdictional conflict at all, but instead to find an institutional mechanism capable of moderating the degree of anger and bitterness which such disputes engendered. To divert the attention of the protagonists away from their irreconcilable differences, Meany suggested that procedure take precedence over principle. He advocated what came to be called the "short way" to merger. Each affiliate would enter the Federation with its membership intact. All jurisdictional disputes would then be resolved by machinery that the new Federation would establish. [8]

Since the two groups of unions were unable to resolve their substantive disputes, they were hardly more likely to find mutually agreeable machinery for arbitrating them. By taking the "short way," Meany was hoping to buy time to develop strong enough attachments to the new organization on both sides, so that both groups would be willing to make concessions on the jurisdictional issue. The creation of such institutional loyalty is a slow process, and Meany was in no hurry to put it to a crucial test. But six years after the merger was consummated, Walter Reuther made it clear that he would no longer tolerate delay on the question. Unless the 1961 Convention established coercive machinery for solving jurisdictional disputes, he planned to quit the Federation and take his former CIO colleagues with him. " 'We merged,' " he said, " 'but we did not unite.' " [9] The 1961 Convention was thus to be the test of whether the AFL-CIO was in fact an institution for the preservation of which its members would sacrifice important interests.

When Meany's compromise plan was presented, Reuther protested its lack of coercive power and attempted to split the Federation by staging a walkout. He rose from his chair. For a tense moment, the future of the Federation hung on whether or not his former CIO colleagues would rise with him. They sat. After further changes of language, both the industrial unions and the building trades representatives on the Executive Council endorsed the compromise jurisdictional plan. The founding of the merged organization had at last been successfully completed.

STABILIZATION

Meany's success in stabilizing and maintaining the size and power of the AFL-CIO was the result of his ability to recognize the opportunities inherent in the seemingly adverse conditions which the organization faced during the 1950s and 1960s. The stability of the Federation was severely threatened by two groups. The automation of basic industry drastically reduced the number of jobs available in the sector that had accounted for labor's rapid expansion in the 1930s. The defection from the Federation of its two largest affiliates, the United Auto Workers (UAW) and the Teamsters Union, deprived the organization of one-quarter of its membership. Although he might lack concern for the plight of the unorganized worker per se, Meany knew that the economic and political strength of the Federation required a steady increase in the number of dues-paying members. He was, therefore, obliged to find new sources of membership growth and to prevent other affiliates from following the example of the UAW and the Teamsters.

Expansion

Recognizing the futility of trying to organize workers in those sectors where any slight rise in wages or benefits would simply result in the displacement of workers by machines, Meany sought to concentrate the Federation's energies in the sector of the labor market most resistant to automation, public employment. In contrast to the industrial sector, this work force was growing rapidly at all levels of government. Since computers and data-processing equipment have not as yet been granted the franchise, public officials have displayed a far greater reluctance than their counterparts in the private sector to substitute such equipment for men and women who are capable of going to the polls. The AFL-CIO's success in fostering unions among public employees is primarily responsible for its continued membership expansion despite the onslaughts of automation in heavy industry.

Besides their simple ability to pay dues, Meany found the affiliation of public employees to be particularly desirable for two additional reasons which relate directly to his strategy of leadership. Since these employees come from a sector of the work force outside the traditional scope of union organizing activity, the effort to organize them did not serve to rekindle the acrimonious jurisdictional disputes among existing unions—still the greatest source of tension within the union movement. The dependence of public employees upon the largess of municipal, state, and federal governing bodies renders them far more sympathetic than their comrades in the private sector to the AFL-CIO's staunch support of "Big Government." They have proven far more willing than the average union member to participate in the Federation-sponsored voter registration and campaign activities upon which labor's political power depends.

The successful organization of public employees was a direct by-product of Meany's reliance upon political action. The greatest obstacle to recognition of public employee unions had been the intransigent hostility of governmental bodies at all levels. Public employees were barred by law from using the weapon which their counterparts in the private sector had relied upon to overcome employer opposition, the strike. Although such legal restrictions did not always prevent them from engaging in work stoppages, the heavy fines, which such illegal strikes inflicted upon them, served as a strong deterrent. For unionization of public employees to succeed on a large scale, a major change would have to take place in the legal and political context in which public employee unions functioned.

Such a transformation did occur as a result of an executive order issued by President John F. Kennedy in 1962. The order endorsed the concept of federal employee unionization and proscribed federal agencies from placing obstacles in its path. By legitimizing the concept of public employee unionism, the President's action greatly facilitated the recognition of such unions by local and municipal governmental bodies which were technically immune from the order. Meany termed Kennedy's action "the equivalent of a Wagner Act for public employees." The executive order came as an acknowledgment of the possibility that Kennedy may well have owed his victory, in the closest presidential election in history, to the massive voter-registration drive conducted by the AFL-CIO and to its vigorous support of him during the 1960 campaign.

Schism

Meany could not avert the departure of the two largest affiliates, the UAW and the Teamsters, from the Federation. He was, however, able to prevent the leaders of those two mammoth unions, Walter Reuther and James Hoffa, from establishing effective, rival national labor organizations. He succeeded in preserving the role of the AFL-CIO as *the* voice of organized labor because, of the three men, he alone fully recognized that a national labor spokesman must maintain a careful balance between the conflicting expectations of the labor constituency itself and the public at large.

Hoffa's spirited defense of the principle of autonomy may have warmed the hearts of his building trades confreres, but coming as it did in the face of congressional revelations of widespread union corruption, it made him look like a common thug to the public. Meany was thus able to convince the old AFL'ers that the alternative to disciplinary action by the central body was not a return to their beloved autonomy, but rather, severe censure and regulatory action by the government.

Although the constitution of the merged Federation granted the Executive Council the right to investigate charges of union corruption and to suspend any affiliate which was found guilty of *corruption,* it was by no means clear that the former AFL affiliates, who deeply cherished the principle of individual autonomy and who had acquiesced most grudgingly in the corrupt practices provision, would actually permit a suspension to occur. Meany used the shocking revelations concerning labor corruption unearthed by Senator John L. McClellan's committee as a wedge with which to crack the wall of support for union autonomy. Thomas Brooks aptly describes Meany's opportunistic use of public opinion for the purpose of strengthening centralized control:

> Meany in a sense skillfully used the corruption issue as a tool to reshape the Federation into his concept of what the labor movement ought to be. . . . The McClellan revelations . . . enabled George Meany and his supporters to convert what might have been a splintering off into a casting out of Devils. Not only did the expulsion [of the Teamsters] avert a split, but it forestalled any attempt by Hoffa to become the John L. Lewis of today. Once the AFL had been stamped "clean" by the McClellan Committee, the unions

expelled for corruption could not conceivably form still another federation of labor as Lewis did the CIO. . . .[10]

Reuther made his grievances against the Federation known in a set of letters, sent to UAW members during the early months of 1967. The general character of this charge is aptly summarized by the following quote from the first of these letters.

"The AFL-CIO . . . suffers from a sense of complacency and adherence to the status quo and is not fulfilling the basic aims and purposes which prompted the merger. . . . The AFL-CIO lacks the social vision, the dynamic thrust, the crusading spirit that should characterize the progressive, modern labor movement. . . ." [11]

Significantly, this diatribe was released to the press and sent to a long mailing list which did not include George Meany and other AFL-CIO officials, who were thus put in the humiliating position of learning of their sins from the newspaper. Thus began a consistent pattern of public attack, unaccompanied by any effort to gain redress of UAW grievances through existing Federation machinery.

Reuther's specific demands were incorporated into an omnibus resolution, for which he demanded consideration at a special convention called explicitly for that purpose. If Meany refused to call such a convention, the UAW would have no option but to withdraw. Meany agreed to hold such a convention, provided the UAW promised to attend, and provided the UAW pledged to abide by the convention's decisions. Reuther demanded that the convention be held with no preconditions and announced that the UAW would withhold per capita payments to the Federation unless its demand was met. Meany responded by suspending the UAW for nonpayment of dues. Reuther reacted to the suspension by announcing on July 1, 1968, that the UAW would disaffiliate from the Federation.

In contrast to the apocalyptic tone of Reuther's indictments, his specific demands were relatively modest and amenable to debate and compromise. He asked for a ninety-million-dollar, six-year organizing drive, with one-third of the ninety million earmarked for farmworkers and one-third for the "working poor," more coordination of collective bargaining efforts on the part of different unions, the establishment of an electronic data processing center, and a strengthening of the Executive Council committee system. This discrepancy between tone and substance served to heighten suspicion among Reuther's former CIO allies concerning his real motives for provoking a clash with Meany.

By acceding to the demand for a special convention, Meany was in effect committing himself to accept enough of Reuther's demands to make the convention a success. Reuther's refusal to pledge himself to accept the convention's decisions revealed that his major objective was not "progress," but civil war. Reuther's preference for confrontation rather than accommodation irretrievably impugned his credentials as a national labor spokesman. His willful violation of the expectations of his labor constituents did as much to solidify Meany's position of leadership as did Hoffa's attempts to thumb his nose at the public.

CIVIC EDUCATION

Like Madison, Meany recognized that the type of institutional system he had established required a certain sort of citizenry to support and defend it. Most importantly, it required a membership sufficiently calm, patient, and tolerant to accept the tutelage of its national representatives and yet interested enough in public affairs to campaign and vote for labor-endorsed candidates. The civic education, which Meany's strategy required, involved focusing the rank and file's public vision away from its preoccupation with the local union and toward a concern for the national social welfare goals which the Federation's political and lobbying staffs were seeking to promote.

Such a detached and rational approach to public affairs did not come naturally to the Federation's constituency, which was more inclined to adopt the parochial, emotion-laden perspective of neighborhood, parish, or ethnic group. To infuse such members with norms of liberality and tolerance, therefore, required an educational effort of major proportions. The Federation has established a large and well-staffed public affairs bureaucracy for the purpose of performing this immense task. Its two regular publications, *The American Federationist* and the *AFL-CIO News*, are largely devoted to the sort of favorable coverage of social reform and public welfare issues that members are least likely to get from television news shows and local newspapers which form the rest of their public information diet.[12] In addition, the Federation provides local affiliates with a raft of pamphlets, films, and other sorts of propaganda designed to present its legislative program in a favorable light.

Such educational vehicles can inform, but they cannot teach. The task of changing minds, rather than simply enriching them, must be carried out in a more personal, direct, and evocative manner. Far more than any other leader in contemporary American life, George Meany has accepted the challenge of providing such education to his members. He has spoken out boldly and bluntly on matters that are highly controversial within the ranks of labor and has relied upon a straightforward appeal to principle as an antidote to prejudice and narrow material interest.

We shall never really know to what degree Meany's advocacy of forced school busing and his unconditional support for the Vietnamese refugees changed the "hearts and minds" of the large number of union members who opposed both those policies. But it is clear that his unequivocal endorsement of those programs, when opposition to them had reached its most vehement and emotional pitch, dramatically improved the climate of opinion in which deliberation about them took place.

The refugee airlift came at a time of serious economic recession, with unemployment in excess of 8 percent. A Gallup poll revealed that a majority of Americans opposed allowing the refugees to settle in the United States. Of even greater significance, important molders of liberal opinion who could ordinarily be counted on to lead a fight for the war victims were, at best, grudging in their support. Edmund Brown, Jr., governor of California, proposed that the jobs of Americans be protected against an influx of the Asian horde and that the refugee aid bill be amended to ensure that available jobs go to Americans *first*.[13] Senator George McGovern was quoted as saying that 90 percent of the newcomers would be better off returning home and that a high priority should be accorded to providing planes and ships to facilitate their return.[14] Senator James Abourezk stoutly maintained that the refugee ranks contained "thousands of trained political assassins," and Congresswoman Elizabeth Holtzman advocated "screening the refugees in order to remove 'undesirables.' "[15]

In view of the devastating effects which the recession was having on his members, Meany could easily have justified joining such distinguished representatives of the liberal community in demanding that the refugee program be curtailed. Instead, he issued a statement announcing his unconditional support for the program and his hope that all Americans, including the representatives of labor, would do all within their power to make the refugees' transition to American life as smooth and pleasant as possible.

We are a nation of immigrants. And to turn our backs on people who are fleeing from oppression, fleeing for their lives, and say to them that "we are going to dump them in the sea"—this to me is about as contrary to American tradition as anything that I ever heard of. . . . And we look at 120,000—whatever the number is of South Vietnamese refugees—there will possibly be 30,000 of them looking for jobs. . . . Yes we have nine percent unemployment . . . and if this country can't absorb another 30–40,000 people and try to find some way for them to make a living, then I feel that, in a sense, we are denying our heritages.[16]

Meany's strong support for the refugees was echoed by many leading newspapers and political figures of both right and left. Public enmity towards the Vietnamese quickly abated, leaving the refugee program unharmed. However, had Meany, as the spokesman of American labor, chosen to join the chorus of opposition led by such prominent members of the liberal left, the storm of public indignation might well have reached hurricane proportions.

The situation was even more problematic with respect to school busing, in that affiliates of the Federation in Kentucky and Massachusetts were actually directly engaged in anti-busing activities. To remove this threat to established Federation policy in support of busing, Meany combined the sort of appeal to the consciences of the membership that he had employed in the refugee case with an ultimatum to the leaders of the Kentucky and Massachusetts state federations that continued disobedience of Federation policy would result in disciplinary action. He informed the Massachusetts State Federation of Labor that should it fail to rescind its anti-busing resolution, he would have no choice but to expel it from the Federation. The Massachusetts state body reversed itself immediately.[17] While it would be naive to assume that Meany's forthright action transformed the attitudes of the members on this emotion-laden issue, it no doubt succeeded in depriving the anti-busing forces of potent political allies.

Studies of the political attitudes and behavior of union members have demonstrated the positive effects of the civic education effort: (1) Despite his or her lack of educational attainment (the variable which most highly correlates with liberal attitudes), the average union member is at least as liberal as the average person at large with respect to most political issues, and a bit more liberal with respect to matters of race, aid to the poor, and support for foreign aid and the United Nations. The union members' views have remained remarkably stable over the past two decades and have grown increasingly tolerant with respect to the race issue.[18]

(2) Members are willing to abide leaders whose views are significantly more liberal than their own. An unpublished poll, taken by a large international union, revealed that the delegates chosen to represent the rank and file had significantly more liberal views on racial matters than did the membership at large. The views of the full-time national staff of the union were far more liberal than those of either the rank and file or the convention delegates.[19]

(3) While union membership per se does not correlate with rate of political participation, exposure to political issues within the union context does. Those members who reported discussing political issues in their

union exhibited significantly higher levels of political participation than those who did not.[20]

As valuable as these positive accomplishments have been, they are dwarfed in importance by a great negative achievement. Union members have been kept from succumbing to the blandishments of those who would seek their vote on the basis of senseless passion and blind prejudice. While the rest of the nation was being entranced by the military grandeur of General Dwight Eisenhower, union members delivered a solid majority to Adlai E. Stevenson. Despite George Wallace's attempt to exploit blue-collar America's supposed distaste for "pointy heads" and "welfare chiselers," he received a mere 15 percent of the union vote in 1968.[21] Clearly this form of civic education has succeeded most in that aspect which is most distinctly Madisonian. When making their political choices, union members have followed their leaders' advice and displayed an uncommon distaste for zealotry and bigotry and a great respect for moderation and rationality.

NOTES

1. James O'Gara, of *Commonweal* magazine, quoted in Derek C. Bok and John T. Dunlop, *Labor and the American Community* (New York: Simon & Schuster, 1970), pp. 31–32.
2. George Meany interview, *New York Times*, 31 August 1969.
3. Walter Reuther's approach to leadership was quite similar. This essay concentrates upon Meany rather than Reuther because, of the two, Meany adhered more consistently to Madisonian tenets. Although Reuther espoused the goal of unity, he continually took positions calculated to alienate the craft-union sector of the Federation. As evidenced by the UAW's withdrawal, his adherence to merger was tactical and temporary.
4. George Meany interview, *New York Times*, 31 August 1969. Emphasis mine.
5. George Meany interview, *U.S. News and World Report*, 21 February 1972. Emphasis mine.
6. Joseph C. Goulden, *Meany: The Unchallenged Strong Man of American Labor* (New York: Atheneum, 1972), p. 397.
7. Goulden, *Meany*, p. 186. Emphasis mine.
8. The best discussion of Meany's role in the merger is contained in Arthur J. Goldberg, *AFL-CIO: Labor United* (New York: McGraw-Hill, 1956), pp. 85–86.
9. Goulden, *Meany*, p. 287.

10. Thomas R. Brooks, *Toil and Trouble: A History of American Labor* (New York: Dell, 1964), p. 235.
11. Goulden, *Meany*, p. 389. Substantially the same account of the Reuther-Meany feud appears in Frank Cormier and William J. Eaton, *Reuther* (Englewood Cliffs, N.J.: Prentice-Hall, 1970), pp. 405–19.
12. Bok and Dunlop, *Labor and the American Community*, p. 35.
13. *New York Times*, 2 May 1975.
14. Ibid., 11 May 1975.
15. Ibid., 6 May and 9 May 1975.
16. George Meany press conference, Executive Council Meeting, Washington, D.C., 6 May 1975.
17. *New York Times*, 25 November 1975. Also, letter from George Meany to Joseph Warren, President, Kentucky State AFL-CIO, 23 October 1975.
18. Bok and Dunlop, *Labor and the American Community*, p. 47.
19. Ibid., p. 134.
20. Sidney Verba and Norman H. Nie, *Participation in America: Political Democracy and Social Equality* (New York: Harper & Row, 1972), p. 193.
21. Bok and Dunlop, *Labor and the American Community*, p. 47.

Chapter Six

Dr. Martin Luther King, Jr.
The Politics of Sounds and Feelings

REVEREND WILLIE K. SMITH

EDITOR'S INTRODUCTION

Martin Luther King, Jr., was a leader with unique resources. His rhetoric, his culture, and his training combined to give him special access to his followers and to allow him to deviate dramatically from the mainstream of American leadership. The Reverend Willie Smith's discussion of these resources in this essay offers a similarly unique glimpse at the style and the substance of King's leadership. Eschewing the more traditional academic modes of analysis, Smith presents a moving and insightful "story" of the feelings, the symbols, and the language employed by one of America's most remarkable leaders. King's language, in marked contrast to the banality of so much of our public discourse, addressed with clarity and force both the emotional and the material needs of his people.

Simple and direct in his appeal, King nonetheless confronted and addressed the most complex political-philosophical issues of his age. His rhetoric was dominated by the particular symbols and traditions of his people, yet it stirred the national conscience and transformed the national political agenda. Rev. Smith argues that these successes can best be understood through recognizing that King spoke in the tradition of the Old Testament prophet. Rev. Smith's "story" eloquently captures these prophetic qualities and the emotional responses which they evoked. His "story" is then placed in analytical and historical perspective by Ed Schwartz, who compares King's prophetic style with the organizational style of Cesar Chavez. There are, argues Mr. Schwartz, limitations to the prophetic style, limitations that must be confronted if we are to understand the possibilities of political leadership as political education in contemporary America.

I want to tell the story. Let me explain something. If a black minister is asked to preach away from his congregation in any one of 90 percent of all black churches in America, he could begin this way, "I don't want to preach this morning; I just want to tell the story." Most black folk, involved in black religious services, know that this brother minister is going to talk about *deliverance*. The sermon or talk may take on a variety of forms and utilize numerous illustrations. While the examples are too numerous to list and are not necessary for our purpose, the theme is the same: *deliverance*.

THE TRADITION

Black ministers, from slavery to last Sunday morning, standing in pulpits in the sprawling urban metropolis and in rural, dusty Southern counties, have been preaching *deliverance* from the early days of the Republic, the slave Republic, to the automated, mechanized society of urban America. Said the preacher, often in less than clearly constructed sentences and the best of diction, "Go down Moses, way down to Egypt land and tell old Pharaoh to let my people go." When the preacher didn't say it, the choirs, often without pianos and organs, would sing it to the beat of their own pulse and rhythm. As the choir sang, the congregation would stir. It's hard to explain! Within minutes the entire church would be singing. No pianos, no organs—just shining, smiling faces lifting their voices to a universal tune of freedom, singing again and again, "Go down Moses, way down to Egypt land, tell old Pharaoh let my people go." Nobody stopped to take the time to write a dissertation on freedom. Freedom was in the air. The preacher, moved by his people, stood and yelled, "Set the captives free." While in the midst of all the shouts of jubilation and joy, the church kept singing, "Let my people go."

Dr. Martin Luther King, Jr., was born into this tradition, the tradition of black religion, of singing, of shouting, of testifying, of preaching, of deliverance. King's father, Martin L. King, Sr., was a preacher. Martin's mother was a musician; she knew the "sweet songs of Zion" and taught others how to sing them. Mama King's (as Martin's mother was affectionately called) father was a black Baptist preacher and for forty years served as pastor of the Ebenezer Baptist Church. The Reverend A. D. Williams gave the hand of his daughter, Miss Alberta Williams, in marriage to Martin Luther King, Sr., who later succeeded his father-in-law as pastor of the Ebenezer Baptist Church. Martin Luther King, Sr., remained pastor of this church for thirty-one years, until his voluntary retirement in 1975. His wife, Mrs. Alberta Williams King, was felled by a sniper's bullet in June 1974 while carrying on her Sunday morning activities.

Dr. Martin Luther King, Jr., did not drop from thin air. He was born into a black Baptist church and a preaching tradition. Yet Dr. King made a difference where other black (and white) preachers did not. What was this tradition and how did King make a difference? The two questions are the subject of my essay.

Having been born into the black community, into the black Baptist Church preaching tradition, King knew certain "secrets" about the black heritage that are only grasped by living in the community rather than formally studying it. Most people who live in the black community—who regularly attend church—would have trouble if they were asked to explain what constitutes the black community and its traditions. It's often difficult to articulate associations and relationships so near at hand.

A first secret is that the common denomination in the black tradition is faith in God, or that God is supreme. Obviously, not all black people profess a formal belief in God or attend church services on any regular basis. Yet there is an overarching spiritual dimension in black communities that cannot be measured. God is present in the black community and He resides as a spiritual presence in the soul of every black brother and sister. This is partly why black people refer to each other as "having soul." Soul is not primarily the outward manifestation of eating collard greens, ham hocks, corn bread, and black-eye peas; nor is it solely expressed in the way black people dance, crack jokes, love, and enjoy themselves; nor is soul fully the body movements of black athletes when they hit each other's hand after scoring a touchdown, or putting in the last point in a tight basketball game, or breaking an Olympic record.

By living in the black community and by coming from a warm Christian family, Martin Luther King, Jr., knew that the black community had a spiritual foundation. This community is headed by God himself as represented by his preachers. The day of celebration is Sunday. The day of jubilee is that day when the weary cease working and the troubled, beaten farmers, factory hands, and slaves can once again spit up their anxieties, channel their cares, and find meaning and hope for another week of toil and suffering. They come to the church on Sunday and together meet their God, head of the intangible community. They tell God all about their troubles, through songs and prayers and testimonies, and He tells them all about His kingdom through scriptures, sermons, and closeness. Look at a line of this typical song: "Take your burdens to the Lord and leave them there."

King knew another "secret" that most black people take for granted. That God is the ultimate source of honor, prestige, and social status is assumed. Such a belief may not be so strong in 1976, since many blacks have found props to self-esteem either in their vocations or along social lines. Nevertheless, as a general rule, this "secret" remains a dominant part of the black tradition. While conditions around us are terrible and difficult to take from day to day, we are saved from automatically resorting to feeling like nothing and acting like nobody. Most black people believe that God has ensured and guaranteed their dignity and worth. Consequently, King knew that his appeal for dignity in suffering and kindness toward your enemy would fall neither on hardened hearts nor deaf ears. "I am somebody," says Reverend Jesse Jackson, Director of Operation PUSH (People United to Save Humanity), and he asks his mixed audience to repeat after him, "I am somebody." The next line expresses greatly a faith in God's command of dignity, "And before I'll be a slave, I'll be buried in my grave, and go home to my Lord and be free." That God is the giver of dignity and honor is as black-American as peach cobbler.

By growing up in the black church among the so-called middle-class blacks and the poor and the rest, Martin knew still another secret: that black people had a common destiny. Black people, regardless of class, status, or honor, accepted their destiny. God was in charge! Only luck and education separated the highly affluent from the lowly. They placed their future in the hands of God. Their destiny was God's destiny. Thus, what the black community believed about God and His activities in the world greatly influenced how they interpreted their conditions, past, present, and future. Black people have never been without a history, a faith, and a hope. They viewed themselves as a collectivity, tied together by at least one friend, God, and by at least one enemy, segregation. Day after day, week after week, year after year, they cried out to Him in groanings, murmurings, and whispers, "Oh Lord, how long? How long? How long?" Black churches and their preachers helped to find an answer.

Any person entering a Free Baptist congregation, or churches that were organized by blacks themselves, such as the Baptist and A.M.E. Zion, will notice many exchanges of personal affection. In general, there is talking, hugging, kissing, ticket-selling, and common meals. In particular, the warmth of the people expressed in these ways takes on a significance almost as great as the service of worship. Often greater! King knew this secret, too. I talked with Mrs. Edith Savage about Dr. King. She was one of Dr. King's associates and remains a close friend of the family. Time after time, she called attention to the "personal touch" of Dr. King and how he generated warmth. Dr. King grew up in a feeling and hearing community. These senses played a major role in shaping the black tradition. Open display of affection and warmth created an almost unbelievably new world which is still evident in the black churches today.

That new world, created from hearing and feeling the Word, or the truth about life, is the world of transcendent reality. It seems that one course of human nature, under harsh conditions, is to rise above the circumstances and find momentary relief from suffering. The ridicule heaped on black churches and their preachers fails to acknowledge the subtlety in the "pie in the sky" theology that black ministers were preaching—to speak of "a better day" was not entirely a cop-out. It was not the passive acceptance of a marginal, second-rate existence in their world for the sake of the milk and honey of heaven after death. Herein lies the fifth secret. The capacity to endure unbearable suffering is limited, particularly when no end is in sight and when one's existence is so provisional. Physical, psychological, and spiritual suffering is more bearable when a cut-off point is known, and when the inflictors of pain make an effort to meet basic human needs. It fell to black churches and their preachers, not only to remind blacks that their present condition was not the end, but that God was preparing a better place for them, "the promised land," "the new Jerusalem," "a Kingdom not of this world."

I doubt that all the black preachers knew the tremendous effect of their message. The constant preaching brought temporary relief from suffering by focusing heavily on the promised state, call it what you will. This process enabled those receiving the message to hear the Word, to imagine the new existence, to experience it with deep emotions, and to gain relief from suffering through shouting and moaning—an adaptive process of psychological catharsis, temporary transcendance, and future hope. As most preachers are aware, King knew that one secret of black preaching was providing temporary relief from suffering, but he knew as well that the preacher provided much more. W. E. B. Du Bois argued:

> The preacher is the most unique personality developed by the Negro on American soil. A leader, a politician, an orator, a "bass," an intriguer, an idealist—all these he is, and even too, the center of a group of men, now twenty, now a thousand in number. The combination of a certain adroitness with deep-seated earnestness, of tact with consummate ability, gave him his preeminence, and helps him to maintain it.

When I speak about the "secrets" of the black tradition, I'm not suggesting that such matters are locked in the hearts of black people and the keys thrown away. I am referring to living styles and techniques and practices that are common to the black experience. These styles may be seen by the outside world, but they cannot be observed. Most white American visitors will leave a black church service with a good impression of the singing and a fascination with the dramatic, moving speech of the preacher. Yet they have neither understood nor observed what is happening when the congregation sings:

> Amazing Grace, how sweet the sound,
> That saved a wretch like me;
> I once was lost but now am found;
> Was blind but now I see.

Every cultural group develops a way of knowing and communicating. The black tradition emphasizes the senses of hearing, feeling, and touching. Most white Americans are not accustomed to the black way. Too many whites have lost touch with feelings as a direct means of communicating. Most blacks—not all—are different.

King knew this. Every Sunday morning, Sunday afternoon, and Sunday evening, he participated in some aspect of this tradition. Most black people know about this tradition. Only the outside world looked on in wonderment and ridicule: "What are those niggers doing?" They didn't discover the secret until the cat got out of the bag in Montgomery, Alabama, in 1955. By then it was too late. The choices had narrowed: Join it! Fight it! Step aside!

THE MOVEMENT EXPERIENCE

The cat got out of the bag in Montgomery, Alabama, on December 1, 1955. Sister Rosa Parks, a well-respected, dignified black woman, made a decision that confronts all black people, from time to time, in the depths of their humanity—"I just can't take any more." On the face of it, hers wasn't an earth-shaking decision. Yet Rosa Parks spoke to reclaim black humanity from all the years and incidents of degradation attached to a black skin. "I can't take any more." Sister Parks didn't move and her act of not-moving moved the world. Normally, we are taught that moving is associated with assertion and that restraint is akin to passivity. The black experience, however, turned these personal and social dynamics around, as they drifted from white usage to black realities. What some take for granted, others use for revolution.

The black movement is neither secular nor sacred; it reflects the best in the Judeo-Christian heritage, together with the unique tradition of black people. I put black people in a "unique" category because we are a part of the Judeo-Christian heritage, while possessing a tradition that takes into account an African ancestry. Since the days of slavery, blacks have experienced a dual identity. We are both Christian and largely Protestant, as well as Christian and unmistakably African. These African beginnings no doubt contributed to the way black people appropriated

Christianity. Blacks always felt closer to the Judeo-Christian heritage of viewing religion as a deliverance-oriented, minority-culture phenomenon, seeing God as a totally active personality in history. For blacks, biblical history was the story of minority people and how God saved them. In this respect, the ground of religion becomes the ground of the movement, namely, the underpinnings of hope and deliverance. The movement gained strength and motivation from religion because a faith was all the people had. Blacks had God and themselves *only*. There was no debate as to where to begin the struggle. The beginnings were the people themselves. They had absolutely nothing other than the sacred intangibles gained from their religion—spirit, faith, courage, hope.

> I ain't gon' let nobody turn me round
> Turn me round
> Turn me round

So the black movement was the stirrings of black people, hanging on to their God, believing in the ideals gained from their religion, and lovingly asserting themselves in a battle for freedom and justice.

When Sister Rosa Parks decided she couldn't take any more, Dr. Martin Luther King, Jr., was there, not on the bus, but in the town. He was there; he was present. Others were there, and I don't mean to slight them. My story is about King, and I'm going to stick with him. The general story of the movement can be found in many volumes. King was present. I repeat myself (like a Baptist preacher) to make sure the point sticks. Dr. King became a leader, not because he created an army, nor because he filled a vacuum. He became a leader because he created a *presence*. He was a presence. The point is that King decided to go to Montgomery when other options were open to him. Little did he know what his decision would mean. King was noticed not merely because of Sister Rosa Parks and the bus incident, but because he didn't allow education and the Northern bright lights to separate him from his roots. As some say, he kept his feet on the ground. He left the North and went home, and thereby placed himself along the route of the impending movement. Martin Luther King, Jr., was there and he didn't have to be. That's all I'm saying.

Secondly, Dr. King not only was present in Montgomery, he responded to a felt need of the community. He was part of the community. His education, family, and church background equipped him with brainpower, savvy, and a love of tradition. Yet Dr. King was not compelled to respond. How often do you and I forfeit our greatness by looking the other way, ignoring a request for help, or simply pretending indignities don't exist. King became a leader because he was decisive.

Deciding to participate in aiding Sister Parks and gaining redress for her specific injury and the general insult to black people was not automatic. King could have acted busy, played sick, or faked a church meeting. It's been done before. Martin heard the anguished cry that echoes across each generation:

> Go down Moses, way down to Egypt land,
> Tell old Pharaoh to let my people go.

King made a difference not because he was called, but because he responded. He was decisive.

Thirdly, although King was in Montgomery and did respond to a call for help, neither his presence nor his response would have meant anything had he not been prepared to handle the situation. The Montgomery incident and the ensuing struggle could have become the biggest massacre in black history. Nevertheless, King's tradition taught him to trust in God and move forward.

Fourthly, if his tradition gave him a deep faith in God and people, together with a trust in himself, the educational institutions he attended had added dimensions to his raw talents. King had a golden voice before he went to the theological seminary. He was preaching for his father in the Ebenezer Baptist Church in Atlanta, and most probably other congregations. Again, this practice is part of the black church tradition: confess your calling and then preach. Obtain a good education, but don't wait until you finish your education to preach.

Dr. King had committed himself to a role within the tradition of the church by accepting the "call" into the ministry and being ordained in the Ebenezer Baptist Church. This was done before he took his degree at Morehouse College. He received a Bachelor of Divinity degree from Crozer Theological Seminary in Pennsylvania. He could easily have left Crozer after graduating and returned to the South. Given his father's prominence, contacts, and influence in the Baptist tradition, young Martin would have had little trouble finding a congregation. And if he encountered difficulty there was always a co-pastorship or an assistant pastorship in his father's church. King decided to continue his education. This decision was the key to understanding the high level of King's participation in the movement.

The point is not that King had a Ph.D., but rather that King had the knowledge and wherewithal to lend a sharp, conceptual analysis to the movement, once he decided to jump. King used his degree in a way remarkably different from any person in the black or white community. Dr. King read widely while in school. He remembered what he read. He experienced the materials and was affected by them. He was aware of both religious and secular philosophies undergirding movements of social change—the Social Gospel movement of Walter Rauschenbusch, the nonviolent struggle of Mohandas K. Gandhi, and many others. King did not drop from thin air with a bullhorn in his mouth. He was ready! Little did King or the world know how tremendous an impact his additional knowledge would have on the affairs of state.

King could teach and preach. Undoubtedly, he could have hit the lecture/speaking circuit and cleaned up. He didn't! He chose to use his knowledge, skills, and titles on behalf of other people. Choosing such a course he became for many "De Lawd." He seems to have chosen the less prominent, less selfish route, and yet he became the most prominent, the most popular, the most effective leader. "De Lawd," they called him. "De Lawd." Later, they were to crowd around borrowed television sets and watch "De Lawd" receive the Nobel Peace Prize. He was their leader, privately loved and publicly acclaimed. Make no mistake about it.

And whosoever shall exalt himself shall be abased;
and he that shall humble himself shall be exalted. —Matt. 23:12

Dr. King humbled himself and he became a leader of people. What kind of leader? What were the specific ingredients that constituted his appeal? Why did people follow him? Why did they refer to him as "De Lawd"?

Let's pause and summarize where we are in the story. First, King was a product of the black church preaching tradition, and he remained faithful to this tradition. Second, the black movement during the 1950s had come to the point of saying, "I just can't take any more." Third, King possessed both the resources of his tradition and the discipline of his learning to lend shape and direction to these cries. Fourth, King made himself available through the series of great decisions discussed earlier, which allowed him to be in the right place at the right time. Fifth, both spiritually and academically Martin was ready. Sixth, the movement was in progress throughout the South, but it had no single voice. Enter Dr. Martin Luther King, Jr.

The nation was on edge. Black people in the South were ready. Martin Luther King, Jr., was present. Sister Rosa Parks sounded the trumpet in Montgomery. The black people gathered. Martin went into action. Someone said, "Let Martin speak," and speak he did. When he finished talking, the smooth fingers of preachers and teachers, the rough hands of farmers and maids and all the rest pointed toward him. "He's the one! He's the one!" Poor Martin, he had caught the tiger by the tail and couldn't let it go—or was it the other way? Let history judge! Was Martin a leader? Well, every place he went thereafter, people said,

"He's the one! De Lawd." When they heard he was coming, they patiently waited for hours, days, weeks. "Where is he and when is he coming?"

Was King a leader? Not like John F. Kennedy: He had no money. Not like Lyndon B. Johnson: He had no political office and no experience in politics. Not like George Meany: He had no organization. Was Martin a leader? Yes! He was a leader because the people proclaimed him a leader. He was a leader because the movement laid claim to him. He was a leader because he couldn't have been otherwise. Martin was a leader in the best sense of his tradition. He followed the models of leadership most familiar to him and to the black tradition. These models were based on the Bible, especially the Old Testament, and the roles that black pastors play in black churches. The movement called him as a *voice* to articulate their groanings and looked to him for moral and spiritual leadership. He transferred his black church experience to the movement and thereby became its pastor, its spiritual head. Consequently, he added another dimension to the movement by relating its leadership functions to the Old Testament models of prophet, priest, and king. Assuming these role models, consciously or unconsciously, made King a formidable leader. Add to these his conceptual analysis of social problems gained from years of study, together with the tradition of general restraint in the black community enforced by lynch laws and mob violence. Link all this to nonviolence and civil disobedience and you get "De Lawd."

THE POLITICS OF SOUNDS AND FEELINGS

When he spoke funny things happened: Despair resurrected herself and put on the wings of hope; hate moved her bridal suite to the threshold of love; fear separated itself from anxiety and was exposed for what it is; violence arose from the psyche and greeted nonviolence with passion; courage became the order of the day, while the wistful lingering of inertia and passivity faded into the distance.

The story is near its end now. There isn't much more to tell, but there is more to witness. Let me tell you what I heard. Let me give you the testimony of one man's experience at a rally during the early days of the movement.

He said: "This man! This man was different I tell you. I can't remember all of his name. He got a long name for a Negro. It's something like Luther King. I was just passing by. I saw all the people gathered and so I decided to see what was going on. I had my overalls on so I slipped in the back door and stood near the side. I never seen so many of us out.

They was all there. Even Uncle John—chewing his tobacco. Of course, he couldn't spit nowhere, being it was the church. But I tell you, that young boy spoke. They said he's some kind of doctor. He went up North and got it. That boy got music in his voice. I understand him. Most of them doctors I don't much bother with cause I can't understand them. But this one spoke plain. He was simple. He said things I've been trying to say all my life. He said, 'Don't hate the white man because that would do something to you.' He say, it take too much time to hate. That hate ain't natural. He said, don't shoot and cut and kill. God is love. Then he went on and told a story about a man from across the water named Khandi or Condi —something like that—how he led a whole nation of them Indians against the British and won independence. He said this man didn't have a gun and wouldn't let his people carry guns or do harm to them British. Then he talked about Jesus and Moses and David. When he stopped speaking everybody got up. You know how we like to carry on. Folk hollering! 'Yes, sir.' 'Tell it.' 'Glory!' 'Keep on keeping on.' Everybody was excited! I thought it was all over—then, people started joining hands and linking arms. I got nervous because I was just off work. I was nasty, and sweaty. Before I could turn and slip out the way I come in, Mr. Clyde Brown, who ain't never been to church, grabbed my left arm and hooked it, and Mrs. Dolly Brown grabbed my right one. I looked up and saw the preacher smiling from the pulpit. Those sitting up there hooked their arms around each other and around him. Then it started. The singing started. I didn't get it all, but it was something about 'overcoming,' 'black and white,' and 'deep in my heart.' People was crying and shouting. Miss Hattie Edwards threw her pocketbook in the air. I got scared. I never saw people carrying on like that, 'cept sometimes in Sunday morning church and revival meetings. All this fella said was:

> Let justice roll down like waters
> and righteousness as a mighty stream.

Now, it wasn't just *what* he said. It was *how* he said it. He said it funny and the people start hollering. What you think he means by words like justice, and some Greek word he used for love called *agap*—something, and that long word he got from across the water, nonviolence? Funny things happen when he talks. I hope Luther King come back. He put into words what I feel and think. He's good! Never heard a man who sounds like I feel."

Dr. Martin Luther King, Jr., Jesus of Nazareth, and Moses of the Exodus were great political leaders without trying to be. They had the knack of "sounding like people felt." I hope he comes back. Luther King. "Never heard a man who sounds like I feel." Martin Luther King was not born a prophet, but he stood in the prophetic tradition. He sounded like people felt. By sounding like they felt he could move them beyond their feelings to embrace new solutions to old problems. Historically, the role of the prophet in the Old Testament was precisely these functions. For example, Amos and Jeremiah "sounded like people felt." They could identify long enough to get a hearing. They could articulate and interpret the internal and external evils of the society and their causes. They would point the way back to God or announce an impending disaster. The people had a choice. They could either heed the advice of the prophet or ignore him.

The role of prophet had been known in the black community since the introduction of Christianity in slave days. The black preacher was looked upon as an interpreter of God's word. Martin's experience and training allowed him to extend this interpreting process to include racial, social, and class questions. Following prophetic tradition, his interpretation was not without a solution, namely, nonviolent struggle in order to bring about change. If the people chose to ignore him and to take the violent route, the consequence would be disaster.

Martin Luther King, Jr., was a leader because he was a priest. He was a priest because he assumed the role of suffering. He stood in the priestly tradition of the Old Testament. He decided to suffer with his people and on their behalf. The role of the priest in the Old Testament is to serve as a mediator between God and people, offering sacrifices to God on behalf of his people, reasserting their sense of communality, reaffirming the covenant. Later, the priest would become the sacrifice. Jesus was such a priest. "He gave his life for me, his precious blood he shed." Martin stood in this tradition. He was willing to risk his life for his people. Time after time, he engaged in campaign after campaign for no ostensibly selfish, profit-making reasons. He himself said, "I've been to the mountain top." The people gave Martin power (and a sense of themselves as *a people*) because he gave them his life. His life was not his own. He walked, talked, and marched for freedom in the supreme role of a high priest. "Nothing matters to me now, I've been to the mountain top."

He had no horses, no chariots of fire, no magic solutions. He got out there. His army was us. We marched, prayed, played, cried, and sweated. He is our king. Every preacher is a king, but Martin Luther King, Jr., was the king of kings.

I followed him. We all did, black and white, Protestant, Catholic and Jew, North and South. Oh, I cried! You don't know how hard I cried—didn't have nothing to wipe my eyes with. I cried, I cried, I cried. I told you, I only heard the boy in person once. They shot him! Martin

Luther King, Jr., is dead. No! My king is dead! My king is dead! I told you after I first heard him—Luther King—"Never heard a man who sounds like I feel."

> For if the trumpet give an uncertain sound, who shall prepare himself to the battle?
> So likewise ye, except ye utter by the tongue words easy to be understood, how shall it be known what is spoken? For ye shall speak into the air.—1 Cor. 14:8,9

Chapter Seven

Cesar Chavez
The Leader as Organizer

ED SCHWARTZ

In an article in *Playboy* magazine for January 1970, Cesar Chavez observed, "Nothing is going to happen until we, the poor, can generate our own political and economic power. Such a statement might seem radical, but it shouldn't." [1] For Chavez, the statement represented more than an obligatory call to the barricades. It summed up his strategy, his way of proceeding, a way that distinguishes him from virtually every major movement leader of the past generation.

Martin Luther King, Jr., exemplified the leader as prophet; Cesar Chavez shows us the leader as organizer. To be sure, there are similarities between the two men. Both emerged from dispossessed minorities. Both succeeded in mobilizing nonviolent movements for social and economic justice. Both espoused and practiced nonviolence—indeed, Chavez may be America's leading practitioner of nonviolence today. Both understood the importance of winning support for their demands from other groups in the population—churches, labor unions, liberals, elected officials. Most significant, both grounded their movements in civic and religious ideals widely shared by the general population.

IN THE TRADITION OF DAVID

These similarities should not obscure the important differences between them, however. King, the prophet, stands in the tradition of Moses; Chavez, the organizer, reflects the tradition of David. The prophet is satisfied when the people listen and respond. The organizer is content only when the people come together within a permanent organization. The prophet addresses large numbers at a time; the organizer works with small groups until they can work together. The prophet demands the center of the stage. The organizer frequently remains in the background. These are obvious points of contrast between the two men.

To the Reverend Martin Luther King, Jr., the message, the demands were the goal. Of course, popularizing the issues required mobilizing people in their behalf, but a movement was only a means to the end. Once one cause was won, a new movement would be built to fight for the next one. Indeed, contemporaries criticized King for raising the expectations of local groups without giving them strong structural support. Organization building was simply not his kind of architecture. He designed philosophies, strategies, not constitutions and by-laws. His personal legacy remains, of course: But, significantly, the Southern Christian Leadership Council barely survives.

Cesar Chavez, by contrast, hopes to leave the United Farm Workers of America (UFWA) as his major legacy. His private work, compared to King's, is minimal. We can think of no Chavez speech comparable to "I Have a Dream"; no Chavez book comparable to *Why We Can't Wait*. What Chavez believes apart from the issues of his own movement is unknown. The movement itself, the organization, the Farm Workers is what we know about Chavez, because this is what he wants us to know.

Chavez' earliest political education grew out of his religious convictions. As a young man in San Jose, he attached himself to a *barrio* priest Father Donald McDonnell, who mixed discussions of social justice with stories from the history of the labor movement. It is Father McDonnell, in fact, who must stand as Chavez' main teacher. A graduate of St. Patrick's Seminary in Menlo Park, California, the priest had resolved to apply the principles of justice in "Rerum Novarum" (Pope Leo XIII) and "Quadragesimo Anno" to the problems of the farmworkers. Joan London and Henry Anderson, two chroniclers of the farmworkers, describe his encounter with Chavez as "perhaps the most important single meeting in the history of the farm labor movement." [2]

Chavez is no less enthusiastic:

> "Father McDonnell sat with me past midnight telling me about social justice and the Church's stand on farm labor and reading from the encyclicals of Pope Leo XIII in which he upheld labor unions. I would do anything to get the Father to tell me more about labor history. I began going to the bracero camps with him to help with Mass, to the city jail to talk with prisoners, anything to be with him." [3]

Father McDonnell later recommended Chavez to the second person who would influence him, Fred Ross.

Ross was legendary in organizing circles for piecing together community organizations from house meetings held throughout a neighborhood. In 1951, he was working in San Jose to establish a Community Service Organization under the auspices of Saul Alinsky. At Father

McDonnell's suggestion, Ross persuaded Chavez to hold such a house meeting. Though he was skeptical at first, the meeting convinced Chavez. As he recalled it several years later:

"So he [Ross] came in and sat down and began to talk about farm workers, and then he took on the police and the politicians, not rabble-rousing either, but saying the truth. He knew the problems as well as we did; he wasn't confused about the problems like so many people who want to help the poor. He talked about the CSO [Community Service Organization] and then the famous Bloody Christmas case a few years before, when some drunken cops beat up some Mexican prisoners down in L.A. I didn't know what the CSO was or who this guy Fred Ross was, but I knew about the Bloody Christmas case, and so did everybody in that room; some cops had actually been sent to jail for brutality, and it turned out that this miracle was thanks to the CSO. . . .

"He did such a good job of explaining how poor people could build power that I could even taste it, I could *feel* it. I thought, Gee, it's like digging a hole; there's nothing really complicated about it! . . . You see, Fred was already an organizer when Alinsky hired him. I guess some of his theories came from Alinsky, but I learned everything from Fred. It was Fred who developed this technique of house meetings—Alinsky never used them.

"Anyway, I walked out with him to his car and thanked him for coming, and then I kind of wanted to know—well, what next? He said, 'Well, I have another meeting, and I don't suppose you'd like to come?' I said 'Oh, yes, I would.' I told the others I'd be right back, and I got in his car and went with him, and that was it." [4]

Thus, the two most important influences on Chavez gave him the political distance from his community that he needed to change it. From Father McDonnell, he acquired an understanding of social justice and labor history that reinforced his native religious and civic idealism. From Fred Ross, he learned how to turn tight *barrio* neighborhoods into instruments of power, then how to translate the common values and concerns of migrant workers into organized communities. This personal synthesis explains the political hybrid that Chavez has since tried to create—between the tactics of economic power and the philosophy of nonviolence; between a bread-and-butter union and a moral crusade. Interestingly enough, it is an amalgam that defies the conventions of its own separate parts. Modern organizers don't often moralize, and it is still the rare church that works to mobilize an economic movement.

To achieve this synthesis, Chavez has had to cultivate a unique style of political leadership—one that also eludes conventional analysis. How can a man become a leader in modern America who is neither a great speaker, nor an artful infighter, nor a brilliant administrator? How can a person who often stays inside a crowd end up at its head? In Chavez' case, the answer lies both in his personal approach to the movement and in his ability to blend various traditions in its behalf. Six themes come to mind—intimacy, example, and sacrifice; continuity, conflict, and participation.

To understand Chavez, we must analyze how these themes reinforce one another.

INTIMACY, EXAMPLE, SACRIFICE

"The main thing in convincing someone," Chavez commented in an article in *Ramparts* in 1966, "is to spend time with him."

> It doesn't matter if he can read, write, or even speak well. What is important is that he is a man and second, that he has shown some initial interest. One good way to develop leadership is to take a man with you in your car. And it works a lot better if you're doing the driving, that way you are in charge. You drive, he sits there, and you talk.[5]

Some leaders teach from the speakers' platform; Chavez conducts an endless series of tutorials. In an age of mass communications, it is hard to imagine that one of the country's leading movements, the United Farm Workers of America, came together one member at a time, but it did. The Reverend Jim Drake, a United Church of Christ minister who worked with Chavez during the early 1960s, recalled that

> "His consistency and perseverance really struck me. . . . A disability case, a worker injured on the job—he would stay with that worker day and night, day and night, until he could locate an attorney who would take the case for nothing, or find some way of settling it that was of benefit to the worker. That's how his union was built: on plain hard work and these very personal relationships. It was a slow, careful, plodding thing; the growers didn't even know he was in town. Even when the strike started they had no idea who Cesar Chavez was, but the workers did." [6]

By cultivating such relationships, Chavez establishes a realistic attitude among people in the movement as a whole. He views leadership as " 'like taking a road over hills and down into the valley; you must stay with the people. If you go ahead too fast, then they lose sight of you and you lose sight of them.'"[7] He is a realist. "'Anyone who comes in with the idea that farmworkers are free of sin and that growers are all bastards has never dealt with the situation or is an idealist of the first order,'" he told one reporter. "'Things don't work that way.'"[8]

Indeed, Chavez expresses contempt for any image of the farmworkers built upon a naive view of human nature:

"In the beginning, there was a lot of nonsense about the poor farm-worker: 'Gee, the farm worker is poor and disadvantaged and on strike, he must be a super human being!' And I said, 'Cut that non-sense out, all right?' That was my opening speech. 'Look, you're here working with a group of men; the farm worker is only a human being. You take the poorest of these guys and give him that ranch over there, he could be just as much of a bastard as the guy sitting there right now. . . . Remember that both are *men*. In order to help the farm workers, look at them as human beings and not as some-thing extra special, or else you are kidding yourself and are going to be mighty, mighty disappointed. Don't pity them, either. Treat them as human beings, because they have just as many faults as you have; that way you'll never be in trouble, because you'll never be disappointed.'"[9]

He is equally hard on himself. "'Don't let the public part fool you,'" he says.

"Me, here, I am just a plain human being, and I am reminded of this constantly at home. My wife sees me as the same old guy, you know. She has the advantage, she is removed from the public part and she lets me know very definitely who I am. I think that sometimes, al-though I don't enjoy being taken down, it is a good thing, that re-minder at home. . . ."[10]

If Chavez doesn't "enjoy being taken down," he enjoys even less any signs of adulation from his supporters. He is constantly stifling their ovations for him.

Thus, unlike leaders who set themselves apart from their followers, Chavez values intimate, frank relationships with each of them. "'Chavez gave me attention that I had never had before,'" a migrant from the Rio Grande observed.

"I don't know how to describe it. . . . Cesar had the direct atten-tion for us, not like the politician that shakes your hand and says,

'How are you?' and pats you on the back and is gone. . . . Cesar gave his attention to me." [11]

Most politicians today cannot even persuade the voters that they care about people like them, but Chavez has no such problem.

Intimacy creates the possibility of loyalty to the movement; setting an example reinforces commitment to its ideals. Chavez places a high premium on adhering to the principles that he espouses. If he preaches tolerance of human weakness, he practices it. When he demands hard work, he sets the pace himself. When he calls upon others to take risks, he places himself in the most vulnerable position. " 'We don't let people sit around the room crying about their problems,' " Chavez says. " 'No philosophizing—*do* something about it.' " [12]

Of course, at the center of this teaching by example is a strict adherence to nonviolence. It is far more than a tactic: " 'We are firm believers, you know,' " he told a biographer.[13] In the tradition of Mohandas Gandhi and King, he argues that violence, even violence in a good cause, destroys the perpetrator as well as the victim. "We must respect all human life, in the cities and in the fields of Vietnam," he explained in an article in *Look* magazine.

> Nonviolence is the only weapon that is compassionate and recognizes each man's value. We work to preserve that value in our enemies—or in our adversaries, as President Kennedy said more gently, more rightly. We want to protect the victim from being the victim. We want to protect the executioner from being the executioner.[14]

Yet if nonviolence is not merely a tactic, it is a powerful educational tool that Chavez uses to teach farmworkers many other important values of the movement. Nonviolence requires courage. Following a particularly brutal confrontation with the Teamsters union, for example, members of the Longshoremen's Association volunteered to retaliate with their own "goons." Chavez rejected the offer. " 'They would have run the Teamsters out of town,' " he explained.

> "They've done it before, in Puerto Rico and Chicago. . . . Maybe we would have won the strike that way, but we would have lost a lot too. See, every time the Teamsters beat up on one of our guys, they lose. The whole idea of nonviolence is you are not afraid; if you become afraid, you start doing things you are not supposed to do. Violence is a trap. We convert the farmworkers and they can see our strength." [15]

Nonviolence demonstrates discipline, self-control. " 'It takes a lot not to strike back,' " Chavez admits, " 'not that you don't get the feeling sometimes. The reaction, I guess, is built in us.' " [16] On more than one occasion, he has had to intercede between the angry farmworkers and a grower after a particularly harsh instance of brutality against picketers. Once he even warned a mob that, if it was going to "get" a driver who had run down a striker, it would have to get him too.[17] On another occasion, he threatened to resign if union members embarked on a vigilante expedition. That incident, particularly, showed how Chavez persuades by example rather than rhetoric:

> "You can vote right now to arm yourselves—" Chavez began, but before he could complete his threat of resignation, a woman stood up and spoke in his behalf. Concluding, she turned in a semicircle to plead with the brooding audience. "The whole world supports Cesar," she entreated, "just *because* of his nonviolence." A man stood up. "I offer words from the Bible," he said. "Justice of God cannot be won by the sword. We must resist temptation to violence, especially when victory is certain."
>
> The audience fell silent. Chavez, too, was silent. His tired face reflected anything but the certainty of victory. When it resumed, his voice came quietly, as if he had been speaking all along and only now had become audible again. "If you want a guard, and nobody wishes to guard it without arms, then I will guard it myself." He spoke very simply, and he meant it. "If they burn it, we can build again. But if a man is killed, who can revive him?" [18]

The group came around.

Practicing nonviolence also reflects a much subtler, but broader way that Chavez teaches by example—namely, by cultivating gentleness at all times. He is gentle to his wife—to all women, in fact—in conscious contrast to the vaunted *machismo* of Mexican-American men. He is gentle in his criticisms of other people—sometimes, say his critics, too gentle. While he sets exacting financial and administrative standards for his staff, he is careful not to abuse them. His co-workers appreciate the approach. " 'When someone rebukes you heavily,' one told a reporter, 'you remember it, you carry a scar; Cesar did it so softly that I couldn't focus on it while it was happening. I feel bad, but I won't carry a scar.' " [19]

By far the greatest value that Chavez hopes to promote by example, however, is a principle as important as nonviolence itself—sacrifice. " 'Our lives are really all that belong to us,' he once said, 'I am convinced that the finest act of courage, the strongest act of manliness, is to sacrifice ourselves for others in a totally non-violent struggle for justice. To be a man is to suffer for others. God help us to be men.' " [20]

Chavez dramatizes his own personal sacrifice for the movement through periodic public fasts. The first of these, in 1968, lasted 25 days and attracted national attention. Its public purpose was to galvanize support for the grape strike. It had a deeper significance, however, related to the internal politics of his movement.

Nineteen sixty-eight was the year when violent elements challenged advocates of nonviolence in every movement for social change. The confrontation forced Martin Luther King, Jr., into the streets of Memphis, Tennessee, to lead the marches of sanitation workers that cost him his life. Similar upheavals on the campuses drove former Congressman Allard Lowenstein, architect of the "Dump Johnson Movement," to shift from denouncing the war to condemning violent student protests—a shift that cost him much of his student support.

Chavez chose to respond personally. Jerry Cohen, a staff member at the time, explained:

"Cesar was mad. There had been a lot of loose talk about violence. He had told them the life of one man or woman was worth more than the success of the cause, but they were not listening, so he decided he had to find out who had the balls, and he showed them. *He scared the hell out of them.* He didn't say, 'I'm not going to eat until you guys shut up your mouths about violence;' he just said the union was committed to non-violence, then started fasting. The people responded like, 'God, what is this guy doing?' The people were scared and frustrated, they didn't know what to do with him." [21]

Certainly, the impact of the fast exceeded even Chavez' expectations. Workers from all over the country sought audiences with him—opportunities that he used to discuss their individual organizing problems. Supporters conducted rallies in his behalf. He received media attention every night. Senator Robert Kennedy joined him at the conclusion of the ordeal for a brief public ceremony in San Jose. The fast resolved the question of who and what would lead the Mexican-American movement once and for all.

Yet, if Chavez succeeded where the Reverend King and Congressman Lowenstein failed, it was because his style of organizing made success possible. His supporters were more than an audience—they were his students, his friends, who rushed to his side when he needed them. He had shown them how to follow his example in general; it was only a small step for them to understand the meaning of this particularly dramatic act of moral witness. His whole career had embodied sacrifice. It was easy for others to believe that he was prepared to offer the ultimate sacrifice, if the integrity of his vision depended upon it. They had to choose—if they wanted Chavez, they had to live up to his ideals. Cesar Chavez, thus, became the only nonviolent leader of the 1960s to outwit his violent opponents. For his physical survival, he must thank God. For his political survival, he deserves much of the credit himself.

CONTINUITY, CONFLICT, PARTICIPATION

One of Chavez' favorite stories is how he and his brother developed the Farm Workers' flag:

> "I wanted desperately to get some color into the movement, to give people something they could identify with, like a flag. I was reading some books about how various leaders discovered what contrasted and stood out the best. The Egyptians had found that a red field with a white circle and black emblem in the center crashed into your eyes like nothing else. I wanted to use the Aztec eagle in the center, as on the Mexican flag. So I told my cousin Manuel, 'Draw an Aztec eagle.' Manuel had a little trouble with it, so we modified the eagle to make it easier to draw.
>
> The first big meeting of what we decided to call the National Farm Workers Association was held in September, 1962, at Fresno, with 287 people. We had our huge red flag on the wall, with paper tacked over it. When the time came, Manuel pulled a cord—ripping the paper off the flag and all of a sudden it hit the people. Some of them wondered if it was a communist flag, and I said it probably looked more like a neo-Nazi emblem than anything else. But they wanted an explanation, so Manuel got up and said, 'When that damn eagle flies, that's when the farmworkers' problems are to be solved.' " [22]

If the flag symbolizes the Farm Workers movement, the story reflects how Chavez is putting it together—a synthesis of various traditions that creates more energy than the sum of its parts. For the flag, Chavez drew upon the wisdom of ancient Egypt, just as Christianity is the ultimate source of authority for the movement. The Mexican-American symbol, the Aztec eagle, stood in the center, reflecting the centrality of Mexican-American history to the Farm Workers' cause. The design confronted the workers, in the way that the Farm Workers themselves are supposed to confront established institutions. Yet the flag was accessible. Manuel

Chavez drew the eagle so that others could replicate it, just as Cesar Chavez builds his organization so that anyone can participate in it. These three elements—continuity, conflict, and participation—are the ingredients that hold the United Farm Workers of America together.

It is the Catholic tradition, even the Church itself that serves as the ultimate source of authority for the movement. Religious symbols infuse the Farm Workers more directly than almost any other social cause in America, and certainly more than any other union. The religious connection is all the more unusual in that Chavez himself is not a priest. To be sure, his political education was theologically inspired, but more than one politician has had an equivalent education without applying it directly to his work. Indeed, if we had to identify just one characteristic that distinguishes the Farm Workers from other economic uprisings, it would be this religious orientation.

Yet the Catholic appeal has been critical to winning support from the workers themselves. Chavez' first major march in 1966—from Delano to the California statehouse in Sacramento—brought this point home even to skeptical observers. It was not merely a march, but a *pereginación*, with the theme of "Penitence, Pilgrimage, and Revolution," and a climax on Easter Sunday. Along the way, workers paraded under the Mexican patron saint of the *campesinos, la Virgen de Guadalupé*. When some of the volunteers objected to this heavy religious motif—including masses every night and morning—Cesar Chavez took a vote. Dolores Huerta, a Farm Workers leader, summed up the results: " 'We put the Virgin to a motion, and virginity won.' " [23]

Later, William Kircher, an AFL-CIO organizer with the Farm Workers, explained the march's tactical significance:

> "The march was obviously an organizing tool. New. Radical. Different. A crew of people walking along the highway carrying the banner of Our Lady, calling meetings at night which attracted farm workers out of the fields and towns, opening with 'De Colores' [a song about the colors of spring in the fields], maybe a prayer. The whole thing had a strong cultural, religious thing, yet it was organizing people." [24]

Indeed, the Catholic appeal has succeeded with the Farm Workers where all other traditions have failed.

Beyond the religious imagery, Chavez evokes memories of Mexican-American history. "We are men and women who have suffered and endured much and not only because of our abject poverty, but because we have been kept poor," he wrote in an open letter to the California Grape and Tree Fruit League in 1969.

The colors of our skins, the languages of our cultural and native origins, the lack of formal education, the exclusion from the democratic process, the numbers of our slain in recent wars—all these burdens generation after generation have sought to demoralize us, to
break our human spirit. But God knows that we are not agricultural
implements or rented slaves, we are men.[25]

The letter merely echoed a point that Chavez had made to the Farm
Workers from their very first meeting—their cause was part of a history
that extended back to the worker rebellion in Mexico more than 155
years before.

Chavez' third appeal is to American civic ideals, particularly when he
addresses non-farmworker audiences. " 'What we demand is very simple,' " he told a Senate subcommittee hearing, " 'we want equality. We do
not want or need special treatment unless you abandon the idea that we
are equal men.' " [26] In an article in *Look* magazine he noted that

It may be a long time before we get justice under the law, because
the law is on the side of the growers. As Robert Kennedy said to
the Delano Sheriff during the Senate hearings on Migrant Labor
—he was amazed to find that our people were arrested because they
might commit a crime,—"I suggest that the Sheriff read the Constitution of the United States." [27]

Reference to specific civic ideals are not made so often by Chavez as
they were by Martin Luther King, Jr. Certainly, religious and Mexican-
American imagery is more prominent. Nonetheless, like all leaders of
Mexican movements, Chavez sees himself as holding the country accountable to its own professed ideals.

Appeals to tradition do more than rationalize the demands of the Farm
Workers; they strengthen the resolve of the Union to fight for them.
Nonviolent or not, Chavez understands that his movement is engaged in
a sustained battle with established interests—not just the growers, but the
"Banks and railroad companies and big corporations that run agri-busi-
ness, a $1 billion industry in California." [28] Indeed, he sees the move-
ment as being "locked in a death struggle against man's inhumanity to
man" in the food industry, "And this struggle itself gives meaning to our
life and ennobles our dying." [29]

The problem of leadership lies in involving workers directly in the
process of conflict. Chavez believes that the picket line serves this purpose well:

"If a man comes out of the field and goes on the picket line, even for
one day, he'll never be the same. The picket line is the best possible

education. Some labor people came to Delano and said, 'Where do you train people? Where are your classrooms?' I took them to the picket line. *That's* where we train people. That's the best training. The labor people didn't get it. They stayed a week and went back to their big jobs and comfortable homes. They hadn't seen training, but the people here see it and I see it. The picket line is where a man makes his commitment, and it's irrevocable; and the longer he's on the picket line, the stronger the commitment. The workers on the ranch committee who don't know how to speak, or who never speak—after five days on the picket lines they speak right out, and they speak better." [30]

By speaking of defending ideals and preserving traditions, however, Chavez engages in this sort of conflict without trying to subject the growers to humiliating defeat. "Let them have their pride," he says,

"What we want is the contract. This is what they fail to understand. We are not out to put them out of business, because our people need the work; we are out to build a union, and we'll negotiate half our lives to get it. If we can get better wages and conditions for the workers, we are willing to give up something. But the growers choose to make it a personal fight, so we have to do something to save their face. . . . So things can't look as if we are getting a victory and they are not." [31]

The key to the success of their process, thus, lies in the participation of the workers themselves. Every step that Chavez takes—from his personal contacts with the workers to his insistence that they join the picket lines—aims at providing the direct involvement upon which personal dignity and political democracy depend. "We don't need perfect political systems," he says, "If you don't participate in the planning, you just don't count." [32]

It is on this point, primarily, in fact, that both the growers and the Teamsters now resist Chavez. " 'The companies wanted to come direct to *La Paz* and have us straighten out the problems,' " he explains, " 'but we can't do that.' " [33] Instead, the Farm Workers union gives powers to individual ranch committees, both to manage their internal affairs and to participate directly in contract negotiations. The procedure is cumbersome, but Chavez defends it:

"We have to preserve the ranch committees. They must have direct representation at the convention. They not only have the right, but the responsibility to deal with their own internal problems. They deal with the members directly. They are involved at all levels of grievances but they must be responsible for the first and second steps of the grievance procedures." [34]

This is participatory democracy with a vengeance, but Chavez believes that the future success of his organization depends upon it. Why spend so much time with individual workers, if not to prepare them for self-government? Why set an example of courage, if the workers themselves never feel the pride that comes from displaying it? What good is gentleness if a community's members never relate to one another? How can a congregation fulfill God's will, if the parishioners never take responsibility for their decisions? What purpose is served by endless conflict, if it leads only to the replacement of one boss by another? These questions dictate a single answer to Chavez—the workers must participate in their union, or it will not be their union.

THE ORGANIZING OF DEMOCRATIC IDEALISM

In *The Federalist Papers*, James Madison warned, "A zeal for different opinions concerning religion, concerning government, and many other points," had, "divided mankind into parties, inflamed them with mutual animosity, and rendered them much more disposed to vex and oppress each other than to cooperate for their common good." [35] The possibility that private groups within a democracy might promote public values never entered the Madisonian equation. The only way to guard against the "evils of faction" was to design a government sufficiently complex to prevent any one group from gaining ultimate control.

Writing about America forty years later, Alexis de Tocqueville came to exactly the opposite conclusion:

> Among democratic nations . . . all the citizens are independent and feeble; they can hardly do anything by themselves, and none of them can oblige his fellow men to lend him their assistance. They all, therefore, become powerless if they do not learn voluntarily to help one another. If men living in democratic countries had no right and no inclination to associate for political purposes, their independence would be in great jeopardy, but they might long preserve their wealth and their cultivation: whereas if they never acquired the habit of forming associations in ordinary life, civilization itself would be endangered. [36]

Cesar Chavez would agree with Tocqueville. Many observers see in the Farm Workers only a new "interest group," using extraordinary tactics to achieve essentially private goals—economic security, higher wages, collective bargaining. Chavez views the process in reverse. To him, demands for economic improvement are beginning steps toward the over-all improvement of the workers' lot—toward their gradual assumption of democratic rights and responsibilities. Even now, the union runs co-operatives, health clinics, and community centers. It sponsors voter regis-tration drives and supports candidates. It trains student volunteers to work with farmworkers, while it sends farmworkers to work on the boy-cotts in the major cities. It is already a cause. The question now is whether it can evolve into a full-scale, democratic culture.

By any standard, of course, Chavez' success has been improbable. Farmworkers could not be organized, but he is organizing them. Door-to-door canvassing has vanished in the electronic age, but Chavez makes it work. Today, idealistic leaders either sell out, give up, or get shot, but Chavez has preserved his principles over twenty difficult years. Tradition, particularly religious tradition, is losing its force everywhere, but Chavez is bringing people into his movement on the strength of its appeal. Most Americans have lost confidence in politics, but the Farm Workers are devoting their lives to it. Modern organizations cannot sur-vive unless they bureaucratize, but Chavez is creating ranch com-mittees and democratic conventions. From this perspective, it is not sur-prising that the Farm Workers face problems. It is astonishing that they exist at all.

Yet Chavez' accomplishment should tell us something about the power of this kind of political leadership. The prophet worries about the vision; the organizer tends to the community itself. The people learn to love him, so that through him, they can find one another and the common pur-poses that will sustain them. It is a Populist leadership; and although Chavez is a Mexican-American, he has become our major spokesman for the Populist tradition—that unique synthesis of religious idealism, economic radicalism, and political democracy that modernity was sup-posed to have crushed. Chavez knows better than anyone what a Popu-list faces today—corporate dominance of the economy, bureaucratic domi-nance of the polity, and materialist perversion of our basic civic values. Chavez should have lost to the growers and the Teamsters long ago, as surely as David should have lost to Goliath. His success should re-mind us that when Divine inspiration brings a people together, even their slingshots can become powerful weapons.

NOTES

1. Cesar Chavez, "Sharing the Wealth," *Playboy*, January 1970, p. 127.
2. Joan London and Henry Anderson, *So Shall Ye Reap* (New York: Thomas Y. Crowell, 1970), p. 143.
3. Ibid., pp. 143–44.

4. Peter Matthiessen, *Sal Si Puedes: Cesar Chavez and the New American Revolution* (New York: Random House, 1969), pp. 45–46.

5. Cesar Chavez, "The Organizer's Tale," *Ramparts*, 5 July 1966, p. 44.

6. Matthiessen, *Sal Si Puedes*, pp. 57–58.

7. Ibid., p. 172.

8. John Gregory Dunne, *Delano* (New York: Farrar, Straus & Giroux, 1971), p. 171.

9. Matthiessen, *Sal Si Puedes*, p. 115.

10. Ronald B. Taylor, *Chavez and the Farmworkers* (Boston: Beacon Press, 1975), p. 212.

11. Ibid., p. 215.

12. Matthiessen, *Sal Si Puedes*, p. 115.

13. Taylor, *Chavez*, p. 139.

14. Cesar Chavez, "Non-Violence Still Works," *Look* 33 (1 April 1969): 52.

15. Taylor, *Chavez*, p. 300.

16. Ibid., p. 140.

17. Matthiessen, *Sal Si Puedes*, p. 88.

18. Ibid., pp. 147–48.

19. Ibid., p. 116.

20. Taylor, *Chavez*, p. 229.

21. Ibid., p. 225.

22. Chavez, "The Organizer's Tale," p. 46.

23. Matthiessen, *Sal Si Puedes*, p. 128.

24. Ibid., pp. 127–28.

25. Cesar Chavez, "Letter to the Growers," reprinted in Paul Fusco and George D. Horwitz, *La Causa: The California Grape Strike* (New York: Macmillan, 1970), p. 14.

26. Matthiessen, *Sal Si Puedes*, p. 126.

27. Chavez, "Non-Violence Still Works," p. 57.

28. Ibid., p. 52.

29. Ibid., p. 14.

30. Matthiessen, *Sal Si Puedes*, pp. 83–84.

31. Ibid., pp. 105–6.

32. Chavez, "Sharing the Wealth," p. 20.

33. Taylor, *Chavez*, p. 20.

34. Ibid., p. 20.

35. James Madison, Number 10, in *The Federalist Papers*, ed. Clinton Rossiter (New York: Mentor, 1961), p. 79.

36. Alexis de Tocqueville, *Democracy in America*, ed. Phillips Bradley (New York: Vintage Books, 1954), 2:115.

Part 3

Public Power
and
Private Values

EDITOR'S INTRODUCTION

Political leaders elected at all levels have been put on the defensive in the twentieth century. Pressure applied by nongovernmental leaders has in many cases forced elected officials to respond to their initiative and to judge among their policy alternatives. Political leaders, to be sure, have attempted to establish positions independent of these private leaders. Their successes and failures in these endeavors have determined the course of the American polity and will continue to do so. The four leaders examined in part three have all confronted great pressures. Mayors James Michael Curley and John V. Lindsay both faced the pressures of disparate ethnic groups, labor unions, and business forces of urban America. Each attempted to establish an independent and forceful direction for his city. At the same time, each realized the need to maintain close and personal contact with his constituents. Likewise, on the national level, John F. Kennedy and Lyndon B. Johnson recognized the need to balance demands from a wide variety of pressure groups with the requirements of national political leadership.

James Michael Curley and John V. Lindsay provide sharply different images of urban political leadership. Their circumstances were, of course, very different; but their styles and policies, their successes and failures, present a wide range of possibilities to present and future leaders. Dennis Hale depicts the late mayor of Boston as a figure far more

intriguing than the character modeled after him, Mayor Frank Skeffing-
ton, in Edwin O'Connor's *The Last Hurrah*. To speak of Curley solely as
"the Mayor of the Poor" is to lose sight of the breadth of his achievements
and the doggedness of his determination. Working within the strict limitations of the "Boston Reform Charter" of 1909, Curley created "a local
Democratic Party that anticipated by twenty years the party put together on a national level during the New Deal." Curley created a
vigorous local politics, the likes of which few urban centers in the twentieth century can match. Mr. Hale suggests that in this vitality there is
"revealed what modern politics sorely lacks; a dimension of humanity
that the most efficient welfare state will never approach."

William D'Arrienzo paints a picture of a very different urban leader.
A man whose attachment to the people of his city was more symbolic
than real, John Lindsay also lacked a clear, substantive policy direction
that might have won him the support of those people from whom his
background and his style constantly separated him. John Lindsay, urges
Mr. D'Arrienzo, "was a combination of a moral leader, who rejected
consensus politics as well as the role of prudent statesman, and a man
who was committed to the modern techniques of governing, i.e., scientific management and public relations." Lindsay was, in the end, a
victim of his own techniques. It may be, as City Club members suggested, that he was more "interested in theory than action," but there
is no indication that there was anything "political" about it. "Theorize he
did," concludes Mr. D'Arrienzo, "but not sufficiently about *homo politicus.*"

The differences between John F. Kennedy and Lyndon B. Johnson
are illustrative of the range of problems confronting an American President who would offer decisive leadership. "No recent American leader,"
argues Bruce Miroff, "has so clearly—and effectively—laid claim to excellence as John F. Kennedy." It was, however, an excellence that is
hard to capture, for by its very nature it "required a certain distance between leaders and followers. Leaders had to be wary of the force of
popular passions and mass demands." That sense of distance, Miroff
argues, can be found throughout his term in both foreign and domestic
policy. It was a distance that produced more successes in foreign than in
domestic politics, but the claim of excellence and the sense of distance
that accompanied it were constants. In conclusion, Mr. Miroff suggests,
"claims of excellence similar to those of John Kennedy will be heard
again from the White House. It is crucial that those claims be weighed
and tested." Finally, he suggests, "Democratic excellence should not . . .
involve the monopolization of political activity apart from and above
an admiring people." It should instead be measured "by their capacity
to deepen public understanding and to stimulate public participation."

"The differences between John Kennedy and Lyndon Johnson," asserts Wilson Carey McWilliams, "made them a 'balanced ticket' in 1960. New England Catholic and Texas Protestant, the two were predictably dissimilar in political style. Kennedy, as the public saw him, appeared to personify youthful idealism." Johnson, on the other hand, "was content with the public's contrasting image of him as a shrewd, rather devious political veteran, full of 'human juices'—as David Halberstam later described him—and thoroughly down to earth." Whatever the truth of these caricatures, suggests Mr. McWilliams, "they were also designedly misleading. Few suspected, in 1960, that Johnson a 'Southern moderate,' would be far more militant than Kennedy in combating racial and economic inequality. And, despite the impression he had cultivated, Lyndon Johnson was not a simple-souled 'man of the people.' "

On the contrary, argues Mr. McWilliams, Johnson feared the mass public and saw no "way by which it might be reduced to more human and more educable proportions. Comfortable with a smaller political scale of things, he had also been schooled in the Madisonian tradition which values large states with great power and wealth, able to provide for the private interests of the many." In the end, the conflict between Johnson's public face and private style proved decisive. "Johnson's immediate circle in Washington," concludes Mr. McWilliams, "could not break a mass public into local groups, in which people could be addressed and heard with some respect for their diversity, their dignity, and their individuality."

Caught between the neo-Madisonian and neo-Tocquevillean forces of the private sector, American political leaders have had a difficult task in guiding and educating the American public at the very time when it seems most in need of direction. The examples of these four leaders may help to establish guidelines. *Public* leadership would seem to require the reassertion of a sense of who the people are. The immensity and diversity of the people make the task a demanding one, but the possibilities are there. National political leadership must seek out, listen to, and foster the development of local leadership, public and private. Local political leaders must identify and activate citizen groups. The grass roots of American politics must be revitalized, for, in the end, only the people can tell leaders who they are.

In the absence of such action on national and local levels, the direction of the future of the United States will be left to private leaders. It may be that they will take care of the American people, but then the American people will have little control over such leaders' decisions.

Chapter Eight

James Michael Curley
Leadership and the Uses of Legend

> But if you suppose that any man will show you the art of becoming great
> in the city, and yet not conforming yourself to the ways of the city,
> whether for better or worse, then I can only say that you are mistaken,
> Callicles; for he who would deserve to be the true natural friend of the
> Athenian Demus . . . must be by nature like them, and not an imitator
> only.
>
> —Plato, *Gorgias*

DENNIS HALE

When James Michael Curley died in Boston, in November 1958, his wake
and funeral were the occasions for an unprecedented display of mass
affection. More than one hundred thousand people marched in a quiet
file past his coffin in the State House on Beacon Hill, and nearly one million people—over half the population of the Boston metropolitan area—
lined the streets for his funeral procession. It was, without doubt, the
largest funeral in the state's history, and it was all the more remarkable because it was in honor of a man who had not held office for ten
years, who had served two terms in jail at opposite ends of his career,
who had been excoriated by virtually every respectable citizen in his
state, and who was widely believed to have been a shameless crook.[1]

They scoffed when Jim Curley called himself the "Mayor of the
Poor," but, by the time he was laid to rest, there was no doubting the
sincerity of the common people's approval of that title. From all over the
city, they came to pay respects to "the boss," and to retell the incredible
Curley stories that make up one of the twentieth century's genuine folk
legends: stories of midnight visits to families in distress, of money given
with no hope of repayment, of jobs found where no job had a right to
exist. These stories were the basis of the Curley legend, and there is
no doubt that the vast majority of them were simple, unembellished
truth. "It's hard to find anyone," a Globe reporter commented, "who
really hated Jim Curley." [2] Thousands of Bostonians held a deep love for
this strange man, and to thousands more he was a "landmark." When

he died, it seemed to many as if something impossible had happened, and the crowds at the State House and in the street were orderly as only the dazed can be. One reporter, one of many who had fought Curley, remarked, "Boston will hardly seem the same anymore without him." [3]

There was another response to Curley's passing, however, which was equally noteworthy, if perhaps not so surprising. Political observers were unanimous in the conviction that, with Curley's death, an "era of history" had come to a close. Typical of this reaction were the comments of Senator John F. Kennedy and an anonymous editorial writer for the Boston *Globe.* Kennedy was careful to call Curley "an inimitable part of a memorable era." The *Globe* noted more bluntly that "the day of the former mayor was over several years ago. We can now begin to consider his career in the light of history." John Powers, a Boston politician who had grown up in Curley's shadow, said that "the passing of James Michael Curley closes the door on an era of history." The *New York Times* weighed in with "the last of the big-city bosses." [4]

In the years since his death, these perceptions have hardened, so that today Boston displays a curious ambivalence toward its most notorious statesman. There is a Tobin Bridge, a Fitzgerald Expressway, a Storrow Drive, and a Hynes Auditorium, but the only municipal institutions named for Curley are a grade school in Jamaica Plain and a bathhouse in South Boston. An oil portrait once hung in the lobby of Boston City Hospital, bearing the legend, "James Michael Curley, Mayor of the Poor," but it was removed several years ago. A committee of the State Legislature was formed in 1974 to devise a suitable memorial to the former governor, but it has yet to act.

On the other hand, there is a nostalgia in the city, an eagerness to recall the old battles and those who fought them: Curley in particular. The nostalgia is evident in the continued popularity of Edwin O'Connor's *The Last Hurrah,* whose main character is "a pale carbon copy of Curley" (according to Curley). That novel is especially popular among liberals and intellectuals, two voting blocs not previously disposed to politicians of the Curley type. "Eat and Drink to the Last Hurrah!" proclaims an ad for the Parker House, formerly a favorite watering hole for City Hall types, now a kind of political museum where the walls are festooned with photographs of exotic figures in frock coats and derby hats. The local public broadcasting station produced a popular documentary on Curley last year, and a Massachusetts Institute of Technology seminar on his career was so crowded people had to be turned away.

The broad outlines of the Curley legend are fairly well known by now. According to the legend, Curley was a Robin Hood from the Irish slums who used politics as a way out of the ghetto, confounding his Brahmin opponents with political daring and Gaelic wit. In the process, he accumulated a vast army of followers whose votes he could count on in return for jobs, Christmas turkeys, and the boost he gave to their ethnic pride. Finally, a combination of changing times and younger voters brought his career to a timely end. Just in time, in fact, for the end of an era.

That is the legend in its benign form. Among Curley's detractors (and he had lots of them, managing to be the most popular and the most hated politician in Boston at the same time), the story is somewhat different. In this version, Curley was a brilliant but unscrupulous demagogue, who fought his way to the top with a combination of reprehensible campaign tactics and outrageous promises. Once in office, he replaced worthy public servants with incompetent hacks and made himself fabulously wealthy at the public's expense. His behavior finally became so odious that even his supporters turned against him, and he was consigned to well-deserved oblivion.[5]

As is usual in these cases, the truth lies somewhere else, although parts of each legend are true. However, the debate over whether James Curley was a saint or a sinner has long obscured other issues raised by his career, particularly those having to do with his performance as a political leader.

That subject raises a flock of images, most of them unfavorable. Curley's name has gone into the history books under the sections labeled "demagogue" and "boss," two of the most unsavory categories in our political language. He is virtually a model of everything our tradition says a politician should not be. Nevertheless, Curley has earned a subterranean popularity in certain circles, much like that of another famous reprobate, George Washington Plunkitt. It is almost as if the judgment of history were edging toward the judgment of the Boston voters who said that they were planning to vote for Curley, "despite his faults," because they could not bring themselves to vote for any of his opponents.

James Michael Curley was definitely not what James Madison envisioned for his country. He is more like the specter Madison hoped the Constitution would permanently lay to rest. And yet, if Curley's career is looked at in the context of the time and the place in which he operated, it may be possible to see it as something more than a regrettable aberration. It may even be possible to see it as something more than the inevitable expression of an excluded group seeking recognition and status. There are ways in which the constitutional tradition of James Madison made James Curley a necessity, and reasons for believing that his appearance in Boston was a stroke of luck.

To say this is not to deny Curley's faults, nor to gloss over the fact that some of those faults were serious. But our historical memory enforces a double standard, by which the sins of the respectable and the sins of the unconventional are weighed on different scales. That double standard has prevented us from understanding why "bosses" and "demagogues" appear, by blinding us to their accomplishments. Once those accomplishments are understood it will be possible to give the sins the attention they deserve.

The most striking feature of Jim Curley's career was its remarkable tenacity. He was born in 1874, and ran his last campaign in 1955, well within the memory of most contemporary Boston voters. He was an active politician for over half a century, running for his first office in 1899. He ran in twenty-seven major campaigns, winning seventeen and losing ten. He held office without interruption for the first seventeen years of this century, and until the last decade of his life his longest period out of office was only six years. He held one office or another for thirty-five out of his fifty-six years in public life: sixteen as mayor of Boston, eight as a congressman, seven as a member of the Boston City Council, two as governor of Massachusetts, and two as a state representative from Roxbury.

It is clear from this record that Curley was not really a "boss"—at least not in the sense that Tom Pendergast, Frank Hague, and Ed Crump were bosses. Curley controlled no party machine capable of maintaining him in office, and which depended for its survival on his guidance. In Boston, all the bosses were ward leaders: Except for John Fitzgerald and Curley himself (who started out as the leader of Ward 17), the ward leaders were content to influence mayors. They did not seek the office for themselves.

Curley might have remained a ward leader, but several circumstances conspired to push him in another direction. First of all, Curley's was not a personality that throve in the constricted world of the ward hall. He was too expansive and too ambitious. The personality of the successful ward leader is suggested by a favorite maxim of Martin Lomasney, boss of the West End: "Don't speak a sentence if a word will do; don't say anything if you can just nod your head." Curley had also been given reason to dislike ward bosses as a class, having grown up under an especially benighted one, "Pea-Jacket" Maguire, whose policy was to refuse help to any family without a voter in it. As a result, the Curley family was left defenseless when his father died in an industrial accident, and James and his brother John were forced to work long hours before and after school. Curley's first political success was the destruction of the remnants of the Maguire organization in his home ward, and from his distaste for Maguire, it was but a short step to contempt for ward bosses in general.

But there were more than personal factors involved. Curley sensed

at the outset of his career that the days of the ward leader were num-
bered. The ease with which he had overthrown Maguire's successors may
have had something to do with this: The boss's power was after all
nothing more than a magic trick that any aspiring young man could
learn for himself. Curley read the lesson of that defeat and decided
that, if he could do it to Maguire, someone else could do it to Curley.
He wanted a political base less vulnerable to attack.

Maguire's defeat taught another lesson. If one ward boss was vulnerable, so, too, were the others. Boston was a small city, but it was crowded
with ward leaders and would-be leaders. Under the City Charter in
force during the latter part of the nineteenth century, Boston had been
divided into 24 wards, each with its own ward organization, its own
leader, and its own continual intrigues. A loose confederation of ward
leaders known as the "Board of Strategy" attempted to bring order to
this system by picking mayoral candidates and running them on the
Democratic ticket, but, with such a crowded field, defections were inevitable. Moreover, competition for the limited patronage spoils of city
government was fierce. Curley was probably correct in his estimate that
"the institution [of the ward leader] was outmoded by 1911, and was
breeding party strife, petty animosity and cheap political chicanery,
and was a roadblock in the way of enlightened city government." [6]

The Brahmins had their own motives for attacking this system, and
delivered it a fatal blow with the City Charter of 1909 (the "Reform
Charter"), written by a Republican state legislature and forced on Boston over the protests of the Democratic City Committee. This charter
gave Boston a stronger mayor and changed the City Council from a
bicameral legislature with 84 members, chosen by wards, to a unicameral
one with only 9 members, all elected at-large on a nonpartisan ballot.
The mayor was also to be elected on a nonpartisan ballot, and in 1909
the favorite candidate was Republican banker James J. Storrow, candidate of the Good Government Association and the Municipal Citizens
League. It was thought that Storrow could be elected if he did not
have to declare his party affiliation on the ballot, thus beginning a long
reign of business-minded Republican mayors who would owe nothing to
the Democratic ward leaders. But it was too late. Too many Republicans
had already left for greener (but less Irish) pastures, and Storrow was
narrowly defeated by John ("Honey Fitz") Fitzgerald.[7]

The Reform Charter imposed on Boston a set of institutional constraints with which it has struggled ever since.[8] Boston has a reputation
for being a fiercely "political" city, yet the truth of the matter is that its
political life is normally pallid to the point of invisibility. The City Council and the School Committee (also small, also elected on a nonpartisan,
at-large basis) conduct their business well out of sight of a largely

apathetic public. The authors of the Reform Charter, not trusting the Republican Party's ability to control the City Council, gave it very little power. Mayors in the twentieth century have scarcely paid it any attention except to ridicule it. The School Committee's business is fairly routine, and during the past few decades its limited power over educational policy has been steadily eroded by state and federal regulations. Currently it is held virtually in receivership by the federal courts, and has all but disappeared from the news columns.

The mayor under the Reform Charter has substantial power on paper, but the method by which he is elected severely inhibits his use of that power. By destroying political parties, the nonpartisan ballot cuts the mayor off from his sources of support in the local ward organizations, a fact which Mayor Kevin White, first elected in 1967, has tried to correct by establishing "little City Halls" in various neighborhoods. But since the power of the little City Hall is the mayor's power exclusively, he accomplishes little more than presenting a convenient target for neighborhood grievances. He does not gain support for his policies or augment his power in any way.

The "Boston Plan," then, tends to produce weak and often irresponsible city governments. Mayors under this system are usually cautious, low-profile executives; when they try to break out of this pattern, they invariably get into trouble, as Mayor White discovered when trying to exercise leadership during Boston's busing crisis of the past few years.

Curley understood the implications of this charter better than anyone else, and, when he was ready to run for mayor in 1914, he ran a campaign that set the pattern for all his subsequent campaigns. He ran against everybody: the newspapers, the Republican legislature, the Democratic City Committee, and the Good Government Association. He called the chairman of the Democratic City Committee a "barnacle on the ship of state" and gave the Good Government Association a name that was to become a label for reformers everywhere: "Goo-Goo's." He won two-thirds of the city's wards and defeated Thomas Kenny, candidate of the Good Government Association and the Democratic ward leaders (such are the alliances produced by the nonpartisan ballot) by just under six thousand votes.

Curley understood that, under a system such as Boston was given, caution was a fatal mistake. The politician who kept a low profile would very quickly sink out of sight. So Curley cultivated controversy, and if he could not find a scrap to get into, he would manufacture one. Opponents soon found that it was futile to remind audiences that Curley had spent 60 days in jail for taking a civil service exam for a constituent, since Curley supporters in the audience would simply yell, "He did it for a friend." [9] When the Ku Klux Klan stopped burning crosses at Curley

rallies during his 1924 race for governor—they found he was mobilizing
the anti-Klan vote in his favor—he simply instructed his campaign workers to burn the crosses themselves.[10] Shut out of the Al Smith campaign by
his opponents in the Democratic Party, Curley hired a hall in downtown
Boston and announced his intention to add one hundred thousand new
voters to the registration lists, and then came within a respectable distance of that goal, a substantial contribution to Smith's seventeen-thou-
sand-vote majority in the state.[11] Shut out of the Massachusetts delegation
to the 1932 Democratic convention because of his support for Franklin
Roosevelt, Curley managed to talk his way onto the Puerto Rican delegation, under the name "Jaime Miguel Curleo." [12]

Controversies such as these were as much a part of the Curley legend
as his efforts as "Mayor of the Poor." His strategy was simple: Make a
lot of promises, be careful to keep most of them, and make as much
noise as possible in the process. With this strategy Curley was able to
make Boston's moribund political system accomplish what other mayors
found impossible or unwise. During his four terms as mayor and his two
years as governor, the city and state witnessed an unprecedented redis-
tribution of wealth. Slum areas built on swamps were torn down, filled in,
and rebuilt. Cow paths became streets. Auto and subway tunnels were
built or extended, for the first time connecting East Boston (an Italian
neighborhood) with the mainland. The City Hospital received its first
major expansion and overhaul since its construction in the mid-nine-
teenth century. Health units and schools were built in poor neighborhoods. Through the city's power of eminent domain, Curley took unused
waterfront property and turned it into a series of public beaches—the only
ones in Boston. He motorized the police and fire departments and expanded the airport. He built bathhouses, parks, and playgrounds.[13]

All of this construction was expensive, and Curley paid for it by raising taxes on real estate owned by banks, businesses, and newspapers.[14] He
also cajoled wealthy Brahmins into leaving their money to the city when
they died (in return for having their names chiseled in granite), raising
5.5 million dollars this way in one year.[15] And he created jobs. During the
depths of the Depression, as governor, he found jobs for one hundred
thousand people in a single year.[16] Every day he was in office, long lines
of job-seekers and supplicants formed outside his home and in the corridors of City Hall, and Curley would speak with each one, a practice begun during his first mayoralty as a way of undercutting the ward
leaders. He could meet, and probably do favors for, two hundred people a day, or two hundred thousand people during his first term alone.[17]

Curley was also responsible for establishing the principle of a mini-
mum wage for city employees, the recognition of city unions, securing a
48-hour week for employees in state institutions, prohibiting the prac-

tice of attaching wages for repayment of debt, major reforms in the Workmen's Compensation laws and the Old Age Assistance Act, the first credit union and the first retirement fund for city workers, the reduction of gas and electricity rates, and the establishment of planning boards for both the city of Boston and the state. William Green, president of the AFL, said of Curley's term as governor, "More laws in the interest of the worker were enacted in 1935 in Massachusetts than in any 10-year period in the history of the Commonwealth." [18]

The final element in Curley's strategy was his personal generosity. As his critics rightly pointed out, he was often generous with other peoples' money, but that hardly mattered to the beneficiaries. It is impossible to estimate how much money he gave away during his career, but certainly it must have amounted to a small fortune. He gave away hundreds of dollars a day during his walks to and from City Hall, and he boasted that he gave 20 percent of his salary to the poor, challenging his businessman opponents to do likewise. In flush times he gave away his entire salary, and he was a master of the perfectly timed donation: When he returned to office after his prison term for mail fraud in 1947, he donated his entire salary to the prisoners at the Deer Island county jail.

Where all this money came from was the object of considerable speculation, and if the Boston Finance Commission was never able to prove corruption charges against Curley, one reason may be that he never held onto money long enough to get caught with it.

There was method in this madness, of course. Curley's munificence made him extremely popular, not so much because the silver dollars he gave away actually raised anyone out of poverty (although there were times in Boston when a dollar went a long way), but because of what the giving meant. Curley was fond of comparing the methods of the traditional welfare agencies with what he called "Curleyism." The charitable associations and the city welfare departments, he said, did not care about their clients, did not understand them, and, above all, did not respect them. Curley, on the other hand, by his generous and unquestioning gifts of jobs and money helped his constituents without hurting their pride. He was their chief, and it was his responsibility to help them through the hard times. That was the natural way. Moreover, they could pay him back for his help. They could give him their support, and that made all the difference. Curley was not shy about asking for repayment. "If Curley has been kind," he said in a radio broadcast, "if Curley has been generous, if Curley has helped the unfortunate in their time of need, then you clearly have a duty to perform on election day."

The proof that Boston voters felt obliged was demonstrated in 1941. The Massachusetts Supreme Court in that year upheld a judgment against Curley sought three years before by Mayor Frederick Mansfield, who had sued Curley for the return of money allegedly misappropriated during his third term as mayor. The Court ordered him to pay $42,629 at the rate of $500 a week, or go to jail. This was one of Curley's lean years, and he went home that day fully resigned to another prison term. The next day the usual line of supporters showed up outside his door, but this time they were there to give money instead of seek favors. They came every day for a month, in which time enough money was raised to pay the entire fine.[19]

And yet the obituaries were correct. By the 1950s Curley, like the ward bosses he had replaced, was a figure from the past, an embarrassment to the "new Boston" rising out of the dust of urban renewal. Boston received another "Charter Reform" in 1949, calling for preliminary and run-off elections for mayor, bringing more order, if not more participation, to Boston's elections. Although he ran for mayor in 1949, 1951, and 1955, he was defeated on all three occasions. In 1955, he finished third for the first time in his career.

The coalition that Curley termed "the State Street wrecking crew" was already at work, clearing Martin Lomasney's old bailiwick in the West End to make way for high-rise, upper-income housing, and tearing down Scollay Square to clear space for a new City Hall and a complex of office buildings. The men who occupied the mayor's office during the 1950s and 1960s—John Hynes and John Collins—were judged by press and reformers to be a vast improvement over the old breed: more honest, efficient, and business minded, closer to what Edward C. Banfield and James Q. Wilson have defined as the "public-regarding" ethos once identified with Anglo-American Protestants.[20]

Curley's death seemed, on the whole, to be an obvious symbol for the end of the bad old days. And according to the eulogists, those days were very bad, indeed. Reviews of Curley's career written after his death always stress the raucous, violent, and sometimes terrifying quality of the old-style campaigns. Curley seemed to share that view in his autobiography, although naturally his disapproval is clearly mixed with a great fondness for the past.

All those uproarious years of politics have gone a-glimmering now, but there are chuckleworthy memories. I can still see the boys waylaying the opposition as they delivered eleventh hour defamatory circulars against Curley. I can still hear Bill Gleason asking his South End audience to vote for him as he offered to swear by Holy Scripture that he "socked" Governor Joe Ely the day he threw out the first ball at Fenway Park. That was the campaign issue when Gleason ran for the House of Representatives: Did he or did he not hit the Governor before he was ejected from the baseball park? I sometimes wonder whether the electorate gives as much thought today to fundamental issues as they did in the old days.[21]

Others recall the past with less tolerance. Francis Russell grew up in a middle-class Protestant enclave in Dorchester known as "the Hill," and this is his recollection of the bitter 1921 mayoral campaign:

> To the Hill, the city's personification of evil was its feared and hated mayor, James Michael Curley. I remember the turbulence of his second election, when he was opposed by a reform candidate who carried the "suburbs," Dorchester, West Roxbury, and Hyde Park, but failed ignominiously with the massed voters of Boston proper. The evening of Curley's victory was one of chagrin and frustration for the Hill. Several groups of grown-ups stood with us children near the pignut trees watching Curley's triumphant torchlight parade as it swung down Walk Hill Street below us, a cavalcade of autos with the tops down that wound along toward Forest Hills under the arching elms like a grossly irridescent and enveloping snake.[22]

Judged by contemporary standards, the political life of Boston before the Second World War was a riotous affair indeed. Elections were frequently dishonest and always bitter. In the beginning the "issues" were reduced to one: the anger of the immigrant, the resistance of the native. That anger threatened constantly to erupt in violence, and it was a rare election rally in which someone was not hurt. Nor was the violence directed only at the powerful; it was more frequently the expression of intra-ethnic rivalry for place and position.

Curley was always accused of exploiting this situation, and there is plenty of evidence in the record of his campaigns to support the charge that he was a demagogue. He ridiculed all of his opponents, but he saved his special oratorical gifts for the Brahmins. He impugned their motives and lampooned their traditions, including such favorite patriotic symbols as the Boston Tea Party, which he referred to in a mock-serious historical lecture as "a desperate act carried out by a band of drunks." He liked to remind Back Bay audiences that their ancestors had hanged Quakers and made millions in the slave trade. He called them pirates and skinflints and claimed that Boston hadn't been a fit place to live until the Irish arrived. ("Politicians who cannot rise above ridicule," he wrote in his autobiography, "are sheep for the shearing.")

Yet there was another side to Curley's oratory, and, when he wished to, he could be quite respectful of his opponents' traditions. He frequently referred to "our" ancestors when discussing the state's past, and was always available to deliver an appropriate oration in observance of such Yankee holidays as Bunker Hill Day and Patriots' Day. And he could chide the Yankees in a constructive way as well, as he did during the Harvard University Tercentenary celebration in 1936, when, as Governor of the Commonwealth, he gave an address, in which he attempted to remind the University of its origins as a public school and its obligations to the people of the state.[23]

Curley was bent on deflating the considerable mythology of Protestant New England, but what kept him from being just a "Brahmin-baiter" was his stronger desire to be remembered as "Mayor of the Poor." This led him to attack the "F.I.F.s" (First Irish Families) with a scorn equal to that directed at the wealthiest Brahmins. In fact, it was a largely Irish establishment which he attempted to overthrow in 1914. The coalition Curley put together in his winning campaigns was invariably a coalition of the poorest of Boston's voters, with his heaviest votes coming from low-income Irish, Italians, Jews, and blacks (*see figure 1*). The views he expressed and the policies he supported were designed to appeal to these groups, with the result that he lost great chunks of the Irish vote in the more affluent wards. Irish businessmen were no more anxious than their State Street brethren to hear that "national prosperity is dependent upon a more equitable distribution of the fruits of industry, or in other words, a larger distribution of the profits . . . to labor and a less generous distribution to capital."[24] Nor were Irish businessmen enthusiastic about Curley's tax policies.[25]

What Curley accomplished in this way was the creation of a local Democratic Party that anticipated by twenty years the party put together on a national level during the New Deal. It included virtually every component of the New Deal party except liberal intellectuals, who found themselves separated from the "immigrant Democrats" on a host of issues, from prohibition to the League of Nations. It included Jews, blacks, and Italians at a time when those groups normally voted Republican. And, most importantly, it included new voters registered for the first time by the massive registration drives that were a frequent accompaniment to Curley's campaigns: an important advantage in the days when the turnout for Boston's mayoral elections was as high as 75 percent of registered voters.[26]

Yet, there is no doubt that Curley "played upon" the resentments of his constituents, that he used their anger, their sense of rejection, and their desire for recognition. Without such emotions, it is unlikely that Curley or any other Boston politician could have kept the public's at-

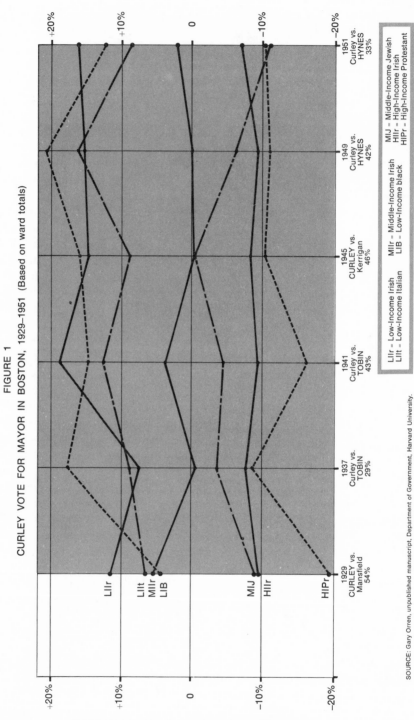

FIGURE 1

CURLEY VOTE FOR MAYOR IN BOSTON, 1929–1951 (Based on ward totals)

Percentage above or below city-wide vote for Curley

LIIr = Low-Income Irish   MIIr = Middle-Income Irish   MIJ = Middle-Income Jewish
LIIt = Low-Income Italian   LIB = Low-Income black   HIIr = High-Income Irish
                                                          HIPr = High-Income Protestant

SOURCE: Gary Orren, unpublished manuscript, Department of Government, Harvard University.

tention for five weeks, let alone fifty years, given the effects of the Reform Charter. That Charter ensured that only the noisiest campaign would awaken the voters' interest in politics, and at this sort of campaign Curley excelled. The setting he liked best was the campaign rally, where he could keep a huge crowd in thrall for hours with his booming voice, his archaic, nineteenth-century orator's accent, and a full panoply of stage props and carefully tutored shills. These events were great entertainment, and, in the old days at least, provoked a certain amount of audience participation. "Those were rough days in the political arena," Curley recalled in his autobiography, "and the gloves were off in every fight. Political rallies often degenerated into gang fights in which the guided missiles were sticks, stones, bricks and brass spittoons." [27]

But in the midst of the buncombe and the theatrics, the issues of the day managed to get mentioned with surprising regularity, and a political coalition of sorts was growing up around whatever issues touched the audience most deeply. These ranged from the League of Nations, an emotional issue in Boston because of the Irish question, to prohibition and the 40-hour week. Curley sought the most controversial of these issues, and often took stands that were unusual, given his constituency, taking advantage of his credits built up on previous occasions. Thus, he urged voters in 1919 to support the League of Nations by voting for the Democratic candidate for President, James M. Cox, who was campaigning on Woodrow Wilson's record.[28] He told the Boston Irish that Al Smith, however grand a man, could not be elected President because of his religion, and that they should support a Protestant aristocrat from New York, instead. Never so much of a political lone wolf as he pretended to be, he sought to play a role in the statewide Democratic Party and invariably supported men who had earlier been his bitter enemies, once they received the Party's nomination.[29]

In the end, however, the political quietism mandated by the charter was bound to have its way, aided by changes in the technology of campaigns and the climate of opinion regarding them. Curley was fairly effective on the radio, but he knew television would defeat him.

At a street corner rally you might gain votes if you said your opponent was built like a South Boston hydrant. . . . but this line of attack is not considered *comme il faut* by the network vice-presidents. . . . Impromptu speeches, prepared gesticulations, histrionics and other oratorical displays are as dated as an old-fashioned melodrama like "Bertha the Beautiful Sewing Machine Girl." Even Daniel Webster would have difficulty holding an audience today for more than an hour, unless he took time out, every ten minutes, to give away a frigidaire or an automobile.[30]

But before this happened, Boston's immigrant communities had found the voice that the 1909 Charter had attempted to deny them. Curley must be given part of the credit for the fact that those communities were able to dictate so many of the terms of their acceptance by the natives. Above all, Curley made the natives pay attention.

The story of Boston, unfortunately, does not have a happy ending. The city is still little more than a collection of ethnic neighborhoods without a center, and it will continue to be so, until it gets a government in which it is possible for citizens to participate at some level deeper than reading about it in the back pages of the newspaper. In that sense, Boston is an important test of the models of leadership under review in this book. The Madisonian model was expressed, however inadequately, in the Reform Charter, whose provisions echoed a time when Boston had been a small, homogeneous community capable of being governed by a public-spirited elite. But, in the very different circumstances of twentieth-century urban politics, "reform" possessed limitations, which Alexis de Tocqueville prepared us to understand. First, by ignoring the fact of gross social and economic inequality, "reform" left the city vulnerable to a tremendous explosion of bitterness at some point in the future. Second, by separating the city government from the roots of its popular support, "reform" denied to government the force and the energy that a more democratic politics could have given it.

Tocqueville predicted "strange vicissitudes" for a Republic whose governing institutions had lost contact with a vigorous local politics. Those troubles have been much in evidence of late, not only in Boston, but in all cities where local government has become isolated and purely defensive. With no visible means of support, modern politicians have become cautious, afraid to move beyond the extremely limited commitments they make to their constituents. They are then driven further into the company of the experts and the bureaucrats, whose loyalty they are sure of, and whose language and values they adopt as their own. Meanwhile, serious problems are left unattended, until an alienated populace comes face to face with a reality it can no longer avoid. That confrontation is bound to be explosive.

It is tempting to speculate on what Boston would be like today had there never been a James Michael Curley. The most likely pattern would have been a string of isolated mayors presiding over a series of powerless City Councils, leading to a virtual paralysis of local government or its capture by the city's powerful private institutions. But the real damage would have been done to the city's social fabric. Curley's reign amounted to a "Founding" of sorts for Boston's ethnic communities. Without him, the defensive isolation of the city's ethnic neighborhoods would have solidified much earlier. Certainly, none of Curley's successors has been able to duplicate his broad base of support among the "working poor" of those neighborhoods, a resource that contemporary politicians desperately need.

Modern politicians, then, might contemplate the career of Jim Curley, not in order to imitate it, but simply to learn from it what the possibilities are for an urban political leader. By accomplishing what he did against great odds, Curley proved that great accomplishments are still possible, even if they must be achieved in other ways, with other methods. By leaving behind a legacy of gratitude and genuine affection, he revealed what modern politics sorely lacks: a dimension of humanity that the most efficient welfare state will never approach.

NOTES

1. Attendance figures from the Boston *Globe*, 14, 15, 16 November 1958, p. 1.
2. Boston *Globe*, 13 November 1958, p. 5.
3. Ibid., p. 1.
4. Ibid., pp. 20, 28; *New York Times*, 13 November 1958, p. 1.
5. Various versions of the Curley legend can be found in the following: James Michael Curley, *I'd Do It Again: A Record of All My Uproarious Years* (Englewood Cliffs, N.J.: Prentice-Hall, 1957); Alfred Steinberg, *The Bosses* (New York: New American Library, 1974), chap. 3; J. Joseph Huthmacher, *Massachusetts People and Politics, 1919–1933* (New York: Atheneum, 1973); William V. Shannon, *The American Irish* (New York: Macmillan, 1963), chap. 12; Reinhard H. Luthin, *American Demagogues: Twentieth Century* (Gloucester, Mass.: P. Smith, 1959), chap. 2; Francis Russell, *The Great Interlude* (New York: McGraw-Hill, 1964); Joseph Dineen, *The Purple Shamrock* (New York: Norton, 1949).
6. Curley, *I'd Do It Again*, p. 114.
7. Since that time, Boston has had only one visibly Republican mayor, Malcolm Nichols, 1926 to 1930.
8. The city went back to a council elected by district in 1924, but switched to the at-large system again in 1949. It has kept the nonpartisan ballot without interruption. Cf. Edward C. Banfield and James Q. Wilson, *City Politics* (New York: Vintage Books, 1966), pp. 94, 154.
9. Curley, *I'd Do It Again*, pp. 69–71.
10. Steinberg, *The Bosses*, p. 161; Curley, *I'd Do It Again*, p. 183.
11. Huthmacher, *Massachusetts People*, pp. 176–77; Curley, *I'd Do It Again*, 191–92; Steinberg, *The Bosses*, 164–65.
12. Steinberg, *The Bosses*, p. 170.

13. Ibid., pp. 157–58, 150–51.
14. Ibid., p. 158.
15. Ibid., p. 163.
16. Ibid., p. 178.
17. Ibid., p. 150. A survey taken during the 1945 mayoral election showed that 10 percent of the voters declaring their intention to vote for Curley claimed to "know him personally." That works out to nearly twelve thousand people. Jerome S. Bruner and Sheldon J. Korchin, "The Boss and the Vote: Case Study in City Politics," *Public Opinion Quarterly* (Spring 1946):16–17.
18. *Addresses and Messages to the General Court, Proclamations, Official Addresses, Correspondence and Statements of His Excellency Governor James M. Curley for the Years 1935 and 1936* (Boston: Commonwealth of Massachusetts, 1936), pp. 13, 14, 24, 26, 28, 55; Curley, *I'd Do It Again*, pp. 65–66.
19. Steinberg, *The Bosses*, p. 186.
20. Banfield and Wilson, *City Politics*, pp. 138–50.
21. Curley, *I'd Do It Again*, pp. 158–59.
22. Russell, *The Great Interlude*, p. 183.
23. *Addresses*, p. 407.
24. *Addresses*, p. 9.
25. While it would be stretching a point to call Curley a Populist, his economic views were consistently radical, even during the New Deal, when he resisted the blandishments of Father (Charles Edward) Coughlin and others to mix his attacks on Roosevelt with a reactionary economic philosophy. His Administrations also had a remarkable hybrid quality, embracing such historically opposed goals as publicly elected utility commissions and the restoration of partisan elections.
26. *Annual Reports*, Board of Election Commissioners (Boston: City Printing Office, various years). In 1917, the turnout was 75.9 percent of registered voters; in 1921, 78 percent; in 1925, 78.7 percent. This compares to a turnout of roughly 60 percent in the 1950s and 1960s.
27. Curley, *I'd Do It Again*, p. 51.
28. Huthmacher, *Massachusetts People*, p. 40.
29. Ibid., p. 203.
30. Curley, *I'd Do It Again*, pp. 339, 340–41.

Chapter Nine

Symbols and Increments
The Political Leadership of John V. Lindsay

WILLIAM D'ARRIENZO

The democratic regime is always tenuous, for it has great difficulty in getting citizens to attend to its daily needs. The danger that it will degenerate into chaos is exceeded only by a still greater danger—that the chaos will be stilled by a tyrant. The tyrant will succeed because, in Alexis de Tocqueville's words, "the vices which despotism produces are precisely those which equality fosters," [1] i.e., civic indifference, suspicion, envy, and self-indulgence. Consequently, the task of political leadership in a democracy is to guide the citizenry so as to offset these tendencies. A major remedy is to encourage the practice of political liberty. The exercise of political liberty joins people together, nourishing sensitivity, concern, and pride in the performance of civic duties. This pride, in turn, nurtures a desire to continue, and the activity, over time, becomes habit and then "manners." Therefore, public activity in public institutions performs an integrative function which tempers the isolating effects of equality.[2] However, Tocqueville was cautious, if not pessimistic, about democracies achieving a balance between liberty and equality. Both human nature and history warn against an easy and stable union; [3] in addition, civic commitment must be practiced consistently over time before it can become a habit, or part of the "manners" of a people.[4] Thus, "Political liberty bestows exalted pleasures from time to time upon a certain number of citizens. Equality every day confers a number of small enjoyments on every man." [5]

This tension between liberty and equality will concern us first, in terms of decentralization and community control in New York City under John V. Lindsay's leadership. Our thesis is that his failure to understand this inherent stress, and his tendency to substitute rhetoric and hope for a sound understanding of the political culture, exacerbated an innately tenuous situation.

Our second concern will be to explore specific political problems arising from the conflict between the management and planning goals of experts in the bureaucracy and the more personalized problem-solving approaches of local interest-groups and community organizations. A structural concomitant of this conflict was the centralization of bureaucratic functions and the decentralization of planning and services, the latter being more symbolic than real. The values of management experts often were substituted for those of the community, while the mayor's knowledge depended more often on what managers told him rather than on what he could discover for himself. An operational type of leadership emerged, in which "style" and "the impression of maneuverability" became paramount.[6] This was especially the case in circumstances of community unrest—successful leadership was determined by "the affective response of political groupings in particular situations."[7]

Finally, the value framework under which John Lindsay operated will be explored. In general, the values of socioeconomic equality were primary, with little attention paid to political and spiritual values. Concessions to political aspirations were often secondary to the social and economic goals that Lindsay sought to achieve. Therefore, because of a lack of planning as to the role local political units should play, unstructured and chaotic political situations often resulted. A serious inattention to long-term political goals and to the overall character of the political culture of New York City seemed to be at the root of this disorder. There was never any vision of how to effect change while integrating the varying subcultural communities and independent interest groups into a common consciousness. As we shall see, there was a self-righteousness about the Lindsay Administration that drew serious political liabilities along in its wake. Too often "reform" failed and rhetoric succeeded. If there were gains, they were more often incremental than far reaching. The genesis and development of these three aspects of John Lindsay's leadership will be analyzed here. We shall begin with this last category, by exploring Lindsay's political values.

VALUES, PERSONALITY, AND POLITICAL STYLE

John Lindsay was educated in the tradition of noblesse oblige where championing the cause of the disadvantaged and public service were considered as moral obligations. At St. Paul's, where he received his secondary school education, he characterized the training and educational philosophy of the school as teaching the "gospel of responsibility." [8] He took both his undergraduate and law degrees at Yale, where his senior thesis was written on Cromwell and the quest of the Puritans for religious toleration. That study marked the beginning of a clear commitment to civil libertarianism, which was to characterize his posture during his days in Washington as an assistant in the Justice Department and as a congressman; his devotion to civil liberties had, as a natural concomitant, a concern for the underdog and thus for civil rights.[9] What is perhaps even more interesting about his thesis, however, was its failure to discuss the significance of the Puritans' quest for political community. Of course, it is an omission for which he can scarcely be indicted academically. Still, commitment to principle (in this case, commitment to religious toleration) could not, for the Puritans, be separated from political community. Perhaps John Lindsay's failure to perceive the absence of political community (what Aristotle would have called *polis*) in New York City would seriously impair his attempts at change.

John Lindsay was always more interested in procedural questions, however. He emphasized social and economic variables as being the critical determinants in the decay of urban life, and spoke of their importance for the founding and stability of the Republic. His use of historical sources was, however, often strained. For example, he often identified with Thomas Jefferson and Abraham Lincoln in terms of the founding and maintenance of the Republic. His characterization of these two leaders was, however, somewhat curious. On one occasion, he spoke of the "Jeffersonian theme" as part of the founding tradition. America was, in these terms, seen as a haven for "poor Europeans," driven by the squalor and vice of industrialized cities to come to the new Arcadia.[10] By some curious circumlocution, he saw the cities as the new islands of hope and believed his attempts to resuscitate the cities arose from an ideology comparable to and compatible with Jefferson's. Needless to say, Jefferson's rejection of the city as a healthy political community had nothing to do with the historical moment called eighteenth-century Europe, but was based on a more classical and permanent pasture. The cities, because of their size, structure, and manufacturing, were sources of corruption, and such an atmosphere made community and individual responsibility difficult to attain.[11] Tocqueville, in a brilliant pre-Marxist analysis, foresaw the alienating and dependent effects that the rise of a manufacturing class promoted vis-à-vis the worker, and argued that this was a real threat to democracy.[12] Where else would the manufacturing class take hold if not in the cities? What clearer justification for Jefferson's Louisiana Purchase, in spite of his previous intimations that such executive initiative was contrary to the spirit of the Constitution? [13]

Lindsay's identification with Lincoln was equally strained and, once again, reflected a limited perspective on the founding and continuation of the Republic. Lindsay justified his association with the Republican Party in these terms:

> It's the party of Lincoln, of civil rights, the protection of the person and his liberties against the majority, even against big business or the federal bureaucracy.[14]

> I am Lincolnian . . . in that I believe when an individual or locality can't help itself, it is the function of the Federal Government to help it. . . .[15]

> Lincoln forswore both power for its own sake and motion for its own sake. When he used Presidential power aggressively and bluntly, he publicly acknowledged regret at having to do so.[16]

His "devotion" to Lincoln is clearly underlined by one of his biographers; Lindsay himself stated that he is a Republican by choice, not by inheritance or family tradition.[17] His attachment to Lincoln is something more than a necessary symbol brandished for political advantage. An examination of his understanding of Lincoln, what he correctly identifies as being in the tradition of Lincoln and what he alters or omits, is thus helpful in understanding his own public character.[18]

In arguing for passage of a civil rights bill in 1960 on the floor of the House of Representatives, Lindsay ended his speech with a quotation from Lincoln's speech at Springfield, in 1857, to the effect that the Signers of the Declaration of Independence "intended to include all men." [19] Again, during the mayoral campaign of 1965, he suggested that the Emancipation Proclamation was a great humanitarian edict and that Lincoln was concerned, primarily, with civil rights when he issued it.[20] Yet an examination of Lincoln's words does not support this. Moreover, in the Peoria speech, Lincoln clearly indicated that his criticism of Stephen A. Douglas was limited to the question of the extension of slavery and that he was not "contending for the establishment of political and social equality between whites and blacks." [21] In the Springfield speech, he agreed with Douglas that intermarriage was something which should be avoided and he supported a general separation of the races.[22] Consequently, his notion of equal rights did not include the *social* equality which characterized Lindsay's commitment and that of the Civil Rights Acts of the 1960s. This is not to argue that Lincoln did not believe in his pronouncement that the guiding principle of America was the Declaration of Independence and the ideal that "all men are created equal." However, political prudence, the mark of great leaders, dictated several considerations starkly absent from Lindsay's perception of political leadership: first, the separation of the individual from the office, and second, that policy should attempt "to remove evils without shocking the prejudices that support them—allowing time and circumstance to wear down the prejudices." [23]

Lincoln's restraint in refusing to identify the public interest with his own private beliefs is widely known. In a famous letter toward the end of his days he wrote:

> I am naturally anti-slavery. If slavery is not wrong, nothing is wrong. . . . and yet, I have never understood that the Presidency conferred upon me an unrestricted right to act officially upon this judgement and feeling.[24]

This disposition has exceedingly important consequences. It kept Lincoln from the self-righteous pronouncements and policies that can support good principles and bad politics. The modesty of this restraint makes it difficult for critics to challenge an individual for seeking personal and political advantage.

One of the major criticisms of John Lindsay, in this regard, was his tendency to identify himself (in a pre-Nixon fashion) with the office and to project an aura of self-righteous indispensability to his aides and advisors. He once criticized the press for continuing to question him, in a manner that he considered to be personally demeaning, by responding, "Remember, I am the Mayor!" In another instance, he argued for the need to bring "dignity" to the office, after he had experienced a brusque cross-examination by a citizen at a City Hall hearing.[25] An analysis of his speeches, both in Congress and out, shows a marked use of "I," rather than "We," in describing proposed political solutions.[26] In short, the "I-am-the-Mayor" perspective reflects what one commentator called Lindsay's "magisterial conception of his office." [27]

His attitude of noblesse oblige led one biographer to state that "he doesn't seem to know what he doesn't know," [28] and that he actually "believes in right and wrong" and attempts "to do what is right." [29] Implicit in all of these observations is a potential for the failure of the political art, the art of the possible, a sense of proportion in accommodating what is right to the sensibilities of one's fellow citizens. Lindsay had failed to learn the most important lessons taught by his hero.

Finally, Lindsay's attempt to portray Lincoln as apologetic in his exercise of extreme executive power is not accurate. Lincoln made no apologies for his use of extreme executive power.[30] His actions were always guided by prudence, but he could and did defend the temporary suspension of civil liberties when the defense of political equality demanded it. The point is that his prudent use of extreme executive power was always directed by substantive principle. It was the character of the law in its implicit respect for human equality that gave it its specific value. There was, for Lincoln, a spirit underlying the letter of the law without which the letter of the law was empty. If that spirit died, then so would the Union. Lincoln sought to use his power to preserve that spirit and that Union, while still maintaining a sensitive understanding of the diverse segments of that national population which he served. To do that, he had to remove the evil (slavery) without shocking the prejudices that support them (that some human beings are not equal to others). The Emancipation Proclamation represents such a strategy, for it casts no moral aspersions, nor does it lecture; it merely establishes a legal right.

In dealing with his own problems of racial inequality, Lindsay had no such perspective. He seemed to lack an understanding of both power and prudence. He could neither "exercise extreme executive power" nor speak sensitively to the diverse audiences of Fun City. Granted he was well meaning, but his policies and attitudes were such as to alienate the white middle class during his first term, and thus cause him to spend his second term trying, as he admitted,[31] to bring its members back from their disaffection. As we shall see, this was the result of a lack of clear direction, of a failure to consider the whole community, and of a self-righteousness that failed to grasp that there can be no moral leadership in politics without prudence.

The absence of a clear substantive direction often resulted in what Lindsay criticized in other Presidents: "motion for its own sake." In a 1967 interview, Lindsay, in discussing political leadership, distinguished between symbolic and actual leadership. Symbolic leadership is needed, he said, to produce "the feeling of leadership";[32] the mayor, he argued, must "move around with style."[33] As Sid Davidoff put it, there is a need to develop "a sense of movement" or a "feeling of movement," and another top aide, in criticizing the Wagner Administration, asked why "things didn't move" when Wagner was in office.[34] This prevailing preoccupation with motion may reflect an inordinate concern with style and image, and it suggests an inability to effect a transition from campaigning to governing, or from general promises to specific policies. To come full circle, Lindsay's Lincolnesque stance is marked by an absence of concern with political education. Nowhere do we find reference to Lincoln's speech of 1838, "On the Perpetuation of Our Political Institutions," where he calls for a political religion built around the Fourth of July, the Declaration of Independence, and the heroes of the Founding.

POLITICAL LEADERSHIP AND
THE QUEST FOR COMMUNITY

Lindsay's campaign was clearly directed to the problems of the poor and the fashions of the rich. A good deal of emphasis was placed upon housing, jobs, giving more political control of the poverty programs to the communities, and revamping the city bureaucracy.[35] One theme which was to recur again and again was Lindsay's promise not to give in to the "power brokers" of the city.[36] Who they were was never made clear, although Lindsay never tired of saying that "they know who they are." [37] Following Peter Maas [38] and the timing of Lindsay's accusations, we may conclude that one such "power broker" was the Transit Workers Union and its leader, in 1965, Michael Quill. The transit strike was an important benchmark, for the union was representative of those very ethnic and social class groups which Lindsay would soon exasperate. The conflict with Quill was, for Lindsay, a question of principles and, for Quill, a question of style. Lindsay fired the first salvo by accusing the union of "blackmailing" the city, and at a press conference, at the height of the strike, vowed not to bow to the "power brokers." Quill countered by calling Lindsay a "pipsqueak" and characterized his Anglo-Saxon heritage as a form of arrogance. However, Quill's threatened strike was not a new technique; Robert Wagner had managed it for a number of years without an actual incident. Consequently, as a bargaining tactic, it had a strange kind of acceptance, if not legitimacy, in New York City politics. Yet Lindsay, a minority mayor, sought, with resounding rhetorical flurries, to change the accepted patterns of expectations without giving anything in return. The result was a settlement considerably higher in cost than would have been the case had Lindsay been willing to meet with Quill and settle on a package.[39] Perhaps, more importantly, the high settlement was then used by the uniform services (police, fire, and sanitation) in later negotiations over their raises. By pontificating on a spurious principle, Lindsay not only helped to escalate contract demands throughout the ranks of city workers, but also set himself against those groups whose interests he simply *declared* to be illegitimate. From the city workers' point of view, Lindsay's confrontation with their unions was simply a confrontation between two classes and ethnic groupings.

The transit strike of January 1966 and the teachers strike of September 1968 are separated only by time; both reflect the beginning of and, then, the most severe point in the dissolution of civic commonality. Only the controversy over scatter housing approximated in intensity the severity of the wounds and scars left by this confrontation.

The decentralization controversy began on a racial note which persisted to the end. A strike by parents, at the site of the new Intermediate School 201 in Harlem, over the quality of education and de facto segregation precipitated the action. The strike soon generated support in other ghetto districts, and a special task force appointed by the mayor recommended a decentralization experiment—three districts, in three different parts of the city (upper Manhattan, lower Manhattan, and Brooklyn) would be set up with a degree of administrative autonomy. It is important to note that Lindsay was not on record as supporting decentralized, participatory administration of education. In fact, as we will discuss later, there is some question as to whether his "commitment" to participatory processes in social action programs was symbolic or real.

In his 1965 campaign, Lindsay had promised teachers, among other things, continued job security. The advent of these experimental districts posed a serious threat to these traditionally held values. Soon firings were begun by school board administrators who argued that quality education demanded the removal of some teachers. This was especially true in Ocean Hill–Brownsville. The racial issue began to define quality education. Teachers who were found not to be "sensitive" to minority children were often labeled "racist" and removed. It became impossible to challenge these removals without being accused of racism. The problem was made more acute by the absence of clear lines of fiscal, personnel, and policy jurisdictions.[40] Lindsay's commitment to the social goal of equality had made it impossible for him to resist the claims of the ghetto districts and their leaders. One consequence of this was a default of leadership, for there were no central political lines of authority through which directives could be issued. Since Lindsay had been elected on a "fusion" ticket, the political clubs of the city (in these traditionally Democratic ghettos) could not be used as authoritative lines of communication or as centers for political education. Thus, there was little preparation on the part of the participants for civic responsibility, and the mayor and his Administration were equally unclear as to what direction to take.[41] The independence of the public school superintendent and the board of education exacerbated the situation, for, under the City Charter, they were not subject to the mayor's will. The final difficulty arose from Lindsay's miscalculation of the enormous power and cohesion of the United Federation of Teachers (UFT) and the Central Labor Council; the latter had threatened a general strike if the teachers' contractual rights were not restored.[42] Lindsay failed to consult with the UFT. The plan for experimental decentralization became thus a double affront: it was imposed without real consultation and did not include a single white middle-class school district! The vicious racial and ethnic epithets which were hurled through the streets of the city were testimony to the total deterioration of the situation.

Lindsay did attempt to find common ground, but the appeal was to "orderly, due process"[43] rather than to civic virtue. The appeal to the law is traditional in American politics, but it is effective only insofar as the people feel that justice has been incorporated into the law. The UFT felt that the firing of teachers was a violation of the law, while the Ocean

Hill–Brownsville school leadership felt that the nature of public education was substantively and procedurally unjust. Thus, the conflict was precipitated by contrary definitions of what the public weal required. Certainly, public participation by both the UFT and the school districts could have provided a common denominator. However, Lindsay's concept of participation was a function of his concept of social equality, and political participation would take its character from the nature of social policy rather than being the source from which the social policy emanated. For example, bringing in the Ford Foundation to formulate a decentralization plan reflected, once again, his belief in the superiority of his own judgment (or that of *his* experts) on matters of social equality. It also reflected his commitment to public policy engineered by policy experts, and not formed by public participation.

The entire question of decentralization and participatory democracy is open to reevaluation. Both James Madison and Tocqueville saw positive, albeit different virtues in such administrative structuring and political activity. But in their analyses, the localities were real communities, and not districts created by political pressures or the drawing of administrative lines on maps. Thus, especially for Tocqueville, civic virtue was possible. The districts used for both school boards and community corporations were often amalgams of territory without a traditional neighborhood or community identity. In addition, there had been little chance for political tutelage, which, in the absence of the habit of participation, would have been a way to begin to develop civic consciousness. If voter turnout is any indication of the success of the participatory idea, the facts point to the artificiality of this experiment in local democracy: school board elections in the City seldom bring out more than 5 percent of the eligible voters, and in one election, for an antipoverty community corporation in Manhattan, the board of directors was elected by less than one percent of the eligible voters.

Although Lindsay admitted his error in his Second Inaugural and in his book, *The City*, he seemed unable to translate his awareness into policy. By 1971, he had begun to work on one of his top priorities, public housing. He again assumed that the white middle class would readily accept the idea of scatter housing. The virtue of the concept was that it broke away from building public housing in ghettos or creating new ghettos through the building of massive projects. It also provided a way to achieve a gradual integration of white communities.

The sites picked for the projects were in areas of the city which were cool—if not hostile—to the Mayor. This apparently was not intentional, but, nonetheless, it appeared vindictive to the residents. If there had been prior consultation, perhaps this could have been avoided. However, neither the borough presidents nor the communities affected were brought into the planning; again, policy experts choose the sites. At the public hearings, black homeowners joined Jewish and Italian homeowners in protesting that fear of declining property values and crime were the reasons for their opposition. Thus, racial balance was not a prevailing concern, and no attempt was made to develop it as such. As one commentator suggested, there was no real sense of civic duty, and Lindsay and his advisors seemed to assume that to do what was right was all that need be done. Again, Lindsay's failure here was a function of his tendency to plan policies around "abstract notions about democracy and social justice." [44] Ironically, the borough presidents, through their seats on the Board of Estimate, were able, not only to stop the projects, but to hold hearings and prevail against the mayor in the name of the people. The Board of Estimate (at least the borough presidents) thus became the true "representatives of the community" and could claim that participatory democracy was at work and that democratic sentiment had prevailed! [45]

BUREAUCRATIC REORGANIZATION AND THE PUBLIC INTEREST

A review of John Lindsay's public communications shows an inordinate concern with bureaucratic problems. For Lindsay, the bureaucracy was the real battlefield, where, if the battle were won, victory against urban decay would soon follow.

The battle was to be waged on two fronts, as outlined in the Sviridoff Report of June 1966. The first entailed the reorganization of the fieflike bureaus into ten superagencies, with the Health Resources Administration serving as model, and with Mitchell Sviridoff as its first administrator. The second sector was the decentralization of and participation in community services by the people affected by the service.[46] The reorganization into the superagencies would make it possible to institute Planning Programming Budgeting System (PPBS) management techniques; PPBS would, it was argued, bring more efficient bureaucratic planning, hiring, and spending practices to city government. Unification along functional lines would, it was hoped, reduce the mayor's span-of-control problems and eliminate overlapping jurisdictions and duplication of services.[47] In addition, the forward-looking approach would appeal to young professionals, who would be lured from the private sector or Washington to New York City. In many instances, their hiring would require the creation of special appointment lines or provisional appointments as a way to by-pass civil service regulations; [48] this was done as a matter of course. In addition, consultantships, using outside personnel, were frequent. On the neighborhood level, the mayor's office and the agencies' staffs helped to develop various planning, antipoverty, and human development organizations in the communities. With organizations such as the Urban Action Task Force and "Little City Halls," the communities were also put in closer touch with Lindsay's Administration. Thus, community control, communication, and bureaucratic efficiency would help to solve the problems of urban life.

The Lindsay approach reflects an attempt at joining Populism and efficiency in a broad package of reform. "The legacy of reform is the bureaucratic state." [49] The bureaucratic state seeks to replace the political influence in policy and staff development with the principles of scientific management. In so doing, it may find itself in tension with its avowed purpose of also increasing citizen participation. The increase in participation may, however, make political considerations rather than efficiency the crucial variable in policy determinations. The result is too often a participatory program, which is more symbolic than real, and it raises a question whether Populism and efficiency will always remain "uncomfortable" allies." [50] The difficulty is often resolved in favor of the professional bureaucrats. Their strength rests in their belief in their superior wisdom, in contrast to the appointees who are receiving political rewards for their support of the candidate. Thus, the "bureaucratic agencies are not neutral"; they are only independent from community and, often, executive control.[51] Commissioners in agencies often lose touch with the constituents whom they are to serve—certainly, the scatter housing plan reflects this.[52] Without the political clubhouse links, "politics remains, but loses its popular base." [53] Lindsay often went to the streets, perhaps, because he didn't live there. In addition, the functional power exercised by the professionals may be more difficult to control than the political power of the old patronage appointees, for the former may be able to collect satellites of power based on his "superior" knowledge and stature. Finally, if "reform" is meant to eliminate *corruption* from politics, the bureaucratic state may simply effect a shift in corruption "from the politician to professionally oriented or career civil servants"; [54] certainly, the Lindsay Administration had its share of administrative scandals.[55]

In his attempts to shake up old-line bureaucrats Lindsay not only created the superagency, but also surrounded himself with a host of special assistants. These aides often had the inside track to the mayor, especially in crises, and this created a good deal of resentment among the line commissioners. The tremendous turnover in commissioners (some 13 between 1966 and 1969) reflected the feeling that they had lost access to City Hall and the mayor, either because of the superagency structure,[56] or because mayoral aides and special committees were backed by Lindsay over the line commissioners.[57]

The concept of community control emerged from the participatory democracy movement, as reflected, for example, in the Port Huron Statement of 1962, and the "maximum, feasible participation" guideline in antipoverty legislation. However, the question remains as to whether the participation was of equal import with the substantive goal, the elimination of poverty. In addition, the mayor had a good deal of leverage in determining the administrative structure of the program. Although the community corporations, because of Office of Economic Opportunity (OEO) guidelines, had to be elected, their boundaries and responsibilities were not clearly defined. Lindsay's scheme, as we indicated earlier, moved in two antithetical directions: The Community Development Agency was set up to monitor and plan for the corporations within the Human Resources Administration, but monies were to be distributed by the Committee on Poverty (COP) with an appointed staff. COP was thus placed outside of HRA and had the role of validating corporation elections, defining communities, and reviewing and judging programs. The effect was to centralize control of the antipoverty program.

The fact that the corporations were elected did not necessarily increase their policy leverage or effectiveness in combating poverty. In fact, it was never clear whom or what they represented. Participation, in the Lindsay style, was more symbolic than real. In the words of one observer, "it was probable . . . that Mayor Wagner's anti-poverty program would have had greater productivity and less excitement without the involvement of the poor." [58] This same observer concludes that the participatory element was limited in its success, not only because of the continued centralization of policy, but also because COP was often unable to arrive at a satisfactory delineation of a community, and thus it was often "social militants," rather than the poor, who were able to define the community by their action and will; it was also the militants who were usually elected.[59] Again, the absence of a natural community (or of Lindsay's ability to identify one) affected the character of civic participation and the exercise of political liberty.

CONCLUSION

John Lindsay's approach to political leadership was a combination of a moral leader, who rejected consensus politics as well as the role of prudent statesman, and a man who was committed to the modern techniques of governing, i.e., scientific management and public relations. The latter stance led to the creation of his "street mayor" concept in which, "through an increased projection of his own presence, [he sought] to heighten everyone's awareness of his government in the hope that people would feel they were part of the process." [60] The techniques of scientific management too often produced results that coincided with what the commissioners already knew by experience, and often attempts were made to measure things which could not be quantified.[61] How do you measure fear or dissatisfaction?

Solutions were often arrived at by logic, and not from a prudent analysis of the political setting. In one instance, PPBS analysis concluded that new sanitation programs were getting the streets 85 percent clean! [62] This announcement of what was seen as a great success is indicative of the tendency to deal with problems that are manageable and quantifiable rather than those which defy the system. Even so, the measurement of success by percentages obscures the fact (by neutralizing it through numerical insignificance) that many and often the same people are deprived and suffering.

What Lindsay did accomplish was providing the impetus for the emergence of a new generation of black and Puerto Rican leaders.[63] But the cleavages which resulted often remained serious, and, in some cases, rifts were created as a result of one group's seeming to benefit at the expense of another. There was no real attempt at lateral interracial or interclass institutional integration at the community level.

Another serious problem was Lindsay's inability to reach a working agreement with many major interests in the city and his inability to choose his staff and administrators wisely. The unprecedented number of strikes by city workers and the incredible rate of turnover in staff are indicative of real shortcomings in leadership.

Finally, the view of one of Lindsay's top aides, that the essence of politics is "how to distribute inadequate resources," [64] captures the limited and very modern perspective that too often characterized Lindsay's understanding of urban problems; it was thought that the difficulties of city life could be resolved if enough money were made available. This is another variation on the attempt to quantify what are basically qualitative, human problems of a spiritual and political nature, which are not amenable, therefore, to predominately economic and/or administrative resolution. The City Club of New York gently rebuked Lindsay in its evaluation of his first term, as the members felt he was "more interested in theory than action." [65] If they meant speculative theorizing, then, perhaps, they made an accurate assessment, but, if they meant political theory, then they are, it appears, incorrect. John Lindsay did not have a *political* theory drawn from reflecting and acting on the total political dimension. He did not do what Tocqueville and Madison did—act, reflect, and theorize about *politics*. Theorize he did, but not sufficiently about *homo politicus*.

NOTES

1. Alexis de Tocqueville, *Democracy in America*, ed. Phillips Bradley (New York: Vintage Books, 1954), 2:109.
2. Ibid., p. 110.
3. Ibid., pp. 110–11.
4. Tocqueville uses *manners* to mean something more than mores; *manners* are the characteristic sentiments that animate a people and give a people their distinctive identity.
5. Ibid., p. 101.
6. See Murray Edelman, *The Symbolic Uses of Politics* (Urbana: University of Illinois Press, 1972), p. 74.
7. Ibid., p. 75.
8. Nat Hentoff, *A Political Life: The Education of John V. Lindsay* (New York: Knopf, 1969), p. 55.
9. As Attorney General Herbert Brownell's assistant, Lindsay was the chief architect of the 1956 Civil Rights Act.
10. John V. Lindsay, *The City* (New York: Norton, 1970), p. 51.
11. See Thomas Jefferson, Letter to James Madison, 20 December 1787. In *The Life and Selected Writings of Thomas Jefferson*, ed. Adrienne Koch and William Peden (New York: Random House, 1944), p. 436.
12. See Tocqueville, *Democracy in America*, 1: chap. 20, esp. pp. 170–71.
13. Thomas Jefferson, "First Inaugural Address" quoted in *Selected Writings*, p. 321.
14. Daniel E. Button, *Lindsay: A Man for Tomorrow* (New York: Random House, 1965), p. 17.
15. Ibid., p. 30.
16. Ibid.
17. Ibid., pp. 29–30.
18. See his letter to the "Boston Republican Party Leaders," in Walter E. Volkomer, ed., *The Liberal Tradition in American Thought* (New York: Capricorn Books, 1970), pp. 203–4.
19. Lincoln's speech on Dred Scott, quoted in Volkomer, *Liberal Tradition*, p. 199; Button, *Lindsay*, p. 30.
20. William F. Buckley, Jr., *The Unmaking of a Mayor* (New York: Viking Press, 1966), pp. 76–80.
21. Peoria Speech, quoted in Volkomer, *Liberal Tradition*, p. 193.

22. Springfield Speech, quoted in Volkomer, *Liberal Tradition*, p. 201.

23. Harry V. Jaffa, "Abraham Lincoln," in Morton J. Frisch and Richard G. Stevens, *American Political Thought: The Philosophic Dimensions of American Statesmanship* (New York: Scribner's, 1971), p. 135.

24. Quoted in James MacGregor Burns, *Presidential Government* (Boston: Houghton Mifflin, 1963), p. 41.

25. Hentoff, *A Political Life*, p. 88.

26. See, for example, William F. Buckley's discussion of Lindsay's rhetorical style in *The Unmaking of a Mayor*.

27. Steven R. Weissman, "Why Lindsay Failed as Mayor," *Washington Monthly* 4 (April 1972):46.

28. Hentoff, *A Political Life*, p. 108.

29. Ibid., p. 230.

30. "A Letter to Erastus Corning and Others," 12 June 1863, in Andrew M. Scott, *Political Thought in America* (New York: Holt, Rinehart & Winston, 1959), p. x.

31. Lindsay, *The City*, pp. 43, 91.

32. Hentoff, *A Political Life*, p. 89.

33. Ibid., p. 88.

34. Ibid., pp. 135, 156.

35. *New York Times*, 11 October 1965, pp. 17–19.

36. First Inaugural Address, 1 January 1966; Also quoted in Woody Klein, *Lindsay's Promise: The Dream That Failed* (New York: Macmillan, 1970), p. 114.

37. Ibid.

38. Peter Maas, "Lindsay and the Power Brokers," *New York Magazine*, December 23, 1968, pp. 1, 8, 9.

39. Amitai Etzioni, "Image Over Performance," *Wall Street Journal*, 21 January 1971, p. 6.

40. Diana R. Gordon, *City Limits: Barriers to Change in Urban Government* (New York: Charterhouse, 1973), pp. 113–14.

41. Ibid.

42. Jewell Bellush and Stephen M. David, *Race and Politics in New York City* (New York: Praeger, 1971), p. 154.

43. Ibid., p. 124.

44. Ibid., p. 116.

45. Ibid., p. 127.

46. Gordon, *City Limits*, p. 11.

47. David A. Grossman, "The Lindsay Legacy: A Partisan Appraisal," *City Almanac* 8 (October 1973):4.

48. Ibid., p. 10.

49. Theodore Lowi: "Goswell's Chicago Revisited via Lindsay's New

York," in John A. Gardiner and David J. Olsen, *Theft of the City* (Bloomington: Indiana University Press, 1974), p. 422.

50. Ibid.

51. Ibid., p. 429.

52. Nat Hentoff, "An Interview with Mayor Lindsay," in Edward C. Banfield, ed, *Urban Government: Reader in Administration and Politics*, 2nd ed. (New York: Free Press, 1969).

53. Lowi, "Goswell's Chicago Revisited via Lindsay's New York," p. 429.

54. Edward Costikyan, "The Locus of Corruption Has Changed," in Banfield, *Urban Government*, p. 131.

55. These include the indictments of Water Commissioner James L. Marcus and Housing Commissioner Charles Moerdler and the payoffs discovered in the Sanitation Department.

56. Warren Moscow, "The Mayors of New York City," *City Almanac* 8 (June 1973):7.

57. Barry Gottehrer, *The Mayor's Man* (Garden City, N.Y.: Doubleday, 1975), p. 45.

58. Bertram M. Beck, "Organizing Community Action," *Annals of the American Academy of Political and Social Science* 29 (Spring 1969):164.

59. Ibid., p. 166.

60. Weissman, "Why Lindsay Failed," p. 46.

61. Ibid.

62. Ibid., pp. 53–54.

63. Beck, "Organizing Community Action," p. 166.

64. Gottehrer, *The Mayor's Man*, p. 203.

65. *New York Times*, 7 December 1969, p. 62.

Chapter Ten

John F. Kennedy
The Claim of Excellence

BRUCE MIROFF

While American public life has generally been dominated by material drives, major figures in American political history have called attention to a deeper motivation. Alexander Hamilton spoke of "the love of fame, the ruling passion of the noblest minds. . . ." [1] John Adams described "the passion for distinction, . . . [the] desire to be observed, considered, esteemed, praised, beloved, and admired. . . ." [2] From the startling visions of the young Abraham Lincoln's Lyceum Speech, to the self-crowning autobiography of an unhappily retired Theodore Roosevelt, images of greatness and glory have attracted many Americans to political careers.

Personal avowals of a "passion for distinction" are not, however, heard much these days. Such confessions hint at immoderate pride; they suggest preoccupation with the self, even at the expense of the public welfare. Thus, it is more prudent for political actors to couch their ambitions in the language of excellence. To speak of excellence as the unifying characteristic in motive, act, and accomplishment is to assuage popular doubts. It ensures the mass audience that the benefits they receive from action will equal or surpass the rewards garnered by the political actor himself.

No recent American political leader has so clearly—and effectively—laid a claim to excellence as John F. Kennedy. The language of excellence came easily to Kennedy; it came even more easily to his associates and admirers. To quote Theodore C. Sorensen: "John F. Kennedy was a happy President. Happiness, he often said, paraphrasing Aristotle, is the full use of one's faculties along lines of excellence, and to him the Presidency offered the ideal opportunity to pursue excellence." [3]

Kennedy and his aides worked diligently, as Henry Fairlie has shown, to project "images of excellence." [4] Befriending the press and charming the intelligentsia, they inspired numerous testimonials to their Administration's high purpose and commitment to quality. Some of the most serious analysts of politics in America echoed the favorable judgment. Hannah Arendt, for example, commented after Kennedy's death that he had given the political realm "a kind of dignity and intellectual splendor —whatever you may call it—which it never had before, even under Roosevelt." [5] To contemporary observers, the promise—if not the fulfill-ment—of excellence was the keynote of the Kennedy Presidency.

THE PURSUIT OF EXCELLENCE

What kind of excellence did John F. Kennedy cultivate? On one level, his conception of excellence expressed a democratic intent. It evoked the ideal of democratic theory: participation by ordinary citizens in the manifold affairs of their community. Echoing the widespread complaint that Americans were becoming narrow and self-centered in their pre-occupation with material comfort and security, Kennedy seemed to be looking to the prescription of Alexis de Tocqueville—that only the ac-tive exercise of their public freedoms could provide Americans with a renewed sense of community and purpose.

The President and his aides often spoke in this vein about their hopes for improving and elevating the quality of American life. Public interest in the arts was applauded and encouraged, while the status of artists was boosted through presidential patronage. The flabbiness of the "affluent society" was challenged by a campaign for physical fitness; vigorous New Frontiersmen led the way with 50-mile hikes. Most impor-tant, indifference toward political matters, especially among the much-lamented "silent generation," was countered with ringing summonses to public service.

The results of these calls for national excellence were hardly so dra-matic as Kennedy chroniclers were later to claim. The Kennedy Presi-dency did not launch a renaissance in either the arts, physical fitness, or public service. This was not the fault of the Administration; Kennedy and his aides recognized clearly that there were definite limits to what the government could accomplish in any of these areas. Still, gestures toward national excellence remained attractive to Kennedy and his political circle. Whether or not those gestures inspired citizens to pursue excel-lence, they certainly enhanced the stature of the leaders who made them.[6]

That gestures toward national excellence redounded to the credit of the President and his circle provides a clue to the conception of excel-lence that John Kennedy actually held. In Kennedy's view, excellence could not really become a phenomenon of mass life. For its defining characteristic was precisely its uncommonness. Excellence, he believed, was a scarce commodity in any field of activity; it represented the rare

departure from the ordinary and the typical. What was typical in politics, for example, was convention, prejudice, and ignorance of the facts.
What was special was the ability to transcend these limitations; only a
few in politics would ever be self-possessed, objective, knowledgeable,
and creative.

Despite his rhetoric, then, Kennedy's hopes for national excellence
did not revolve around any transformation of the American citizenry.
Those hopes depended, instead, on a core of leaders possessing uncommon qualities; this leadership was the key to the nation's stature. The
American people would be elevated when they enjoyed elevated leadership. The 1960s would be excellent, John Kennedy and his intimates believed, because the decade would be shaped by their own excellence.

By its nature, such excellence required a certain distance between
leaders and followers. Leaders had to be wary of the force of popular
passions and mass demands. They had to serve public needs without
submitting to public feelings. The problem of keeping a volatile constituency at arm's length—while retaining its support—concerned John
Kennedy throughout much of his political career.

Profiles in Courage, Kennedy's 1956 tribute to heroic American senators
and other public men, represented one approach to the problem. This
volume focused on men of political conscience who had accepted defeat
as the price of doing what was right. Kennedy's biographical portraits
were skillfully drawn, and the actions he chronicled were genuinely
admirable. What was noteworthy, however, was the type of heroism
Kennedy praised. He chose to dramatize the acts of men who believed
they were right, irrespective of what their constituents thought, and who
could not bring those constituents around to their position. These men
were excellent because they maintained their distance, remaining aloof
to popular pressures for compliance. They were courageous because they
refused to bow to popular feeling on a matter of principle, even if it
required sacrificing their office.

While Kennedy could write movingly about the courage of men who
took unpopular stands and suffered for them, he was too pragmatic a
politician to follow their example. During his Presidency, critics frequently commented that he seemed to have lost his taste for the brand
of heroics he had earlier celebrated. But those same critics failed to
notice how much of the sentiment of *Profiles in Courage* was carried over
into the Kennedy Presidency. If the lonely act of conscience gave way
to political expedience and electoral calculation, the sense of distance
from the public, along with the sense of superior objectivity and knowledge, remained.

During Kennedy's Presidency this sense of distance was most often
expressed in the language of expertise. At a time when many social com-

mentators were heralding a new era dominated by experts and techno-
crats, Kennedy and his colleagues made much of their privileged access
to specialized information and their superior preparation for the utiliza-
tion of such information. Questions of foreign policy, Kennedy told the
American Foreign Service Association, "are so sophisticated and so technical that people who are not intimately involved week after week,
month after month, reach judgments which are based upon emotion
rather than knowledge of the real alternatives." [7] Questions of economic
policy, he told participants in a White House Conference on National
Economic Issues, demanded a similar expertise:

> The fact of the matter is that most of the problems, or at least many
> of them, that we now face are technical problems, are administrative
> problems. They are very sophisticated judgments which do not
> lend themselves to the great sort of "passionate movements" which
> have stirred this country so often in the past. [8]

The language of expertise was well-suited for restricting political controversy. President Kennedy and his circle of advisers hoped to operate
as much as possible in a rarefied domain where public opinion would
be heard only faintly. They could handle foreign crises or economic
problems or civil rights dilemmas with prudence and efficiency, if only
public emotions and ignorance would not get in the way. They could
pursue excellence, if the public left them sufficient space for action. Thus
Kennedy and his circle devoted extensive efforts to persuading the public
of what they already believed about themselves—that they were the best
of their generation. Awed by the brilliant capacities of these decision-
makers, and chastened by reminders of its own shortage of expertise,
the public might become an ideal audience for the pursuit of excellence.

In the domestic arena, the claim of expertise met with scant success.
Businessmen and partisan Republicans were too intent on reenacting the
battles of the New Deal to heed the talk of unbiased, sophisticated management of the economy. Writers to the left of Kennedy's Council of
Economic Advisers, such as Leon Keyserling and Oscar Gass, com-
plained that this new expertise seemed only to reproduce standard, stale
approaches to economic management. Southern power-holders visibly resisted the Kennedy Administration's quiet, legalistic approach to racial
problems. Civil rights activists insisted on open confrontations with injustice, exploding the Administration's patient timetable for racial progress.

The claim of expertise could not, in short, produce a *consensus* on domestic matters that could be guided by the White House. Kennedy was
too much a political realist to be surprised by this failure. Still, he and his
aides muttered about hidebound conservatives and utopian intellectuals,

all duped by their respective myths; they periodically grew irritated at the civil rights protagonists, fighting, in their view, for all or nothing. But the combination of these forces propelled the President into the public arena, where issues had to be debated. He entered this arena with reluctance, however; nationally televised addresses on economic policy or civil rights were less favored as a response to conflict than private meetings with the parties immediately involved.

If domestic politics would not yield to expertise and excellence, the story was different in foreign affairs. Here Kennedy and his top advisers were able to operate with a relatively free hand. Critics lay in wait on the right, of course; but the Kennedy Administration's own impulses were hawkish enough to keep the Joint Chiefs and the congressional cold warriors on board when it counted. Executive primacy in foreign affairs, combined with the Kennedy circle's special flair for global action, gave the White House indisputable mastery in *this* arena. So, when Kennedy evoked the atmosphere of global crisis, grimly prophesying "the hour of maximum danger," or when he announced that the moment of confrontation was actually at hand, over Berlin in 1961 and Cuba in 1962, few were prepared to question his definition of the situation and his right to act upon that definition.

As the field for momentous action by an unhampered elite, foreign policy became the archetype of Kennedy excellence. The Cuban missile crisis, in particular, provided the model. The most dramatic image of the Kennedy Presidency was that of a bold yet prudent leader, surrounded by a devoted and similarly gifted band of counselors, leading the nation along the edge of nuclear terror to safety and success. That congressional leaders had urged a course of action more rash than the Administration's carefully crafted blockade of Cuba only confirmed the nation's good fortune in having the President in sole command. (It is seldom emphasized that these congressional leaders were only informed of the situation at the last possible moment, and were supplied with neither the full picture nor the time to reflect on the partial picture.)

Other images added to Kennedy's reputation in foreign affairs. He was the determined foe of subversion, creating a much-vaunted corps of counterinsurgency specialists, the Green Berets, to guard the Free World against communist depredations. He was also the benefactor of poor and underdeveloped countries, promising, with such programs as the Alliance for Progress, an American commitment against global privation and injustice. Through such images, John Kennedy largely attained in foreign affairs what was not forthcoming in domestic politics: the leeway to act on the basis of objectivity, realism, and knowledge. Here, where it most mattered to him, he could pursue—and achieve— excellence.

THE ILLUSIONS OF EXCELLENCE

It is difficult, after the debacles of American foreign policy and the revelations that followed them throughout the last decade, not to be disturbed by the freedom of action John Kennedy attained. In less attractive—or less fortunate—hands, Kennedy's methods of handling foreign affairs came to seem irresponsible and even imperial. The evocation of a crisis atmosphere proved to be an easy device for Presidents to use when they needed to silence critics and rally popular support. The readiness to apply graduated force in a "game" of escalation became, after the Cuban missile crisis, the familiar mark of Presidents who insisted that their own violence was a form of restraint. The penchant for secrecy and surreptitious action developed into an obsession that led the White House well beyond the bounds of both prudence and law.

What is most striking in retrospect, however, is not how dangerous were the precedents that Kennedy established, but how dubious was the original claim of expertise that undergirded those precedents. John Kennedy entered the Presidency after scoring the Eisenhower Administration for underestimating the severity of the global communist threat; he began his own Administration with a rhetorical and military buildup designed to meet that threat. Priding themselves on their realistic grasp of international complexity, Kennedy and his advisers proceeded to operate on the basis of an inflated theory of international politics that obscured local intricacies and fused Cuba, Vietnam, and Berlin into a single worldwide struggle between Soviet ambition and American determination. Magnifying the cohesion and aspirations of their adversaries, they simultaneously magnified America's global reach; the might and the will of the United States were considered to be almost without limitations.[9]

Although dwarfed in popular memory by the Cuban missile crisis of 1962, the Berlin crisis of 1961 manifested all the elements of this inflated approach to international politics. Khrushchev's warning to Kennedy at their Vienna meeting in June 1961—that he intended to sign a peace treaty with East Germany—followed a similar warning to President Dwight Eisenhower in 1958. It reflected Khrushchev's concern over the Soviets' increasingly shaky power position in Eastern Europe. But Kennedy paid little attention to the historical precedents and regional implications; in his eyes, Khrushchev's move took on ominous global dimensions. Proclaiming in late July that "West Berlin has now become—as never before—the great testing place of Western courage and will," [10] he asked Congress for $3.25 billion in new defense appropriations, expanded draft calls, and ordered 150,000 reservists to active duty. Further, he requested funds for a stepped-up civil defense program, sparking widespread speculation about the prospect of a nuclear war.

The Soviets soon retorted by building the Berlin Wall (a ruthless move, but one also indicative of their regional preoccupation); Kennedy could do little save dispatch an army unit on an uneventful mission down the Autobahn from West Germany to West Berlin. After each side had finished its moves, desultory negotiations began, and the atmosphere of crisis faded away. The outcome had been inconclusive, but the stage was set for a more definitive confrontation. That confrontation was, of course, to come over the question of Russian missiles in Cuba (a situation in which Kennedy would once again interpret Soviet ambitions as unlimited). Reviewing this sequence of events, many recent studies have concluded that the Cold War reached a peak of danger and distortion during the Kennedy Presidency—and that John Kennedy was more responsible for that danger and distortion than any of his adversaries.[11]

Kennedy's claims of expertise were also problematic in domestic affairs. In the area of civil rights, for example, the President and his aides believed that their coolly objective analysis of the southern situation had led them to a prudent middle course between white intransigence and black impatience. While periodically listening to and mollifying both sides, they assumed that they alone could find practicable solutions to racial conflict. What they failed to acknowledge, however, was that their solutions had been shaped less by the exigencies of the southern situation than by their own political needs. Practical ideas for civil rights action were rejected or sidetracked by the Administration, particularly when political costs threatened to be high.

An incident from the 1960 campaign is illustrative here. Possessing a mediocre senatorial record on civil rights, yet desperately needing black votes in key states, Kennedy worked hard to generate black enthusiasm. One of the most effective moves of his campaign staff, according to Harris Wofford (chief campaign aide in the civil rights field), was to organize a conference on constitutional rights. This event provided the candidate with a stage for demonstrating his commitment to the civil rights cause; black participants in the conference came away impressed. As Wofford notes, "That group went out all over the country saying, 'This man's got it. He's with us.'" [12]

The conference also produced a series of workshop reports that went beyond the Democratic platform's civil rights plank. The Kennedy people wanted the backing of civil rights activists, but they did not want to be identified with the proposals of those activists. Release of the conference reports by the Kennedy organization was thus postponed; civil rights activists were informed that the reports were being held until the final week of the campaign for maximum impact. By that final week, the phone calls that secured Martin Luther King, Jr.'s release from a Georgia jail had solidified the black vote behind Kennedy; the conference reports were discreetly buried.[13]

Such behavior continued into Kennedy's Presidency. The civil rights movement, as I noted earlier, refused to adhere to the Kennedy Administration's timetable for racial progress. With the freedom rides, the Albany, Georgia demonstrations, and the James Meredith affair, the movement intensified the pace of its struggle. Yet the Kennedy Administration, preoccupied with retaining the political support of both civil rights forces and southern Democrats in Congress, consistently failed to grasp either the urgency of black demands or the strength of white resistance. Only when developments in Birmingham, Alabama, made federal action imperative did Kennedy begin to concentrate on the problem. His rhetoric and legislative proposals, in June 1963, were a major advance in his understanding of and commitment to civil rights. Yet, events would almost immediately begin to outrun him once again.

Kennedy's consciousness of the civil rights crisis expanded during his Presidency, albeit reluctantly and imperfectly. In this as in other areas, there were signs of personal and political growth in Kennedy. This growth should not be exaggerated; John Kennedy was scarcely, at the time of his death, the would-be reformer and peacemaker that some recent versions of the Kennedy story have depicted. He was not a fundamentally different President in November 1963 than he was in January 1961. Still, several of his attitudes had been altered by 1963. He appeared, for example, to be less eager for symbolic confrontations with the Soviets, and more prepared for genuine confrontations with domestic problems.

The irony of Kennedy's growth in office is that so much of it resulted from a breakdown in the distance he had sought to place between himself and the public. In the area of civil rights, for instance, Kennedy would have learned very little if his low-visibility legal strategy had succeeded. It was only because that strategy proved ineffectual, and because activists repeatedly thrust more basic civil rights issues to the fore, that a new appreciation of racial problems was *forced* upon Kennedy. Here, expertise could not impose its solutions on a supposedly uninformed and emotional population; instead, that population generated its own solutions and compelled the "experts" to attend to them. Blacks demanding to be heard made a President listen; they taught him lessons that could never have been learned within the circumscribed milieu of the White House.

An analogous process took place in Kennedy's foreign policy. If he had entered office with an extraordinary faith in what American power (em-

ployed, of course, by a tough-minded and far-seeing leader like himself)
might accomplish in the world, that faith had been somewhat scaled
down by the time of his death. While he had not abandoned either the
flexing of American military muscle or the intervention of American military force in global affairs, the fiasco of the Bay of Pigs and the near-
apocalypse of the Cuban missile crisis had been sobering experiences;
each had indicated certain limitations in military solutions to America's
foreign conflicts. Kennedy can be credited with learning here, too. But
his teachers were not so much McGeorge Bundy, Robert McNamara,
or Maxwell Taylor as they were Fidel Castro and Nikita Khrushchev.[14]

Kennedy's learning experience suggests an important point about presidential leadership. Claims of expertise and gestures toward excellence
by a President are likely to mask the sway of a politically effective but
intellectually meager orthodoxy. Extension of such claims and gestures to
a circle of White House advisers serves only to encase that orthodoxy in
a group consensus. Departures from this orthodoxy are likely to come
only with external challenges to what George Reedy has called the President's "monopoly of authoritative answers." [15] The type of excellence
John Kennedy sought—the exercise of uncommon virtues by an elevated
and insulated leader—may actually produce conventional—and even mis-
guided—policies; the possibility of genuine excellence seems to lie elsewhere, in a more humble openness to the dynamics of political life.

CHARISMA AND SPECTACLE

While Kennedy's claim of excellence does not hold up to retrospective
analysis, at the time, it worked political magic. Unexamined orthodoxy
supplied the substance of the Kennedy Presidency; the popular image
was one of boldness and grandeur. *Charisma* became an overworked
term during the early 1960s, as pundits strained to describe John Kennedy's remarkable personal appeal.

A variety of factors contributed to Kennedy's appeal: his youthful
handsomeness, his beautiful family, his charm and wit, his eloquence.
But no single attribute that can be cited was as important as the impression Kennedy conveyed of being *gifted* as a leader. A friendly and
admiring press made much of his "gifts"—such as the rapid-fire presenta-
tion of torrents of facts during speeches and press conferences, or the
aura of vigor and mastery that characterized his decision-making during
moments of crisis. On occasion, more captious journalists noted the shortage of ideas behind those facts, and the preoccupation with action at
the cost of reflection; but such criticism made little headway against the
prevailing view. John Kennedy appeared to tower over ordinary politicians. He seemingly radiated an uncommon power that had been lacking

in the White House since the era of Franklin D. Roosevelt. Kennedy, as I observed earlier, believed in his own excellence; in the congenial and (from the standpoint of the 1970s) ingenuous atmosphere of the early 1960s, it was not too difficult to convince many Americans that they should share this belief.

Believing in Kennedy was not without its satisfactions. His admirers reveled in public performances that surpassed the image-making activities of his political contemporaries and assumed the character of a spectacle. Two elements were essential for this spectacle: the possession of genuinely attractive personal qualities, and the masterful manipulation of the political setting to transform those qualities into potent symbols for mass consumption. It has often been remarked that John Kennedy was the first effective television President, but it has seldom been noted that his television skills had less to do with public persuasion than with self-dramatization. On the television screen Kennedy's attractive features could be made into heroic virtues. His cautiously selected and carefully prepared appearances become thereby a continuing symbolization of expertise, energy, and courage, suffused with grace and sanctified by grand purpose.

The pleasure of watching Kennedy in action was enhanced by his periodic summonses to the audience to join in his political adventure. Actually, Kennedy's calls for commitment and sacrifice on the part of the American people were mainly rhetorical; the people were seldom asked to *do* anything. When the President was questioned by reporters as to how Americans might serve their country, he could never come up with an effective reply. Nonetheless, lofty invocations of popular participation served Kennedy well. They encouraged identification with presidential heroics, while keeping the public at a respectful distance from the actual sphere of decision.

Some did take Kennedy literally, and entered the Peace Corps or the federal bureaucracy. But most people accepted him as their surrogate. They looked to him to act in their name and for their betterment; they looked to him, too, for color and excitement. If the political realm had seemed reassuring but dull under President Eisenhower, it now seemed romantic and even a bit risky. Little matter that this was a spectacle in which few Americans could play any active part. In the Kennedy years, most Americans were persuaded that it was sufficient to be in the audience when a great political actor held the stage.

Kennedy's *charisma* had a powerful impact, but that impact had little to do with narrowing the *political* distance between the Presidency and the public. Some writers have attributed the participatory politics of the 1960s to John Kennedy's exhortation and example. Their causal logic is faulty, however. The flowering of the civil rights crusade and the first stirrings of the new left occurred between 1961 and 1963; yet neither movement traced its inspiration to the White House. Indeed, both frequently found themselves at odds with the Kennedy Administration. Outside of these movements, the politics of the early 1960s was not much more lively or critical than the "silent" 1950s. The dominant feature of these years was not vigorous public controversy over questions of foreign and domestic policy; more notable was the hush that fell over the nation as the President grappled with the fearful possibilities of nuclear war.

It was only during the Administrations of Kennedy's successors—whose lack of charisma left them no shield against policy disasters—that the public began to exercise its voice. Survey data has pointed to a major increase in citizen awareness and activisim since 1964, as well as to a dramatic rise in mass alienation.[16] Recent Presidents have had to contend with a public that is simultaneously more knowledgeable and more skeptical. The Kennedy Administration stands out as the last in which most Americans remained in awe of the President. It was the last time that a presidential spectacle captivated—and pacified—the American people.

In light of the Presidency's fall from grace since Kennedy's death, his brand of *charisma* is now regarded with some ambivalence. A surfeit of inflated rhetoric and hollow gestures has produced widespread skepticism toward presidential performances. Yet the longing for a President who can excite the imagination and touch the emotions is still strongly felt. A fresh claim of excellence, powered by a drive for political mastery, while sweetened by personal charm and grace, could still be staked in these supposedly disillusioned times.

It remains to be seen whether such a claim could be received as uncritically as was the claim of John Kennedy. The shocks of Vietnam and Watergate have enlightened as much as they have jarred. They have produced incontrovertible evidence that definitions of reality issuing from the White House are no more trustworthy than the arguments and facts advanced on their behalf. These experiences have also enhanced the credibility of alternative definitions of reality, as opponents of the President's "monopoly of authoritative answers" repeatedly demonstrate their superior candor and insight. A decade ago, scholars typically described the President as the chief moral leader and educator of the American people. Vietnam and Watergate have testified to the illusions—as well as the ironic truth—contained in that description.

A restoration of charismatic leadership in this environment would be difficult, but by no means impossible. Much depends on those who write about and analyze political affairs. If journalists and scholars adorn contemporary claims to excellence with the same colorful and hopeful imagery that John Kennedy enjoyed, if they eschew hard analyses of political and economic structures or painful recollections of recent injustice and violence in order to concentrate on optimistic political leaders intent on restoring "trust," the path for those leaders will be substantially cleared. If political commentators join presidential politicians in calling for a new *consensus,* embodied in a new hero, the public's new-found inclination to question and analyze presidential pronouncements will be severely tried.

Claims of excellence similar to those of John Kennedy will be heard again from the White House. It is crucial that those claims be weighed and tested. It is equally crucial for the *meaning* of excellence to be subjected to public examination. Above all, we need to begin considering the requirements for an authentically democratic excellence.

Democratic excellence should not, I would suggest, involve the monopolization of political activity by superior leaders standing apart from and above an admiring people. The excellence of leaders might be measured instead by their capacity to deepen public understanding and to stimulate public participation. It might be tested by their capacity to learn from citizen associations which have developed the confidence and strength to voice their own views and press their own grievances. If we care about democratic excellence, we might look for it in the fullness and clarity of the dialogue established between leaders and citizens, and in the political growth on both sides that such a dialogue fosters.

Excellence of this sort will be found more often in social movements or communities than on the national political scene. The obstacles to achievement of democratic excellence in presidential politics are particularly great. Conventional wisdom teaches Presidents to bend their major persuasive efforts toward members of the political elite and to gratify public opinion with rhetoric and style. Structural relationships ensure that corporate interests are heard far more easily and frequently by the White House than ordinary citizens. In the wake of Watergate, Presidents have to take account of popular suspicions and make gestures toward a plain and honest communion with the American people. But many resources remain at their command to evade the creative tension of dialogue and to produce new spectacles of presidential *charisma.*

NOTES

I wish to thank James Miller and William Galston for their helpful comments and suggestions.

1. Alexander Hamilton, James Madison, and John Jay, *The Federalist Papers* (New York: New American Library, 1961), p. 437.
2. *The Political Writings of John Adams,* ed. George A. Peek, Jr. (Indianapolis: Bobbs-Merrill, 1954), p. 176.

3. Theodore C. Sorensen, *Kennedy* (New York: Bantam, 1966), p. 410.
4. Henry Fairlie, *The Kennedy Promise: The Politics of Expectation* (New York: Dell, 1974), pp. 170–90.
5. Quoted in A. Alvarez, *Under Pressure* (Baltimore: Penguin, 1965), pp. 104–5.
6. It is not possible in the brief space of this essay to provide full documentation for my analysis of Kennedy. Most of the evidence for this analysis is contained in Bruce Miroff, *Pragmatic Illusions: The Presidential Politics of John F. Kennedy* (New York: David McKay, 1976).
7. John F. Kennedy, *Public Papers of the President: 1962* (Washington, D.C.: Government Printing Office, 1963), p. 533.
8. Ibid., p. 422.
9. On Kennedy's inflated view of world politics, see Miroff, *Pragmatic Illusions*, pp. 35–63.
10. John F. Kennedy, *Public Papers of the President: 1961* (Washington, D.C.: Government Printing Office, 1962), p. 534.
11. See Richard J. Walton, *Cold War and Counterrevolution: The Foreign Policy of John F. Kennedy* (New York: Viking Press, 1972); Louise FitzSimons, *The Kennedy Doctrine* (New York: Random House, 1972); Fairlie, *The Kennedy Promise;* Miroff, *Pragmatic Illusions.*
12. Harris Wofford, Oral History Interview, 22 May 1968, Kennedy Library, p. 53.
13. Ibid., pp. 28–29, 53–55.
14. See William Appleman Williams, *Some Presidents: From Wilson to Nixon* (New York: New York Review Books, 1972), pp. 101–4.
15. George E. Reedy, *The Twilight of the Presidency* (New York: New American Library, 1971), p. 55.
16. See Richard W. Boyd, "Electoral Trends in Postwar Politics," in *Choosing the President,* ed. James David Barber (Englewood Cliffs, N.J.: Prentice-Hall, 1974), pp. 175–201.

Chapter Eleven

Lyndon Johnson and the Politics of Mass Society

WILSON CAREY McWILLIAMS

The differences between John F. Kennedy and Lyndon B. Johnson made them a "balanced ticket" in 1960. New England Catholic and Texas Protestant, the two were predictably dissimilar in political style. Kennedy, as the public saw him, appeared to personify youthful idealism. Elegant, aloof, and eloquently sincere, he seemed untouched by the seamy side of life. It pleased Johnson to emphasize Kennedy's relative youth; he often referred to his running mate as "this boy." Evidently, Johnson was content with the public's contrasting image of him as a shrewd, rather devious political veteran, full of "human juices"—as David Halberstam later described him—and thoroughly down to earth.[1]

There was a good deal of truth in these perceptions, as there is in all caricatures, but they were also designedly misleading. Few suspected, in 1960, that Lyndon Johnson, a "Southern moderate," would be far more militant than Kennedy in combating racial and economic inequality. And, despite the impression he had cultivated, Lyndon Johnson was not a simple-souled "man of the people."

Feeling, memory, and all the powerful experiences and associations of early life bound Johnson to the "plain folks" he had grown up with. His concern for the poor and the excluded was more personal and passionate than Kennedy's rather distant compassion. But Lyndon Johnson was a powerfully ambitious, exceptionally able man who had spent almost all of his adult life in national politics. As a part of that larger world with its broader horizons, he would have felt penned in by the narrower limits of the world "down home." Johnson was a man caught between two worlds, attached to both and at home in neither.

Lyndon Johnson admired, envied, and courted the elite intellectuals, with their Ivy League diplomas and their well-mannered arrogance, and he resented and regretted the fact that the intellectual "establishment" regarded him as an interloper. Unlike Kennedy, Johnson observed, "I wasn't friends with their friends," and it made matters worse that Johnson succeeded, where "their friends" had failed, in getting cherished projects enacted into law. Vietnam gave patrician intellectuals a justification for their hostility, but their antipathy to Johnson predated the war.[2]

When he felt slighted or treated ungratefully by liberal intellectuals, Johnson found comfort in identifying with the people at large. When he called himself a Populist, as he did from time to time, it was partly because "some liberals" used the term contemptuously in referring to "progressives who come from the Southern and Western parts of the nation." Moreover, Johnson suspected that "modern liberal politicians" were relatively indifferent to the poor, in contrast to his own "Populist" commitment to help poor Americans to "find their voice and improve their lot." [3] Similarly, because Johnson was certain that Franklin Delano Roosevelt truly cared about the poor, Johnson could refer to Roosevelt as having a "touch of the populist." [4] But Roosevelt was an aristocrat, and by identifying FDR with his own beliefs, Johnson indicated that "populism" in his usage implied *helping* and *caring for* the people, but did not necessarily entail a sense of *being with* them.

"Relations of power," Johnson asserted, rest on an implicit "contract" between leaders and followers, by which leaders agree to pursue the "interest" of their followers (or, at least, what the followers believe to be in their interest). Johnson framed this argument to demonstrate that, "except at knife-point," obedience is always voluntary and power rests on consent.[5] But the terms Johnson used also suggest that leaders and followers have different motives for entering the "political contract," with leaders seeking "power" and followers maximizing "interest." Only political leaders, then, act from public or political motives; ordinary citizens are concerned with private ends. In this very Madisonian image, politics exists to further private "interests," to provide the public with goods and services.

Certainly, Johnson did not share the classical view that human beings are political animals who need political life. In that ancient view, political participation—both ruling and being ruled—was vital for human happiness and a crucial element in moral education. Consequently, classical political philosophers argued for the small state, the *polis*, where public life and active participation were accessible to all citizens. Johnson, by contrast, seemed to see no value in participation itself. Small units of local government were simply outdated, "built around archaic horse-and-wagon conditions," and were unsuited to efficient administration. To be sure, Johnson regretted that the people—contrary to the Framers' assumption, according to Johnson—did not "take a keen and continuing interest in the art of government." And Johnson urged that Americans give more attention to teaching the "art of statecraft." The arts of state-craft and government, however, were not *politics:* they were identical, in Johnson's mind, with public administration. Undoubtedly, Johnson's devotion to "big government" in the New Deal tradition made excellent administrators a necessity. But that emphasizes Johnson's belief that gov-ernment existed to pursue "interests," to advance goals and values estab-lished in private life. Moral education was the task of "society"; public administration was the job of the state. Electoral politics, winning con-sent and constructing the bonds between rulers and ruled, was a part of leadership, but it was essentially a distraction from what Johnson asserted to be the real tasks of government. Hence, Johnson supported a four-year term for the House of Representatives and a six-year term for the President who would then be ineligible for reelection. An im-proved "quality of life" demanded better service by better administrators and more autonomous representatives; it did not require citizens at large to deliberate or to be involved in political life.[6]

It was up to political leaders to link private citizens and public govern-ment, making administration responsive and winning consent. As John-son saw it, leadership required power and power derived from serving the interests of others. The price of leadership and power alike was a leader's willingness to subordinate his own private needs and desires to the demands of his public vocation. Political leadership was taking care of others; the leader's role made it difficult or unlikely for him to be cared *for*—nurtured, protected, freed from or allowed to share the burden of responsibility. Power and leadership were a kind of sacrifice in which the self was denied in order to be glorified.

In this image, political leadership is an "inner worldly asceticism" similar to that described in Max Weber's *The Protestant Ethic and the Spirit of Capitalism.* Johnson had been reared in the traditions of mili-tant "border state" Protestantism, a religion and a culture which were rooted in agrarian, not mercantile society. Capitalism itself was not greatly respected, and it seemed relatively impractical as a career; the "inner worldly asceticism" of Johnson's tradition expressed itself in politi-cal or social life.

In part, the Protestant culture in which Johnson grew up was shaped by the teaching that self-seeking is a mark of sin, and that human beings must be taught to suppress the demanding, greedy, necessitous side of their nature. They must be trained as children to be considerate and giving, instead.

That moral teaching was reinforced by a society and culture in which neediness was regarded with horror. The economic environment for

southern "common whites" was insecure and frustrating, and for most
people poverty was never more than a step away.[7] Experience taught
people to depend on inner resources rather than an unreliable external
world, to "overcome circumstances instead of letting them overwhelm
me," as Johnson's mother said of herself.[8] The inner self had to be for-
tified against the needs of the body and even against the social needs
and affections that could tie the individual to a world which was only
too likely to inflict pain. Need and dependency were acknowledgments
that one had not "overcome" but had been defeated. A confession of
economic, emotional, or social need was also, to some extent, a confession of moral weakness. Dependency, moreover, put one "in debt"
and at the service of another, to some extent weakening personal
autonomy.

Hospitality and lavish giving were a part of that culture, but they
flowed from competition and anxiety as much as from genuine generosity. The giver established that he was not needy, that he had more than
necessary. The recipient could demonstrate that he also was independent only by returning the favor. If he could not, the recipient
would be admitting need, debt, and inferiority. The giver of the greatest
gift "wins," establishing dominance and independence; in a cultural para-
dox, those who get, lose.

But one can only give what one *has*. Giving presumes saving and ac-
cumulation, the amassing of those resources that permit generosity. As
Weber realized, however, saving on a grand scale is possible only for
the "inner worldly ascetic" who works hard but who regards money as
"filthy lucre," suitable only for purchasing the inferior goods of this world
and for doing "good works" among the unfortunate.

What money was to Weber's protocapitalist Protestant, power was to
Lyndon Johnson. For years, Johnson worked to accumulate "political capital," acquiring "credit" through favors, services, and the discipline of
political self-denial. He played down or concealed his own broader and
more liberal aims and ideals, cultivating the narrower interests and
adapting to the prejudices and the greater conservatism of his congressional district and his state. Curbing his own ambition and his desire for
the limelight, Johnson deferred to more conservative patrons like Speaker
of the House Sam Rayburn and Senator Richard Russell. Such senior legislators could advance Johnson's career and help him "get results," but
Johnson also sensed that this dutiful willingness to "wait his turn" and
play by the rules would lessen resentment at his success. Johnson's political apprenticeship provided him with many warm memories and satisfactions, but the great theme of those years was the sacrifice of short-
term gratifications in the interests of long-term gains as, repeatedly,
Johnson swallowed his own pride and bent under pressure. Frustration

and inner fury, in Johnson's experience, were the price of "political capital." [9]

It is hardly surprising, then, that Johnson changed so quickly from a leader devoted to accumulating "capital" to a President hastening to spend it. Every frustration and felt indignity which Johnson had endured in the pursuit of power heightened his appetite for love and admiration. As Doris Kearns wrote,

> His personality did not fade and become indistinct, as personality often does in most men who must continually adapt to others; instead, even though it bent enough to seduce and reshape other wills, Johnson's own will became stronger. Yet Johnson often seemed as discontent in conquest as he was eager in pursuit. [10]

Power, for Johnson, was never an "end in itself"; it was a means to respect, affection, and fame. [11] Johnson knew that he was dissipating his "political capital" in his multifronted wars against poverty, racism, and insurgency in Vietnam, and he acknowledged that he might have attempted "too much too soon." [12] Johnson explained that the checks-and-balances system gives the advantage to those who wish to resist change; a President's enemies inevitably will manage to coalesce, especially since a President's term is constitutionally limited, forcing any President to be in something of a hurry. [13] All of these observations were correct, but such calculations do not explain Johnson's passionate zeal for "doing good," his impatient quest for greatness. Trained to regard material self-interest as contemptible, Johnson was drawn to politics, where serving the interests of others seemed a means to advancing the psychological interests of the self. Taught to fear dependency and his need to be loved, Johnson sought political power as a means of "earning" love. It would be *owed* him by citizens, as a debt to be collected rather than as a gift to be received. Johnson understated the case when he wrote that, "Power can lose its charm when a man has known it as many years as I had." [14] Only the vision—an illusion, as it happens—of a love without dependency made the discipline of power endurable.

Reflecting on his relationship with Robert Kennedy, Johnson remarked that he "almost wished" that RFK had become President, and had been forced to wrestle with the real problems of ruling, so that the country would see the Kennedys as they really were—not in "the storybook image of great heroes who, because they were dead, could make anything anyone wanted happen." [15] Johnson felt a measure of envy for the assassinated Kennedys, who seemed to have won fame cheaply and easily, without the travail and self-abnegation inherent in the leader's vocation. Martyrdom was a kind of cheating, winning without paying the price.

Johnson's decision not to seek reelection in 1968 was, in a sense, only the ultimate gesture of self-denial, the conscious surrender of power in pursuit of the public's regard and good remembrance.[16]

This pattern of service and self-denial meant that Johnson had to struggle constantly against the side of himself that felt needy, neglected, and angry at frustration, that was hurt or enraged by slights or lack of appreciation, and that yearned to be cared for and freed from too great a burden of responsibility. That internal struggle, however, made Johnson acutely sensitive to the strength of feelings of rage, indignity, and resentment in the public at large. Johnson hated poverty with a very personal intensity, and he was concerned with the *moral* cost of poverty as much as with its material deprivations. The "moral and economic fiber of the entire country" was weakened by poverty, especially because poverty bred arrogance in the rich and tempted the poor to violence. But poverty was only one of the "roots of hate." [17] Indignity and unjust discrimination nurtured hatred and violence, even where weakness or other calculations led the victims to keep their resentment "under wraps."

> "We'll never know how high a price we paid for the unkindness and injustice we've inflicted on people—the Negroes, Mexicans and Jews— and everyone who really believes he has been discriminated against in any way is part of that great human price. And that cost exists where many people may not even think it does." [18]

And, in the same sense, Johnson knew that feelings of personal insignificance and despair undermine the basis of self-restraint and moral responsibility.

Johnson understood such demoralization because he combated it in himself. He also had more than a little recognition of the fact that resentful and necessitous people find it difficult to feel deep gratitude and affection for their benefactors, especially if they feel hopelessly dependent.[19] As Thomas Hobbes put it,

> To have received from one, to whom we think our selves equall, greater benefits than there is hope to Requite, disposeth to counterfeit love; but really secret hatred; and puts a man into the estate of a desperate debtor, that in declining the sight of his creditor, tacitly wishes him there, where he might never see him more. For benefits oblige; and obligation is thraldome; and unrequitable obligation, perpetually thraldome; which is to ones equall, hatefull.[20]

The implication of Hobbes's teaching is that Johnson's pursuit of love through service was bound to be futile—his very helpfulness would inspire hostility—unless he could persuade Americans that he was their "superior," not their equal, or that there was "hope to Requite" the benefits they received. In a country so embued with ideas of equality, superiority is not easily accepted, and Johnson had set himself to strengthen and expand equality in America.[21] But Johnson, fearful of any sort of dependence, did not find it easy to acknowledge his need for public esteem. And in any case, as Johnson rather despairingly realized, in a mass society, genuine feelings of interdependence between rulers and ruled are difficult, if not impossible, to attain.

Johnson often expressed a disdain for "politics," in the sense of appealing to the mass public, and it would be easy to explain that distaste by reference to Johnson's ordinarily drab and hesitant qualities as a public speaker.[22] But Johnson began his career with an impassioned stump speech, which captured local attention, and he could be very eloquent, especially when he discarded prepared texts and spoke, in "evangelical fashion," from his own experience and feelings.[23] Notably, his most memorable speeches involve a sort of attack on his audience, a rhetoric of controlled force very similar to the "Godfather's" offers, which cannot be refused, and designed to suggest Johnson's indifference to the audience's probable disagreement, resistance, and feelings of hostility. Speaking to a Joint Session of Congress, in March 1965, for example, Johnson reminisced about his days as a teacher among poor Mexican-Americans and his despair of ever having a chance to help the poor. "But now I do have that chance," Johnson proclaimed, "and I'll let you in on a little secret—I mean to use it." The second half of that sentence, Johnson's "little secret," was a decorously phrased threat, a warning that the President would brook no interference. Rather more flamboyantly, he told a New Orleans audience, in 1964, that he was more than serious about enforcing civil rights:

> Whatever your views are, we have a Constitution and we have a Bill of Rights, and we have the law of the land, and two-thirds of the Democrats in the Senate voted for it, and three-fourths of the Republicans. I signed it, I am going to enforce it, and I am going to observe it, and I think that any man that is worthy of the high office of President is going to do the same thing.[24]

In still-segregationist Louisiana, the effect was "electrifying," Jack Valenti remarked, because it produced shock and awe; the audience felt dominated, literally compelled, and overwhelmed. Johnson knew very well, of course, that no democratic leader can make a career out of defying or insulting audiences. But he found it difficult to be eloquent in *appealing* to an audience for support, in part, because such an appeal came too close to his powerful desire for approval and to his fear of dependence. Such personal factors aside, however, Johnson had good reasons for distrusting any temptation to cajole or inspire a mass audience.

Large audiences bothered Johnson by their very facelessness and impersonality. He was all too conscious of the indignity inherent in the mass: the blurring of individuality and personal character and the extent to which such anonymity lessens feelings of moral responsibility. An "aroused" citizenry, in LBJ's imagination, was almost indistinguishable from an inflamed mob governed by rage, partisanship, or panic.[25]

Johnson shared the traditional American belief that electoral politics is always to some extent a kind of game ("playing politics"). Fairly stable, small communities, like those where Johnson grew up, able to take their unity for granted and more threatened by boredom than by fragmentation, especially strengthened this view. Such communities delighted in a hyperbolic rhetoric, a "speechifying" entertainment, exciting and evocative but not altogether serious. But the emotions dredged up by such oratory could, and often did, turn ugly: In a world where lynch law was a living memory, it would have been surprising if Johnson had not had some fear of the masses. Politicians who claimed to raise issues to encourage discussion, Johnson thought, were at best engaging in "rambling talk," distinct from the real tasks of legislating and ruling. And these politicians often aroused and moralized from narrow and parochial interests, making it difficult to appeal to or act in the name of the common good. The greatest danger, however, was that the rhetoric would inflame the public's destructive passions, leading to "irrational fights" and "unlimited goals" and freezing leaders—afraid of alienating their constituents—into uncompromising positions.[26]

In Johnson's view, it was the duty of political leaders to limit the terms of public debate, restrain their rhetoric, rule out extreme statements, and to keep the doors to compromise open. In his memoirs, as in many of his public statements, Johnson felt obliged to adopt a ponderously reasonable style, which implied that Johnson himself was serenely above the fray. And while he may have felt that this would add to his own stature, it was at least as important that he hoped that his tone of Olympian moderation would calm public passions and restrain debate.[27] Even when Johnson felt compelled to engage in a "politics of principle," as he did in advocating the Civil Rights Act of 1964, he sought to keep the conflict within the limits of good manners and parliamentary gentlemanliness. If the battle over civil rights necessarily approximated a total war, which demanded unconditional victory, leaders like Senators Richard Russell and Everett Dirksen would work with Johnson to guarantee that it would be "fought with dignity and perhaps with sorrow, but not anger or bitterness." [28]

American political leaders, however, were also political rivals. They could hope to set limits to competition and rhetoric only in a world like the Senate, where their face-to-face relationships with each other counteracted, to some extent, the contentious pressure of party and electoral politics. For that reason, Johnson distrusted parties and took some pride in not having used power "in a political way" to build up a party machine.[29] Johnson's suspicion of parties was partly due to the fact that he had grown up in what was still a one-party state, and he had learned to see partisan organizations as personal followings or loose economic factions with little continuity, not as true vehicles of democratic accountability.[30] But although this "consequence of one-party factionalism" influenced his views, it fitted neatly into his general distrust of mass politics.

As Johnson trusted the smaller, more fraternal world of the Senate, so he felt at ease with personal persuasion, the "private oratory," at which he was a virtuoso. His preference for private discussion had its seamy side: Individual conversations "off the record" allowed Johnson to keep secrets, to divide and conquer, and to be all things to all people. This was especially so, since Johnson felt a desperate determination to persuade—whatever the cost in goods, words, or promises—and always remain in control and at the center of communication.[31]

Johnson's faith in the superiority of private and small group conversation also had a more admirable source. Johnson knew the human "desire for recognition," which was especially strong in political leaders. Being consulted and treated with deference and consideration dissolved many leaders' resistance to Johnson's measures. Felt indignity and weakness drove leaders and citizens alike into a fearful defense of their private interests. Giving them a sense of personal importance and private security allowed them to see beyond narrow self-interest to that "self-interest rightly understood," which, as Johnson conceived it, approached and could be harmonized with the common good itself.[32] But only personal involvement and attention could dissolve alienation and anxiety, and, for most Americans, such personal contact with leaders at the center of power simply was not possible. Strong political parties might have built a bridge between the people in their localities and the government in Washington, but Johnson excluded that alternative. His demand that his public appearances allow time for "touching" his audience was an almost pathetic gesture in the direction of personal contact between citizens and their rulers.[33]

Mass politics made it necessary for Johnson to deal with the mass media. He loathed the newsman's pose of "objectivity," being quite aware that all reporters had a "slant" and acted "under pressure." The media were usurpers; acting in a *public* role, the media were governed by *pri-*

vate constituencies. The electronic media especially (but not exclusively) addressed the public *en masse* in radically oversimplified terms and those appealing to the public's lower feelings and anxieties. And newsmen, taken as a whole, were no better than a mob, scrabbling, anomic, and irresponsible. Only individual reporters and columnists, lifted out of the multitude into positions of personal influence and dignity, could be expected to act from higher motives. In general, the media accentuated the problems of mass politics.

As this concern for personal contact suggests, for all of Lyndon Johnson's contemptuous comments about "playing politics," he valued political participation when it consisted of personal relationships between rulers and ruled. Politics was ubiquitous; private life involved public issues, which in turn required a public forum. People needed to be heard and consulted and to sense that they mattered. Educated in Madisonian principles, Johnson's experience taught him that human beings have political needs. For Johnson, however, that knowledge was a sad wisdom. As Doris Kearns suggests, it wedded his imagination to the older, more personal politics of small communities which he had learned from his father. And still Johnson was convinced that such communities were hopelessly irrelevant in an industrial and technological age.[34]

Johnson worried constantly about the "moral underpinning" of his regime. In part, his worries were personal and accidental; he had come to power by assassination in a country which was prepared to feel "disdain" for any Southerner. But Johnson also recognized that elections conveyed only a tentative mandate, an authorization to *attempt* leadership. The people, in a mass election, inevitably *guessed* about the qualities of a leader who would never know *them* as individuals. The President, he wrote, must "become a leader" in order to acquire a "right to govern," and leadership required that he "attract people who are willing to follow him" further than the limited, tentative consent implied by their vote.[35]

As Johnson set it out, the President should decide what was right, "regardless of the political implications," and then attempt to convince a majority of the Congress and the people that his judgment was correct.[36] But although Johnson realized that small majorities often offered the advantage of tighter discipline and cohesion, he also repeatedly urged the need to aim for *consensus*.[37] Johnson reiterated his desire for unity, "the deepest wish of my heart," so often that the theme became tiresome, but Johnson's meaning was far from banal.[38] Johnson's expression of concern about trust and unity is an indication of his fear that America was losing confidence among its citizens.

In 1957, Johnson argued that citizens were "tired of the kind of political thought that divides Americans into blocs" based on class and interest. They thought of themselves first as Americans, Johnson contended, "and they are perfectly right in doing so." [39] For some reason, Doris Kearns describes this statement as an example of "pluralist thought," reflecting the assumption that, if people do not identify with a "single category," it will follow that "political cleavages will be limited in intensity." [40] In fact, Johnson was insisting that Americans ought to see their "Americanness" *as* an overarching category, an appeal to ideas of the common good which would have horrified most pluralists. Johnson's rejection of "blocs" seems to imply an attack on the tendency of pluralistic political thought to classify persons as members of groups rather than as citizens. But, although Johnson attributed his ideal to the American people, he knew that he was arguing against powerful currents working to fragment the society.

Johnson did not aim at *consensus* because he presumed some monolithic agreement about ends in the United States. He worked to produce massive majorities—despite their fissiparous quality—because he feared the country could not survive serious political disagreement. Only a few political leaders could be relied on to put the common good above their private interests. Johnson was haunted by the suspicion that civic spirit and common beliefs were coming to be outweighed, in mass society, by conflicting interests and privatized feelings. And political unity would then be possible only to the extent that Johnson could persuade the vast majority of Americans that his Administration served *all* their private interests.

It was a shrewd perception, though Johnson's own need to serve may have led him to exaggerate the danger. His fear for American unity, however, made economic growth the ruling political guideline. Growth would permit the poor to reach a decent standard of living *without requiring sacrifice* on the part of the affluent; blacks could advance without loss to whites; Vietnam could be fought without any cost to domestic reform. Only so long as there were no losers, would it be possible to advance both equality and unity. Johnson was extremely reluctant, for example, to agree to an anti-inflationary tax increase during the Vietnam War, fearing the consequences of asking the public for sacrifice.[41] Johnson clung to the idea that he could advance unity by satisfying private interests, buying off resentments against anonymity and weakness with material benefits. It was an historic American illusion, rooted in Madisonian theory, and Johnson may be pardoned for his devotion to it. But it was an illusion. Moreover, even though growth may make it possible for you to advance without my having to lose in *absolute* terms (you *gain* $5.00, while I *lose* nothing), there is no way for you to advance out of the indignity of poverty without my losing ground *relative* to you. When you had $5.00 and I had $15.00, I had three times as much as you;

if we both gain $5.00, I shall have only twice as much. We shall have gained equally in absolute terms, but I shall have lost in relative terms. And that change is crucial to feelings of dignity. Growth is no substitute for the desire for equality, the yearning for the common good, the sense of civic bond. "It is more necessary to equalize men's desires than their properties," Aristotle wrote, "and that is a result which cannot be achieved unless men are adequately trained by the influence of laws." [42] But it was just that sort of civic education which Johnson despaired of.

It is surely one of the great ironies of American history that Lyndon Johnson, so passionately concerned to produce unity in America, should have led the United States into the savage divisiveness of the Vietnam War. His Vietnam policies, however, epitomized Johnson's virtues and defects as a political leader.

Johnson was convinced that he was dealing with a war of aggression, directed or controlled by Hanoi across a de facto international boundary.[43] Moreover, the United States had pledged its word to South Vietnam, and, throughout the world, American promises were fundamental to deterrence and to the security of allies who, if they did not trust American guarantees, might seek to develop their own nuclear forces.[44] Abandonment of Vietnam would invite one act of aggression after another—the "domino theory"—and would open the door to nuclear proliferation and to increased international insecurity.[45]

Johnson insisted, however, that America's involvement be *limited*. The Korean War had been limited in its physical setting and, to some extent, in the weapons which were employed. Johnson went further in Vietnam: he limited the *moral* stakes of the war and the terms of foreign policy debate. In sharp contrast to official statements during the Korean War, Johnson refused to vilify North Vietnam. He suggested, in fact, that if Hanoi would "call off" the war, the United States would be eager for North Vietnam to "take its place in the common effort" of reconstruction and development.[46] As Kearns remarks, no other leader of any other nation would have made Johnson's offer to help reconstruct an enemy state.[47] And surely, it reflects Johnson's determination to keep the moral terms of the war under control.

The dangers of escalation obsessed Johnson, strengthening his determination to limit the war. He feared Russian or Chinese intervention in Vietnam. He worried, too, that American preoccupation with Southeast Asia might encourage aggression in other parts of the world.[48] Most of all, he was anxious about the American people.

Johnson believed, first, the people loved peace, and potential aggressors were always likely to mistake this natural preference for a lack of courage. If, acting on the basis of this mistaken assumption, aggressors actually began a war, they would discover their error, but obviously, this enlightenment would come too late to prevent the war itself.[49] Consequently, a democracy needed "tough" leaders who could counteract the public's apparent weakness. John Kennedy, Johnson thought, had seemed "softer" than he was, and Khrushchev, underrating him, had decided to "test the United States with a new crisis in Berlin." [50] Appearances, not realities, were crucial; Johnson had no doubt of Kennedy's inner toughness. (That rather Machiavellian doctrine hints, however, at the possibility that Johnson's own apparent strength was something he felt to be only a disguise.) The public's apparent pacifism was a constant danger to democratic foreign policy.

Secondly, he thought, the public was too parochial, too indifferent, and too self-centered in matters of foreign policy. Johnson himself felt international interdependence as an almost palpable reality, and he had a strong conviction that almost any injustice injured America, at least in the long run. "In the modern world," he commented, "men and nations have no choice but to live together as brothers." [51] He hated poverty in the rest of the world only a little less intensely than he detested it at home, and he proclaimed an extension of the "war on poverty" into foreign affairs. His compassion was almost fanatical, rejecting all boundaries.[52] The original subtitle of Doris Kearns' study, "The Tyranny of Benevolence," was perceptive. Johnson *was* tyrannized by his sense of his duty to serve others, and his benevolence, shaped by that overpowering need, was sometimes equally tyrannical in neglecting to discern whether others wanted help.[53] Nevertheless, Johnson's sense of international interdependence was certainly well founded, even if he sometimes carried it to extremes. He was convinced, by contrast, that the public lacked an adequate appreciation of human unity. "A patient understanding of others," he wrote, "is a great human deficiency," and people in general were more prone to "destructive" criticism and a lack of compassion.[54] (Johnson's own ambivalent feelings about giving are reflected in the ambiguity of his use of "human deficiency." Johnson's wording could imply that "patient understanding" was a human *weakness*, rather than something humans had too little of, although obviously he meant the latter.) Concerned only with immediate events, devoted to peace, well-being, and self-interest, the public would eventually become aware of dangers and crises. But the people were likely to be shocked and surprised by this sudden recognition. Then, they were prone to panic, and too often were misled by demagogues, especially of the extreme right.

The McCarthy era was always on his mind, and Johnson remained confident that his Vietnam policies had prevented the extreme right from escalating the war. Johnson's fear of super-patriotism had a considerable basis in fact. He was certain, for example, that if he seemed "too weak" in Vietnam, Robert Kennedy would lead a movement against him, appealing to militant anticommunism. For Doris Kearns, it is "difficult to understand how anyone could have believed that Kennedy might be a crusading hawk." [55] Johnson, whose political memory was longer and more reliable than Kearns's, remembered that Kennedy had been an assistant to Joseph McCarthy and had been prominent among the Wisconsin senator's mourners; and, he recalled that RFK had offered to become Ambassador to Saigon in 1964. The decline of Cold War hawkishness in America grew out of the disillusionments of the Vietnam War as Johnson conducted it. Anticommunism was strong at the beginning of the war, and a different kind of war might have perpetuated it. It would certainly have been possible for Johnson to ask Congress—quite compliant until late in the war—to declare war on Hanoi or to accept war measures only a little less drastic. Nor would public support have been a difficult problem: Even in 1968, 60 percent of the voters who supported Eugene McCarthy against Johnson in the New Hampshire primary wanted a tougher policy in Vietnam.[56]

However, despite Johnson's deep commitment to America's involvement in Vietnam, he rejected all arguments in favor of putting the country on a "war footing." To do so, Johnson believed, would pose too great a danger of escalation, and would create unacceptable threats to civil liberties and reform at home. But Johnson also considered that, short of stirring the public's patriotic fervor, there was no way he could win genuine public support for his policies and the sacrifices they were bound to entail. He minimized the real costs of the war, hoping to avoid the need to ask the public to bear its burdens. Even Johnson admitted that he had been too "cautious" in failing to inform Congress and the people about probable enemy offensives before the Tet attacks of 1968. In 1958, Johnson had opposed legislation requiring the President to give an annual report on national security to the Congress, fearing that the President would "feel committed to present to the public a rosier picture than the facts would warrant." It certainly proved to be an accurate self-assessment. And it was public disillusionment with such falsely optimistic forecasts and analyses that fatally wounded Johnson's credit, and that of his policies.[57]

Johnson's deceptions about the costs of the war made sense if he were gambling on a short, quickly negotiated campaign akin to his venture into the Dominican Republic,[58] but Johnson had reason to know that Vietnam would require more than that. His conviction that he could not educate the public trapped him between the poles of escalation and deception, and either way, Johnson's goals were bound to be frustrated.

Nevertheless, Americans owe a considerable debt to the moral convictions that kept Lyndon Johnson from attempting to make the war into an anticommunist crusade. Pericles inspired the Athenian public with what amounted to ideological appeals, and he himself was able to control and use the public's passions. Pericles' successors, however, either could not or did not wish to limit the people, and Athens drifted or was led into total war and disaster. Richard Nixon hinted to the South Vietnamese Government that he would be more sympathetic than either Lyndon Johnson or Hubert Humphrey, and his career makes this seem likely enough.[59] But Johnson's restraint had made the protest movement possible, and had cast the issue in terms of a choice between Johnson's policies and greater concessions in the search for peace. Pericles left a war which could not be limited; Lyndon Johnson left a war which could not be expanded. And that restriction was no small benefaction.

Fearing the mass public, Johnson saw no way by which it might be reduced to more human and more educable proportions. Comfortable with a smaller political scale of things, he had also been schooled in the Madisonian tradition which values large states with great power and wealth, able to provide for the private interests of the many. And, reared in the duty to care for others, he underrated his own need to be cared for. He did not learn to be ruled, a lesson to which the classical philosophers had given priority over learning to rule in the education of political men.

An American political leader needs emotional protection against both his fear of the people and his desire to court them. He needs friends who will reassure him, but who will demand that he do his duty. Johnson found that friendship, to some degree, in Mrs. Johnson and in intimates like Walter Jenkins, both of whom helped him overcome his fear of rejection in 1964.[60] Too often, however, Johnson's need for warmth, affection, and admiration expressed itself in a superficial camaraderie with people he could dominate and under conditions he could control. And even there, as Garry Wills points out, Johnson engaged in desperately seductive performances, acting in ways that he despised in himself and that he feared others would detest in him—hiding from intimacy even as he sought to seem candid.[61]

In any case, Johnson's immediate circle in Washington could not break a mass public into local groups, in which people could be addressed and heard with some respect for their diversity, their dignity, and their individuality. To do that, Johnson would have needed a strong and vital political party, devoted to the kind of talk and partisanship which he misprized. *Party* implies collective responsibility, rather than the lonely dominion that Johnson favored. But a powerful party might also have shouldered part of the burden, which even Lyndon Johnson, a political Atlas, knew himself to be too weak to carry; transforming a faceless mass into a citizen-public.

NOTES

1. Halberstam is cited in Jack Valenti, *A Very Human President* (New York: Norton, 1975), p. 390.
2. Doris Kearns, *Lyndon Johnson and the American Dream* (New York: Harper & Row, 1976), p. 313; see also, pp. xi, 5, 13, 42; Valenti, *A Very Human President*, pp. 154, 156.
3. Lyndon B. Johnson, *The Vantage Point: Perspectives of the Presidency, 1963–1969* (New York: Holt, Rinehart & Winston, 1971), p. 72.
4. Valenti, *A Very Human President*, p. 308.
5. Kearns, *Lyndon Johnson*, p. 112.
6. Johnson, *Vantage Point*, pp. 343–45; all these comments are in a chapter that deals with the "quality of life."
7. The term "common whites" is taken from W. J. Cash, *The Mind of the South* (New York: Knopf, 1941).
8. Kearns, *Lyndon Johnson*, p. 21.
9. Richard E. Neustadt, *Presidential Power: The Politics of Leadership, With Reflections on Johnson and Nixon* (New York: Wiley, 1976), pp. 29–30; Kearns, *Lyndon Johnson*, pp. 76, 91, 103, 105, 113, 173.
10. Kearns, *Lyndon Johnson*, p. 134.
11. Neustadt, *Presidential Power*, p. 31.
12. Johnson, *Vantage Point*, pp. 566, 549, 433.
13. Ibid., pp. 440–41; Valenti, *A Very Human President*, p. 144.
14. Johnson, *Vantage Point*, p. 433.
15. Quoted in Kearns, *Lyndon Johnson*, p. 350.
16. This is especially true since Johnson believed, apparently correctly, that he would have been reelected, had he run in 1968 (*Vantage Point*, p. 549).
17. Ibid., pp. 29, 72, 79; Kearns, *Lyndon Johnson*, pp. 97, 113.
18. Kearns, *Lyndon Johnson*, pp. 305–6; see also, Johnson, *Vantage Point*, p. 167. Since Johnson felt discriminated against because of his southern origin, he was clearly including himself as part of the "human price" (ibid., pp. 95, 155).
19. Kearns, *Lyndon Johnson*, p. 305; Johnson, *Vantage Point*, pp. 167, 172.
20. Thomas Hobbes, *Leviathan*, ed. C. B. Macpherson (Baltimore: Penguin, 1968), pp. 162–63.

21. Johnson, *Vantage Point*, p. 166.
22. For example, see Kearns, *Lyndon Johnson*, pp. 128, 354.
23. Ibid, p. 69; Valenti, *A Very Human President*, p. 206.
24. Johnson, *Vantage Point*, p. 109; Valenti, *A Very Human President*, p. 208.
25. Johnson, *Vantage Point*, p. 451; Kearns, *Lyndon Johnson*, pp. 92, 128, 142.
26. Kearns, *Lyndon Johnson*, pp. 92, 109, 142, 154, 244; Valenti, *A Very Human President*, pp. 153, 155; Johnson, *Vantage Point*, pp. 158, 451.
27. Kearns, *Lyndon Johnson*, pp. 14, 150, 154–55, 355–56.
28. Johnson, *Vantage Point*, pp. 158, 159; Kearns, *Lyndon Johnson*, p. 191.
29. Johnson, *Vantage Point*, p. 433; Kearns, *Lyndon Johnson*, pp. 155, 244.
30. V. O. Key, Jr., *Southern Politics* (New York: Random House, 1949), pp. 254–76, 298–311.
31. Kearns, *Lyndon Johnson*, pp. x, 122, 127, 225; Valenti, *A Very Human President*, pp. 188–89, 193, 199; Johnson, *Vantage Point*, p. 457.
32. Kearns, *Lyndon Johnson*, pp. 92, 120, 181, 184, 221–22; Valenti, *A Very Human President*, pp. 178–79, 189, 200; Johnson, *Vantage Point*, pp. 448, 451.
33. Kearns, *Lyndon Johnson*, p. 88.
34. Ibid., pp. x, xi, 34, 36, 64.
35. Johnson, *Vantage Point*, p. 18; see also, Kearns, *Lyndon Johnson*, pp. 171, 173; Johnson, *Vantage Point*, pp. 19, 95, 155.
36. Johnson, *Vantage Point*, p. 28.
37. Ibid., pp. 27, 35.
38. Ibid., pp. 30–31, 95, 110, 427.
39. Quoted in Kearns, *Lyndon Johnson*, pp. 156–57.
40. Kearns, *Lyndon Johnson*, p. 157.
41. Ibid., pp. 296, 302.
42. *The Politics of Aristotle*, trans. E. Barker (Oxford: Clarendon Press, 1952), p. 64.
43. Johnson, *Vantage Point*, pp. 52, 56, 57, 59–60, 67, 121, 501; Kearns, *Lyndon Johnson*, pp. 95–96, 253, 313, 329–31.
44. Johnson was also rightly contemptuous of congressional leaders who pretended ignorance of the nature of American commitments in South Vietnam. On the commitment issue, see Johnson, *Vantage Point*, pp. 23, 49, 50, 68, 293.
45. Ibid., pp. 61, 135–36, Kearns, *Lyndon Johnson*, p. 330.

46. Johnson, *Vantage Point*, p. 133; see also, pp. 119, 126, 153, 241; Valenti, *A Very Human President*, p. 358.
47. Kearns, *Lyndon Johnson*, p. 267.
48. Johnson, *Vantage Point*, pp. 140, 287, 369.
49. Kearns, *Lyndon Johnson*, pp. 95, 143, 329.
50. Johnson, *Vantage Point*, p. 24.
51. Ibid., p. 249.
52. Ibid., pp. 249, 363–64; Kearns, *Lyndon Johnson*, p. 168.
53. Neustadt, *Presidential Power*, p. 283, n. 8; Kearns, *Lyndon Johnson*, pp. x–xi.
54. Johnson, *Vantage Point*, p. 65; see also, Valenti, *A Very Human President*, p. 133.
55. Kearns, *Lyndon Johnson*, p. 259.
56. Ibid., p. 338; on Johnson's fear of the right, see ibid., pp. 142, 252–53, 282; Valenti, *A Very Human President*, p. 300.
57. Kearns, *Lyndon Johnson*, pp. 141, 282, 302; Johnson, *Vantage Point*, p. 330.
58. Neustadt, *Presidential Power*, p. 9.
59. Johnson, *Vantage Point*, pp. 517, 518, 548.
60. Ibid., pp. 93–97.
61. Garry Wills, "Singing 'Mammy' to Doris," *New York Review of Books* 23 (24 June 1976):8; Kearns, *Lyndon Johnson*, pp. 8, 9, 26.

Contributors

PETER DENNIS BATHORY teaches political theory at Livingston College, Rutgers University. He has co-authored *Political Theory and the People's Right to Know* and *The Nature of Leadership*. He is currently involved in research on political rhetoric and public language.

HENRY A. PLOTKIN teaches American politics at Livingston College, Rutgers University. He is the author of several articles on American political economy and is at present completing a lengthy study of the development of American corporate ideology.

MARC K. LANDY is an assistant professor of Political Science at Boston College. He is the author of *The Politics of Environmental Reform: Controlling Kentucky Strip Mining*. He is currently involved in research on corporate politics and on the politics of environmental decision making.

REVEREND WILLIE K. SMITH has long been active in church and civil rights affairs and teaches community development at Livingston College, Rutgers University.

ED SCHWARTZ is president of the Institute for the Study of Civic Values. He is the author of *Will the Revolution Succeed?* and is currently completing a book on American political education.

DENNIS HALE is a freelance writer living in Boston. He is at present at work on a political biography of James Michael Curley.

WILLIAM D'ARRIENZO has taught political science at the City University of New York and at Rutgers University. He has been active in New York civic affairs for several years.

BRUCE MIROFF teaches American government and political thought at the University of Texas, Austin, and is the author of *Pragmatic Illusions: The Presidential Politics of John F. Kennedy*.

WILSON CAREY MCWILLIAMS teaches political theory and international relations at Livingston College, Rutgers University. He is the author of *The Idea of Fraternity in America*.

195

Index

Abourezk, James, 93
Accountability, 14, 68–69, 73–74, 121–22, 178–79
Adams, Charles Francis, 52
Adams, John, 163
Aggression, 65–66, 188–89. *See also* Human nature, aggressiveness in
American character, Tocqueville on, 29–34, 163
Aristotle, 5
Arnold, Thurman, 75
Associational life, 28, 52–54, 56, 98–102; ill effects of, 179–80, 190–91
Authority: based on expertise, 83, 151–52; in loco parentis, 178–79; as source for defining political questions, 167; Tocqueville on, 19–20, 22–23, 28–29; total state, 68–69, 73–74; tyranny of benevolence and, 189. *See also* Power
Autonomy, 14–21; organizational, 68–75, 85–90

Banfield, Edward C., 139
Beer, Thomas, 48
Bendix, Reinhard, 39, 53
Benign neglect, Tocqueville on, 19–20, 22–23, 28–29
Berle, Adolph A., 66
Black communities, tradition in, 98–102, 119–20, 123–24, 140, 146
Blaine, James G., 41, 48
Blodgett, Geoffrey, 41
Bonds, civic, 4, 8–9; Chavez and, 119–23; Hanna and, 51, 85–88; Madison on, 16–17; strains on,

153–55, 189, 190–92; Tocqueville on, 32–34
Brooks, Thomas, 90
Brown, Edmund, Jr., 93
Bryan, William Jennings, 45–46, 47–48
Bureaucracy, reorganization of, 156–57. *See also* Managerialism; Organization
Burns, James MacGregor, 8
Business, 40–42; attempts to conciliate with labor, 50–52; modern tasks of, 71–72; scale of, 65–66; social accountability of, 68–69

Carnegie, Andrew, 52
Charisma, 8–9, 47, 85, 103, 171–74
Chavez, Cesar, 111–24
Chayes, Abram, 68
Civic education. *See* Education, civic
Civic virtue. *See* Virtue, civic
Cleveland, Grover, 41, 48
Cohen, Jerry, 118
Collins, John, 139
Community, 12–13; control, 158; discourse in, 25–26; excellence, 174, 183–84; founding, 22; organized labor as a factor of, 80–81, 85; as personified in a leader, 106–7; tradition in black, 98–102, 119–20, 123–24, 140, 146
Consensus, 6–8; production of, 24–25, 51–53, 86, 158–60, 161, 171, 186–87
Consent: earned, 186–87; modern view of, 178–80. *See also* Participation